CN0043476A

EDWARD THOMAS was born in London in 1878 and educated at St Paul's School and Lincoln College, Oxford. While still an undergraduate he published his first book, *The Woodland Life*, and married Helen Noble, with whom he had three children. Thomas became a professional author, publishing over twenty prose books, as well as a novel (*The Happy-Go-Lucky Morgans*), a biography of Richard Jefferies, and critical studies of Maurice Maeterlinck, Lafcadio Hearn, George Borrow, Walter Pater, Swinburne and Keats. He also introduced editions of Borrow, George Herbert, Christopher Marlowe and William Cobbett, and wrote hundreds of book reviews and articles. Encouraged by his friend Robert Frost, he began writing poetry in 1914, producing over 140 poems in the next few years. Only a few of these appeared in print in his lifetime, under the pseudonym 'Edward Eastaway'; *Poems* by Edward Thomas was published in October 1917 and the first edition of his *Collected Poems* in 1920, establishing his reputation as one of the most admired and influential poets of the century. Thomas joined the Artists' Rifles in 1915. He was killed on Easter Monday 1917 during the Battle of Arras.

GUY CUTHBERTSON was an undergraduate at the University of St Andrews and then a graduate student at Queen's College, Oxford, where he wrote a doctoral thesis entitled 'The Literary Geography in Edward Thomas's Work'. He has been a lecturer at St Edmund Hall and Merton College, Oxford, and at the University of Swansea; and he currently teaches at the University of St Andrews. He has published a number of articles on Thomas, and he is editing Thomas's Autobiographies for Oxford University Press.

LUCY NEWLYN is a Professor of English Language and Literature at Oxford University, and a Fellow and Tutor in English at St Edmund Hall. She has published widely on English Romantic Literature, including three books with Oxford University Press, and *The Cambridge Companion to Coleridge*. Some of her poems appeared with Carcanet in the *Oxford Poets Anthology*, 2001; and her first collection, *Ginnel*, appeared in 2005. She edited Edward Thomas's *Oxford* (2005); and she is the general editor of the forthcoming *Edward Thomas Selected Prose*, to be published with Oxford University Press.

Branch-Lines
Edward Thomas and Contemporary Poetry

Edited by Guy Cuthbertson & Lucy Newlyn

Foreword by Andrew Motion

Afterword by Michael Longley

Lawrence Toulben,

with love and respect

Judy Drew

Christmas 2007

ENITHARMON PRESS

First published in 2007
by Enitharmon Press
26B Caversham Road
London NW5 2DU

www.enitharmon.co.uk

Distributed in the UK by
Central Books
99 Wallis Road
London E9 5LN

Distributed in the USA and Canada
by Dufour Editions Inc.
PO Box 7, Chester Springs
PA 19425, USA

ISBN: 978-1-904634-35-5

Enitharmon Press gratefully acknowledges the support of
Masatsugu Ohtake and Arts Council England.

British Library Cataloguing-in-Publication Data.
A catalogue record for this book is available
from the British Library.

Typset in Albertina by Libanus Press
and printed in England by
Cromwell Press

Contents

Edward Thomas holding his younger daughter Myfanwy and one of her friends.

Acknowledgements

The editors gratefully acknowledge the assistance of the Oxford English Faculty and Christopher Tower in funding the conference from which this anthology has grown, and Masa Ohtake for so generously enabling the book to come into being.

We are grateful to all those who have contributed to the volume; and to publishers who have granted permission to reprint work already published. (Details of publication are supplied after each poem, unless this is its first appearance.)

We would also like to thank Chris Fletcher, Stuart Lee and Kate Lindsay for their assistance in reproducing manuscripts housed at the Bodleian Library; Paul Williams, Rector of Steep, for his permission to reproduce a photograph of the memorial window as the jacket illustration; and Richard Emeny for supplying many of the photographs, some of which appear in print here for the first time. Colin Thornton, Secretary of the Edward Thomas Fellowship, has responded helpfully to a number of enquiries, and Tom Durham has given his expert advice on the typescript.

Last but not least, we are very grateful to Stephen Stuart-Smith of Enitharmon Press for his enthusiastic support of the project, and for the care with which he has seen the book through the press.

The Thomas family, c.1894–5. Edward Thomas (centre) with his parents and his brothers Julian, Ernest, Reggie, Oscar and Dory (left to right).

Foreword

ANDREW MOTION

Why do so many poets love Edward Thomas, and want to advertise the ways they have learned from him? In some respects the question is easy to answer: Thomas's overall vigilance, his attention to neglectable details, his sympathetic quiet-speaking, his genius for producing poems which appear to think aloud rather than be a means of delivering finished thoughts: all these things make this work intensely alive, even as they prove it to be a storehouse of qualities identified with the 'English line' which runs back to the Romantics (Wordsworth and Clare especially) and forward to Larkin and other more recent poets who are interested in what we now call 'environmental issues'.

But there's something else as well. The story of Thomas's arduous journey towards poetry – not simply the pathos of his frustration in prose, but the patient struggle of his efforts to purify his style and 'wring all the necks of my rhetoric' – describes a process that most poets feel they undertake (on a smaller scale) every time they pick up a pen to write. In other words, he is a poet who feels at once fully-achieved, and permanently involved in the act of becoming. It's therefore hard to read him without feeling at once stabilised and provoked: the ingredients of his poems are reliably nourishing, the open-minded wariness with which he approaches them makes them seem endlessly new.

This paradox is celebrated in virtually every poem printed here, and in the essays preceding them – which means the collection has a double value. It is a celebration of Thomas, and a dignified tribute to his achievement; at the same time it bears witness to his powers of re-generation. For much of the last quarter of the twentieth century, critics and poets felt it necessary to consider Modernist and non-Modernist allegiances as being in stark opposition to one another. Given the formal elasticity of much contemporary writing, not to mention its other manifestations of variety, this antagonism now looks increasingly futile. Thomas has played a vital part in this change. His work crosses boundaries with the same easy determination that it crosses landscapes, without ever compromising our sense that it emanates from an authentic self.

Preface

'all the bards, nearly, of Oxfordshire and where else?'

This collection of essays, poems and critical reflections has grown out of a conference on 'Edward Thomas and Contemporary Poetry', which took place on 12 March 2005. The conference was held at St Edmund Hall, Oxford, sponsored by Tower Poetry and supported by Oxford University's English Faculty. The speakers included sixteen poets, most of whom had connections with Oxford (like Thomas himself); and some poets who were unable to attend contributed *in absentia*. Seamus Heaney, who wrote a poem specially for the occasion, observed that the conference seemed likely to feature 'all the bards, nearly, of Oxfordshire and where else?'. Genially remembering 'Adlestrop', he caught the spirit of the day.

The format was unusual for a conference at a university. In the morning, we heard four academic lectures, but the afternoon took the shape of a poetry reading. Poets had been asked either to write a new poem in honour of Thomas, or to find something they had written in the past in which they detected Thomas's voice. They read these poems out, and commented briefly on them. Our intention was to enable a number of different voices to be heard on the subject of Thomas's influence, and to gain insights into his poetic craft from these practitioners. Thomas was himself both a prose writer and a poet; so it was appropriate that the contributions of our speakers should reflect their own duality, as poet-critics. As a critic, Thomas showed a great understanding of poetry, even before he was a poet, and his prose works were frequently concerned with 'influence' – the influence, on poetry, of places (*A Literary Pilgrim in England*), of women (*Feminine Influence on the Poets*), and, most of all, of poetry (even though he did once complain about 'those books made out of books founded on other books').

Like the conference, the materials collected here combine poetry and prose: the book includes not only the poems and critical comments from the conference, but also further contributions. The essays provide new inroads into Thomas's work and his afterlives. Our aim has been to explore widely, enabling a representative mapping of Thomas's influence. *Branch-Lines* has in one or two cases overlapped with Anne Harvey's valuable anthology *Elected Friends: Poems for and about Edward Thomas*

(Enitharmon, 1992), which had itself followed another collection of poems for and about Thomas, *These Things the Poets Said* (Pear Tree Press, 1935). Even during his lifetime, and before he had started writing poetry, poems were written about Thomas: Gordon Bottomley wrote 'To Edward Thomas' in 1908; Walter de la Mare's 'Longlegs' is in *Peacock Pie* (1913); Clifford Bax and Herbert Farjeon wrote 'Walking Tom' in Venice in 1913.

These Things the Poets Said and *Elected Friends* deal with the conscious reception of Thomas: the poems name and imitate him, often evoking Thomas country. *Branch-Lines* is different in kind, exploring Thomas's appeal and influence. The book contains many poems that are not overtly concerned with him; and it moves further afield, not least geographically. Equally, *Branch-Lines* is not exhaustive. We are aware of numerous other poets we might have approached; and our guess is that many more would have responded gladly to the invitation to contribute. Thomas is often referred to as a 'poet's poet', and his appeal seems to be almost universal. The reasons become abundantly apparent in the pages of this book.

All the poems in *Branch-Lines* are tributes to Thomas, by virtue of having been selected (or written) in response to an invitation to contribute. But they are also tributaries; and in their critical reflections, the poets draw attention to what they bring to Thomas, as well as to what they have been given by him. Gratitude is both an endless debt, and a creatively enabling resource. Poets have welcomed the opportunity to reflect on what they have learned from Thomas, either during one particular phase of their careers, or steadily. The acts of investigating, selecting and framing a critical evaluation, have given rise to interesting insights and recognitions.

Thomas is frequently absorbed at an early age, often as the result of a book handed down or given from an older generation: there is a strong familial (or genealogical) aspect to his reception. Many of the poets remember vividly their first reading of him, treasuring their first copy of his poems and consciously thinking of him as they write. But he himself once wrote that 'the chief influences of our lives are unconscious, just as the best of our best work is'. U. A. Fanthorpe sees how deeply Thomas's love of place-names has affected her, without her knowledge: 'He comes naturally, I think, to writers in English, like grass growing'. James Nash observes that Thomas's world-view has unconsciously 'seeped' into his consciousness; and a younger poet, Esther Morgan, comments, 'I was surprised by how much he's influenced my work, without me even realising it'.

Many of the poets took one of Thomas's poems as a starting point for their own. Their contributions can be read partly as imitations, and partly as 'answers' or 'continuations'. David Harsent, for instance, is inspired by 'Rain'; and Charles Tomlinson's 'Old Man or Lad's Love' is directly modelled on 'Old Man'. 'As the team's head brass' was on Heaney's mind when he 'set [Thomas] walking on the Lagans Road'. Gillian Clarke's 'Nettles' takes 'Tall Nettles' as its point of departure, and speaks directly to its ecological concerns. Paul Muldoon was 'hoping against hope that the spirit of Edward Thomas might have been breathing down my neck' when he wrote 'The Killdeer'. The poems in this category are *performative* tributes to Thomas, in that they consciously observe, echo, and continue his preoccupations, stylistic mannerisms, and tones of voice. They are expressions of deep affinity, and they demonstrate, simultaneously, critical insight and poetic craftsmanship.

'Old Man' is probably the poem by Thomas most often mentioned, alluded to, and echoed by contemporary poets. The influence can be noticed both in verbal reminiscences, and in structural parallels. Some of the reasons for its importance are addressed by the poets themselves; and the poem receives critical attention in the essays. 'Old Man' is also a poem about Myfanwy, Thomas's daughter, who died on 8 March 2005, four days before the conference, and the poems that draw on 'Old Man', Tomlinson's especially, can be treated as tributes to her.

'Old Man' deserves a book of its own. 'Adlestrop', Thomas's most famous and best-loved poem, has one: *Adlestrop Revisited: An Anthology Inspired by Edward Thomas's Poem* (1999), edited by Anne Harvey. As that title suggests, 'Adlestrop' is often associated with going back – Thomas never went back there by train, but he went back by remembering. Hans Ulrich Seeber focussed on 'Adlestrop' when he recently argued that 'the retrospective attitude' is a key characteristic of not only Thomas's poetry but also 'the English tradition', which includes poets such as Thomas Hardy, Edward Thomas, Philip Larkin, Andrew Motion. For this book, poets have gone back to Thomas, and 'going back' is a recurring theme, but *Branch-Lines* shows that 'the English line' of influence traditionally associated with Thomas can no longer be thought of as straightforwardly 'English'. Like a railway line, it has branched out in many different directions, and crossed borders.

'Choose me, / You English words', Thomas writes, in 'Words'; but that poem includes a tribute to the 'sweetness' of the Welsh words he knew and loved. Thomas's significance for Welsh writers is linked to his parentage and lifelong love of Wales; and this branch-line of his influence is well represented in our collection. Dannie Abse, Gillian Clarke, Nigel Jenkins and Owen Sheers are Welsh writers, grateful for Thomas's Welsh origins and conscious of his importance for Welsh culture. We also find echoes of his Anglo-Welsh identity in Andrew McNeillie, Patrick McGuinness, Jane Griffiths, and Jeremy Hooker. The Celtic drift in Thomas's writing may partly explain why he has been important for Irish poets too, especially those living away from their country – Paul Muldoon, Bernard O'Donoghue, Tom Paulin, Peter McDonald, Michael Foley. All these poets have learnt in important ways from Thomas's combination of lyric intensity and idiomatic naturalism.

As Robert Crawford points out, Thomas's 'closeness to the grain of language' makes him 'a poet of international appeal'. His writing is rooted in the local and the particular; yet it is not insular – witness the depth of empathy felt by Carmen Bugan, a poet of Romanian-American origins, with his nostalgia for home. Penelope Shuttle's poem, 'Edward San', honours this paradox. Transposing Thomas to Japan, she imagines his poems translated for a Japanese audience, and read in 'the land of the haiku'.

Thomas has influenced a wide range of poets, in a wide range of ways. The poets in this book vary considerably in age, nationality and background. The poets are not a movement, nor on a single line; they do not all know each other, let alone all read each other: this book has surely created some surprising connections. *Branch-Lines* reminded us of a comment on Thomas made in 1937 by his friend James Guthrie:

> But as he had great numbers of friends among literary people whose work and character were extremely varied, his sympathies must have been very wide. It might, indeed, be harder to unite his friends than it was for him to bind them to himself with that sincere and deep affection which has already outlasted a good many years and is even now ardent and expressive.

Guy Cuthbertson and Lucy Newlyn
Oxford, August 2006

Introduction: Edward Thomas, Modern Writer

GUY CUTHBERTSON

In 1918, an elderly Thomas Hardy 'reflected on poetry': 'It bridges over the years to think that Gray might have seen Wordsworth in his cradle, and Wordsworth might have seen me in mine'.[1] Edward Thomas, who was born in 1878, did not have a long life, but given that he was killed at the Battle of Arras in 1917, there are plenty of people alive today who can say that Edward Thomas 'might have seen me in mine'. Indeed, Thomas's daughter, Myfanwy, lived until 2005. In that and other ways, we can easily bridge over the years. There are still a few surviving members of the armed forces from the First World War; and, as we see in 'The Moustache', Michael Longley's father fought in that war, while Peter Scupham's poem, 'The Map-Maker', is about a map made by his father 'in that crux year, 1916, when he was 12'. Yet Edward Thomas is often seen as a man from a different, distant age. Ivor Gurney's deluded belief that Thomas was killed by that symbol of the modern world, the wireless, actually fore-shadowed many later responses to Thomas.[2] 'It is hard to think one's way back into his world', Peter Levi said in 1987.[3] 'Edward Thomas and his world are gone for ever', according to J. M. Coetzee's novel *Youth* (2002).[4]

England has kept on changing (and not necessarily for the worse): there were many old Englands. Thomas wrote in *George Borrow: The Man and his Books* (1912) that 'Borrow's England is the old England of Fielding, painted with more intensity because even as Borrow was travelling the change was far advanced, and when he was writing had been fulfilled'.[5] Borrow was writing a generation before Thomas was born (but lived until 1881, so he might have seen Thomas in his cradle). It might not be possible to give an actual date to the death of Thomas's world, a death that was surely drawn out over decades, but so many have argued that something important

---

1 Florence Emily Hardy, *The Life of Thomas Hardy 1840–1928* (London: Macmillan, 1962), p. 386. In a chapter called 'Reflections on Poetry'.
2 Helen Thomas, *Under Storm's Wing* (London: Paladin, 1990), p. 240.
3 Peter Levi, 'Notes on Edward Thomas', *The Art of Edward Thomas*, ed. Jonathan Barker (Bridgend: Poetry Wales Press, 1987), p. 25.
4 J. M. Coetzee, *Youth* (London: Secker and Warburg, 2002), p. 58.
5 Edward Thomas, *George Borrow: The Man and his Books* (London: Chapman and Hall, 1912), p. 320.

happened to England (and Wales too) in or around the First World War. In *The Strange Death of Liberal England* (1936), George Dangerfield (his surname is appropriate) saw that in 1911 the old England was dying fast:

> *Dying!* In the streets of London, the last horse-bus clattered towards extinction. The aeroplane, that incongruous object, earth-bound and wavering, still called forth exclamations of rapture and alarm. Country roads, with blind corners and precipitous inclines, took a last revenge upon the loud invading automobile.[6]

Reading Dangerfield's description of England one might recall Philip Larkin's well-known poem 'MCMXIV', where, as so often, the death of old England, and of an age, is represented by the First World War. The First World War sits like a vast grave or trench or No Man's Land (the war offers us so many convenient images) between Thomas and us, between the old and the modern. This is a view that is hinted at by Thomas in, say, 'As the team's head brass', which he thought of calling 'The Last Team', where, with hindsight at least, the fallen elm could be seen as representing the death of the English countryside. The elm was felled in a blizzard (John Freeman noted that a gale 'destroyed scores of elms around Edward's camp at Romford'),[7] but so many trees were cut down during the war for the war. If there hadn't been the war, 'it would have been / Another world' (ll.30–31).[8] Thomas's war diary, though mostly from France, contains entries that prefigure the death of his world, such as 'four or five planes hovering and wheeling as kestrels used to over Mutton and Ludcombe'.[9]

Thomas is frequently connected with what Peter Scupham calls 'the vanished English countryside'. Arguing that Thomas's England was 'doomed', Donald Davie turned to 'that country between the North and South Downs which Thomas experienced as immemorially secret and settled and lonely, where now we barge along bumper to bumper between commuters' homes, to and from Gatwick Airport'.[10] And that was in 1979; there are more roads and more cars now, and the airport has grown. As Richard Ingrams reminds readers in *England: An Anthology* (1990), 'in

---

6 George Dangerfield, *The Strange Death of Liberal England* (London: Constable, 1936), p. 63.
7 John Freeman, *John Freeman's Letters*, ed. Gertrude Freeman and Sir John Squire (London: Macmillan, 1936), p. 177.
8 Edward Thomas, *The Collected Poems*, ed. R. George Thomas (London: Faber and Faber, 2004), p. 116.
9 Thomas, *The Collected Poems*, ed. R. George Thomas, p. 155.
10 Donald Davie, 'Lessons in Honesty', *The Times Literary Supplement*, 4001 (23 November 1979), p. 21.

spite of what you read there is still a great deal of countryside left',[11] but any visit to the countryside that Thomas knew will bring home the changes that have taken place. In *Edward Thomas on the Countryside* (1977), Roland Gant says that he has walked 'along the same tracks over downs, fells and mountains as those followed by Edward Thomas', and adds that 'I often wonder what he would have thought of the changes that have taken place in the landscape'.[12] One change that was taking place was the death of the English Elm, which appears so frequently in Thomas's work but was being killed off by Dutch Elm Disease when Davie and Gant were writing in the late 1970s (the fallen elm of Thomas's poem has acquired another ring of significance).

In *Adlestrop Revisited* (1999), edited by Anne Harvey, some of the contributors note changes to the village of Adlestrop, not least the closure of the station on 3 January 1966. One of the two 'Adlestrop' signboards from the platforms is in the bus-shelter along with a copy of the poem. Of course, the commemoration of Thomas in some places is itself one of the changes to the countryside. At Steep, between the North and South Downs, where Thomas lived, the parish church, All Saints, seems to get more visits from Thomas's followers (Thomists?) than from communicants. The beautiful windows there by Laurence Whistler, which Lachlan Mackinnon mentions in his poem, celebrate not a saint, not Edward the Confessor or Thomas the Martyr, but Edward Thomas (who died on Easter Monday, his body miraculously immaculate, his pocket watch, a relic and 'heart-stopping emblem', recording the time of his death).[13]

In Thomas's time, Steep was 'Grub Village' (to use the title of an article by Philip Larkin on Thomas). At Steep, where the property is now so expensive, Thomas tried to make ends meet by reviewing books, writing books, editing books (he compiled anthologies, but since he would have to ask for permission and possibly pay money, he tried to avoid including his contemporaries).[14] Edward Thomas was, as he puts it in *The Icknield Way* (1913), 'a writing animal',[15] and that writing animal belonged to the old

11 Richard Ingrams, *England: An Anthology* (London: Collins, 1990), p. 12.

12 Roland Gant, ed., *Edward Thomas on the Countryside: A Selection of his Prose and Verse* (London: Faber and Faber, 1977), p. 13.

13 See Jon Stallworthy's poem. Gordon Bottomley 'had nicknamed him Edward the Confessor'. John Moore, *The Life and Letters of Edward Thomas* (London: William Heinemann, 1939), p. 121.

14 'Do tell me one thing, preferably not by a living author'. Edward Thomas, *Letters from Edward Thomas to Gordon Bottomley*, ed. R. George Thomas (London: Oxford University Press, 1968), p. 244.

15 Edward Thomas, *The Icknield Way* (London: Constable, 1913), p. vi.

England, like the countryside of the South Country: in 'Grub Village', Larkin says that Thomas 'was, to put it bluntly, a hack, of a kind unknown in these softer days' (of course, some contemporary writers and critics might disagree).[16] One way and another, the war killed Thomas's career as a full-time writer, and he joined the army in July 1915.

The mistake is to think that if Thomas's world is dead, Thomas's work is dead. As Robert Crawford says in this book, 'Though Thomas is long gone, his best poetry does not seem or sound long gone'. Donald Davie is not convincing when he argues that because Thomas lived in another age and another England, his writing cannot give us all it should, that the pleasure we take in his poetry 'cannot help but be, to a large extent, the soothing pleasure of make-believe', and, while that might be a legitimate pleasure, 'it is certainly not the pleasure that we get from great poetry'.[17] Thomas must offer some people the pleasure of make-believe – Roland Gant says that 'when poppies have been sprayed nearly out of existence', Thomas's work 'reminds us that there was a time when poppies "so desirable in their serenity" still coloured our cornfields'[18] – but it is wrong to think that Thomas's writing simply describes the England of his time. When Edna Longley argues that Thomas has plenty to say to the twenty-first century 'as ecological poet and thinker', she doesn't just mean that he depicts a greener England. Likewise, Thomas's poetry does not deserve the conclusion that Thomas came to about *The Spoon River Anthology* (1915): 'I concluded that it must be liked for the things *written about* in it, not for what it expressed'.[19]

Thomas's poetry has repeatedly been described as modern (even by those who believe that the world changed in or around 1914). F. R. Leavis said that the poetry 'expresses a representative kind of modern experience'.[20] Admittedly, that was back in 1939 (and Larkin described the poetry as 'really fairly modern' in 1941),[21] but, quoting from Leavis's *New Bearings in English Poetry* (1932), Andrew Motion argued in 1980 that 'For all

---

16 Philip Larkin, *Required Writing* (London: Faber and Faber, 1983), p. 188.
17 Davie, *The Times Literary Supplement*, 4001 (23 November 1979), p. 21.
18 Gant, ed., *Edward Thomas on the Countryside: A Selection of his Prose and Verse*, p. 12.
19 Edward Thomas, *Elected Friends: Robert Frost and Edward Thomas to One Another*, ed. Matthew Spencer (New York: Handsel Books, 2003), p. 154. *The Spoon River Anthology* is by Edgar Lee Masters.
20 F. R. Leavis, 'The Fate of Edward Thomas', *Scrutiny*, vii, 4 (March 1939), p. 442.
21 Hull, Brynmor Jones Library, Hull University Archives, The Larkin-Sutton Letters, MS DP/174/2/22, f. 13r.

its singularity, Thomas's "distinctively modern sensibility" was formed by profound familiarity with writers who were, to use his own words in "Lob", "English as this gate, these flowers, this mire".[22] In a chapter called 'Edward Thomas and Modern Poetry' in *Edwardian Poetry* (1991), Ken Millard begins by stating that Thomas is 'a modern poet of major stature',[23] and reaches a pertinent conclusion: 'Whether or not contemporary poets are drawing on pre-Modernist models is not at issue here, but if they were, then Edward Thomas would be an excellent focus for their attention'.[24] In 2003, David Gervais wrote that Thomas can be seen 'as a *modern* poet rather than as a revisionist Georgian'.[25]

John Wain argued that Thomas's poetry captures the characteristics of our world:

> He is perhaps the first, as he is certainly one of the best, of the English modern poets. By 'modern' I mean not chic, avant-garde, having the external trappings of international modernism; I mean reflecting accurately those characteristics of the present-day world which mark it off from the world before.[26]

In fact, the poetry does belong on our side of the 'MCMXIV' watershed, since it was written after the war had started. Furthermore, as Dangerfield revealed, the seeds of the modern world had been sown before the war. More importantly, Thomas's work contains not only the Edwardian or Georgian world, but also Edward Thomas's perception of it and of himself, and it is this that many people have in mind when they refer to the poetry as modern. Leavis called it a 'modern sensibility': 'Thomas records the modern disintegration, the sense of directionlessness'.[27] Wain says that the key modern quality is 'this isolation of unbelief', a loneliness 'far more intense than the loneliness that arises from the mere absence of other human beings'.[28] At the very end of his diary, at the very end of his life, Edward Thomas wrote that 'I never understood quite what was meant by

22 Andrew Motion, *The Poetry of Edward Thomas* (London: Routledge and Kegan Paul, 1980), p. 11. F. R. Leavis, *New Bearings in English Poetry: A Study of the Contemporary Situation* (Harmondsworth: Chatto and Windus, 1932), p. 55.
23 Ken Millard, *Edwardian Poetry* (Oxford: Clarendon Press, 1991), p. 107.
24 Millard, *Edwardian Poetry*, p. 130.
25 David Gervais, '"Cock Crow": Why Edward Thomas isn't Thomas Hardy', *PN Review*, xxx, 2 (November-December 2003), p. 39.
26 John Wain, *Professing Poetry* (London: Macmillan, 1977), p. 353.
27 Leavis, *New Bearings*, p. 57.
28 Wain, *Professing Poetry*, p. 353.

God' (which would almost pass for Anglicanism these days).[29] If Thomas's style also has modern qualities, then surely that is because it is attempting to express this modern sensibility.

So there is something wrong with the argument, the argument that seems to be expressed in *Youth*, that because Thomas and his world are dead, his writing should not influence, nor appeal to, poets younger than him:

> The British magazines are dominated by dismayingly modest little poems about everyday thoughts and experiences, poems that would not have raised an eyebrow half a century ago. What has happened to the ambitions of poets here in Britain? Have they not digested the news that Edward Thomas and his world are gone for ever? Have they not learned the lesson of Pound and Eliot, to say nothing of Baudelaire and Rimbaud, the Greek epigrammatists, the Chinese? [30]

Here, John, the central character and an unpublished poet, is commenting on the poetry magazines of the early 1960s, but no doubt there are some people who would say exactly the same today. Yet Thomas performs the same trick that the Greek epigrammatists and the Chinese perform: he speaks to those who live beyond his own time and place. As Penelope Shuttle mentions, Thomas has been translated into other languages – he has 'travelled'. The Edward Thomas Fellowship will attest that Thomas is big in Japan. And as Wain points out, 'modern' is not necessarily the same as 'modernist' (even though Thomas did believe, briefly, that Pound 'has very great things in him').[31]

To look at Thomas's modernity another way, he is modern because he is still popular, in fact increasingly so. And Thomas is modern because he has influenced so many contemporary poets. Equally, he was modern in the early 1960s because poets, such as Larkin and Wain, had clearly taken his road, and many readers of poetry wanted to read poems like Thomas's (even if they didn't know Thomas's). In a sense, his poetry becomes more modern every time his work gains a new admirer. Perhaps one could even argue that in Britain Thomas is more modern than Pound because more people read his poetry than read Pound's. One

29 Thomas, *The Collected Poems*, ed. R. George Thomas, p. 171.
30 Coetzee, *Youth*, p. 58.
31 Thomas, *Letters from Edward Thomas to Gordon Bottomley*, ed. R. George Thomas, p. 185 [28 April 1909].

could mention too that in a poll to discover the nation's favourite poem, 'Adlestrop' gained more votes than any poem by T. S. Eliot.[32]

Pound and Eliot do not seem to have been among Thomas's greatest admirers. Pound said that Thomas was 'a mild fellow with no vinegar in his veins'.[33] In December 1917, after Thomas's death, and when Thomas's first collection of poetry had already been published, a review of his *The Tenth Muse* (reissued in 1917) in *The Egoist* in December 1917, a review that has been ascribed to T. S. Eliot, stated that 'Thomas was evidently a very nice man, and one who was more interested (as Mr. Freeman half suggests), in the "human" side of poets than in their technique, more interested in poets than in poetry'. The reviewer implies that Thomas could not be a poet. The interests of the reviewer are undoubtedly Eliotic: he says that 'his Donne is inadequate, and of Marvell he fails to mention one of the finest love-poems in the language'.[34]

In the same year, in October, in *The Times Literary Supplement*, another major modernist praised Thomas's work. Virginia Woolf said of *A Literary Pilgrim in England* (1917) that 'Mr Thomas brings the very look of the fields and roads before us; he brings the poets, too; and no one will finish the book without a sense that he knows and respects the author'.[35] In the next war, after her own death, Woolf's *Between the Acts* (1941) was published, and Thomas, who was in many people's thoughts at that time, had clearly been in hers.[36] For example, this moment in the novel has been connected with Thomas's 'Old Man':

32 'To coincide with National Poetry Day 1995, the nation's favourite book programme, *The Bookworm*, conducted a poll to discover the nation's favourite poem.' Griff Rhys Jones, 'Foreword', *The Nation's Favourite Poems* (London: BBC Books, 1996), p. 5.

33 For this comment, and a discussion of Thomas and Pound, see Christopher Ricks's Afterword in *Elected Friends: Robert Frost and Edward Thomas to One Another*, ed. Matthew Spencer, p. 205.

34 Anonymous review of *The Tenth Muse*, *The Egoist*, iv, 11 (December 1917), p. 173. The review is ascribed to Eliot by Donald Gallup in *T. S. Eliot: A Bibliography* (London: Faber and Faber, 1969), p. 200.

35 Virginia Woolf, *The Essays of Virginia Woolf: Volume II 1912–1918*, ed. Andrew McNeillie (London: Hogarth Press, 1987), p. 163.

36 In 1940, Alun Lewis wrote the Thomas-inspired poem 'All Day It Has Rained', which was published in the January 1941 issue of *Horizon*, along with a review by Lewis of *The Trumpet and Other Poems*, the new edition of Thomas's poems (produced for a wartime market). In 1941, Larkin bought this edition and called Thomas's poetry 'really fairly modern'. On 10 March 1940, John Betjeman read out 'Adlestrop' on the BBC Home Service, and on 25 May 1940, Thomas Jones wrote to Gwendoline Elizabeth Davies saying that 'we stopped at Adlestrop, the platform all flowers and foliage, and five schoolchildren got out with their gas marks slung like satchels. I thought of Edward Thomas'. Thomas Jones, *A Diary with Letters 1931–1950* (London: Oxford University Press, 1954), p. 459.

. . . she fairly filled the path, swaying slightly as she walked, and plucking a leaf here and there from the hedge.

'Fly then, follow,' she hummed, 'the dappled herds in the cedar grove, who, sporting, play, the red with the roe, the stag with the doe. Fly, away. I grieving stay. Alone I linger, I pluck the bitter herb by the ruined wall, the churchyard wall, and press its sour, its sweet, its sour, long grey leaf, so, twixt thumb and finger. . . .'

She threw away the shred of Old Man's Beard that she had picked in passing and kicked open the greenhouse door.[37]

Julia Briggs has shown that a typescript of the novel not only mentions 'Old Man' and 'The Cuckoo' but also refers to Thomas by name as 'a poet'.[38]

Further, while Larkin, Wain and other Movement poets, or members of an 'English line', clearly enjoyed Thomas's work,[39] so did their literary opposites and opponents. R. S. Thomas liked Thomas's work, and wrote an introduction to Thomas's *Selected Poems*,[40] but Dylan Thomas liked Edward Thomas's poetry too. Right at the end of his life, he told Idris Davies that he liked Thomas 'very much indeed'.[41] On 29 July 1949 he had given a radio broadcast about Thomas for the Welsh Home Service 'Arts Magazine' – it displays his love of Thomas's work, and also his lack of interest in the biographical details (the talk begins with the statement: 'I do not know how much of a Welshman Edward Thomas was, and it does not matter'). Dylan Thomas says that

The shy, passionate love he breathed into his compassionate and ennobling poems – poems, as Walter de la Mare says, that ennoble by simplification – lives now in a number of people. His love has

---

37 Virginia Woolf, *Between the Acts* [The Shakespeare Head Press Edition of Virginia Woolf], ed. Susan Dick and Mary S. Millar (Oxford: Blackwell, 2002), p. 61.

38 Julia Briggs, *Virginia Woolf: An Inner Life* (London: Allen Lane, 2005), p. 376. As noted by Jem Poster at the 'Edward Thomas and Contemporary Poetry' conference in 2005.

39 For a discussion of Larkin and Thomas see Guy Cuthbertson's essay, and for a discussion of the 'English line' see Lucy Newlyn's essay. See also David Gervais, *Literary Englands: Versions of 'Englishness' in Modern Writing* (Cambridge: Cambridge University Press, 1993); Edna Longley, *Poetry in the Wars* (Newcastle: Bloodaxe, 1986); Hans Ulrich Seeber, 'The Retrospective Attitude in Poems by Edward Thomas and Andrew Motion, and the Construction of the English Tradition in Poetry', *REAL*, xxi (2005), ed. Herbert Grabes, pp. 147–159; John Powell Ward, *The English Line* (Basingstoke: Macmillan, 1991).

40 Jan Marsh discusses R. S. Thomas in *Edward Thomas: A Poet For His Country* (London: Paul Elek, 1978), p. 202.

41 Dylan Thomas, *The Collected Letters*, new edition, ed. Paul Ferris (London: J. M. Dent, 2000), p. 967.

multiplied. […] He has grown, surely and simply and slowly, into our language[42]

Similarly, and grandiosely, Ted Hughes said of Edward Thomas that 'he is the father of us all', at the unveiling of the War Poets Memorial at Westminster Abbey in 1985.[43] One could draw up a family tree with Thomas as the starting point, and poets on every branch-line. Thomas as a father, not least a father to an Edward (Ted for short) and a pair of Thomases, is a powerful idea, and he might have seen the other two Thomases in their cradles.[44] In his poetry, Edward Thomas is frequently a father, a father of three children, and this subject is one that seems to have influenced Hughes and other father-poets. For instance, the well-loved 'Full Moon and Little Frieda' is reminiscent of the equally well-loved poems by Thomas about Myfanwy, poems like 'Snow' and 'The Brook', even though Hughes's poem is not at all in Thomas's style. But these major figures in modern poetry usually discovered Thomas long before they became fathers, when they were little more than children themselves. When he was seventeen, Dylan Thomas wrote an article for *The Herald of Wales* on 'The Poets of Swansea', in which he mentioned that Edward Thomas 'spent quite considerable periods with the late Mr. John Williams, headmaster of Waun Wen School, at Waun Wen' (this was before anyone had written a biography of Edward Thomas).[45]

In his teens, Peter Levi discovered and enjoyed Thomas's poetry, and he 'also read his prose, which in those days was still lying about, and admired it greatly'.[46] The impact of Thomas's prose on the twentieth century is harder to discern, but T. E. Lawrence, for instance, didn't consider it inferior to the poetry: he said that 'Edward Thomas wrote very fine poems, and some almost perfect prose'.[47] Noting that James Joyce owned

---

42 Dylan Thomas, *The Broadcasts*, ed. Ralph Maud (London: J. M. Dent, 1991), p. 208.

43 Seán Street, *The Dymock Poets* (Bridgend: Seren, 1994), p. 155. I am grateful to Richard Emeny for suggesting that Hughes might have been quoting from another writer. Henry James described Balzac as the father of us all. In 'Yardley Oak', a poem that Thomas admired, William Cowper refers to Adam as the father of us all.

44 'In October 1914, in all probability the month in which Edward Thomas at last began to write serious poetry, a baby was born in Swansea where Edward Thomas may even have yet again just visited'. John Powell Ward, *The English Line* (Basingstoke: Macmillan, 1991), p. 168. But we shouldn't think that Thomas was literally the father of them all.

45 9 January 1932. Dylan Thomas, *Early Prose Writings*, ed. Walford Davies (London: J. M. Dent, 1971), p. 98.

46 Peter Levi, 'Notes on Edward Thomas', *The Art of Edward Thomas*, ed. Jonathan Barker (Bridgend: Poetry Wales Press, 1987), p. 25.

47 T. E. Lawrence, *The Letters of T. E. Lawrence*, ed. David Garnett (London: Jonathan Cape, 1938), p. 510.

the second edition of Thomas's *Richard Jefferies: His Life and Work* (1909; second edition 1911), Friedhelm Rathjen has suggested that Thomas's book might have contributed to *Ulysses* (1922).[48] *Richard Jefferies*, which Q. D. Leavis called 'a classic in critical biography',[49] influenced another writer, arguably another modernist, E. M. Forster. *The Heart of England* (1906) and *Richard Jefferies* hover behind Forster's novel *Howards End* (1910), even though Forster dismissed Thomas's prose and poetry as boring – there are links between Forster's perception of Thomas and Forster's Leonard Bast, the boring follower of Jefferies.[50]

We see in this book that Thomas's poetry has a powerful influence on poets who are still living and writing (and many of them discovered Thomas in their teens), and we see, too, that Thomas's prose is important to some of these contemporary poets. Nigel Jenkins says that 'many of his prose treatments of the country, such as *Beautiful Wales*, I find thin on content and heavy on adjectives', but Peter Dale is interested in *Richard Jefferies*, which was the first of Thomas's books that Andrew McNeillie read. Lucy Newlyn's 'Stray' starts with a lengthy epigraph taken from Thomas's *Oxford* (1903). Thomas's autobiographical writings seem to be the most significant: Peter Scupham calls *The Childhood of Edward Thomas* one of 'Thomas's most fascinating prose pieces', and Peter McDonald and Michael Longley have both been inspired by Thomas's war diary. It should also be said that the prose fed into the poetry: Thomas's poems were either directly or indirectly influenced by his prose. Therefore the prose has indirectly influenced so many contemporary poets. Equally, Thomas's poetry has had an impact on recent fiction: in addition to Coetzee's *Youth*, there's J. L. Carr's *What Hetty Did* (1988), which plays with 'Adlestrop',[51] and Pat Barker's *The Ghost Road* (1995), which takes its epigraph, and presumably the spirit of its title, from Thomas's poem 'Roads':

48 Friedhelm Rathjen, 'Edward Thomas/James Joyce: Inventing a Connection', a paper given at the XXth International James Joyce Symposium (11–17 June 2006, Budapest-Szombathely), 13 June 2006.

49 Q. D. Leavis, 'Lives and Works of Richard Jefferies', *A Selection from Scrutiny*, volume 2, ed. F. R. Leavis, (Cambridge: Cambridge University Press, 1968), p. 203.

50 See Guy Cuthbertson, 'Leonard Bast and Edward Thomas', *Notes and Queries*, lii [New Series], 1 (March 2005), pp. 87–89. Also, John Beer has linked *Richard Jefferies* with *Howards End* by arguing that 'when Forster describes Bast's "No" concerning the dawn as "a pebble from the sling" he may, whether consciously or unconsciously, be recalling something that Edward Thomas said about Jefferies at the end of his chapter on *The Story of My Heart*'. John Beer, *Romantic Influences: Contemporary – Victorian – Modern* (Basingstoke: Macmillan, 1993), p. 206.

51 J. L. Carr, *What Hetty Did or Life and Letters* (Kettering: Quince Tree Press, 1988), p. 52.

Now all roads lead to France
And heavy is the tread
Of the living; but the dead
Returning lightly dance [52]

On contemporary prose, the impact of Thomas's poetry is more discernible than the impact of his prose, although Will Self uses *The South Country* (1909) at the start of *The Book of Dave* (2006).

The significance of his life, as told through his own prose and that of his family and biographers, is not ignored. Thomas's career belongs to another age, but it offers lessons to contemporary poets. Donald Davie commented that 'there is so much to say of Thomas's life, so many lessons to be learned from it, that one hardly knows where to start'.[53] A few years earlier, Larkin had seen Thomas as 'a figure whose importance seems to reside not so much in his own talent as in the lesson he embodies for those who succeed him'.[54] Thomas's life must touch anyone tempted by 'the romance of scraping a living from the printed word'.[55] David Constantine turns to 'the hand – this above all, perhaps – the hand "crawling crab-like over the clean white page", brave hand of a writer trying to make a living for himself and his family'. Like David Constantine, Bernard O'Donoghue refers to 'Helen Thomas's magical paired memoirs *As It Was* and *World Without End*', which provide a wife's-eye-view of the writing animal scraping a living. The most positive lesson that Thomas's life offers is that it is never too late. On 2 August 1914, Thomas commented to Eleanor Farjeon that 'I may as well write poetry' before asking 'did anyone ever begin at 36 in the shade?'.[56] How many poets have been inspired or consoled by the thought that a real poet did begin at thirty-six in the shade?

---

52 Pat Barker, *The Ghost Road* (Harmondsworth: Viking, 1995), p. vii.
53 Davie, *The Times Literary Supplement*, 4001 (23 November 1979), p. 22.
54 Larkin, *Required Writing*, p. 188.
55 Larkin, *Required Writing*, p. 189.
56 Eleanor Farjeon, *Edward Thomas: The Last Four Years* (London: Oxford University Press, 1958), p. 81.

Edward Thomas at Oxford in 1899.

Going Back to Edward Thomas

EDNA LONGLEY

My title could mean several things. Broadly, of course, 'Going back to Edward Thomas' is what this book is all about. But the book, like the conference before it, belongs to a series of goings-back. The poets gathered here, in this book, and who gathered at the conference like some great hosting of Irish or Welsh bards, follow in other poets' tracks. And, since Thomas himself looked back – with unusual intentness – to earlier poetry, the tracks recede beyond him, as down one of his forest roads, into the past.

The poem to, for or about Edward Thomas is a unique phenomenon. The elegies after his death at Arras in 1917 established a tradition, even a genre. Anne Harvey's anthology *Elected Friends* (1991) contains seventy-six such poems. An update might hit a century. His special position among poets, including poets who might agree on little else, makes Thomas more than an 'influence' – although he is certainly that too. A true 'poets' poet' is not a rarefied creature whose work is unread or unreadable outside an elite group. The term should be understood as a robust tribute from fellow professionals, like 'engineers' engineer'. Professional tributes combine respect for trade-craft with reverence for trade-mysteries. Thus a 'poet's poet' is one who brings the art's sources and resources into simultaneous focus. At some level, poems about Edward Thomas are always poems about poetry.

Perhaps we should include Thomas Hardy's 'The Fallow Deer at the Lonely House' in their number. Hardy grieved at Thomas's death, and 'The Fallow Deer at the Lonely House' seemingly responds to Thomas's second-last poem 'Out in the Dark', which itself implies Thomas's absorption of Hardy. 'Out in the Dark' begins:

> Out in the dark over the snow
> The fallow fawns invisible go
> With the fallow doe;
> And the winds blow
> Fast as the stars are slow.

29

'The Fallow Deer' begins:

> One without looks in to-night
> Through the curtain-chink
> From the sheet of glistening white;
> One without looks in to-night
> As we sit and think
> By the fender-brink.

'The Fallow Deer at the Lonely House' may be an oblique elegy for Thomas, for 'one without'. The Hardy-word 'haunts' occurs in 'Out in the Dark', and the spooky mutuality between the poems suggests how one poet might haunt another. It also suggests the power with which Thomas's poetry immediately spoke to intelligent poet-readers like Hardy and Robert Frost, if not always to critical opinion-formers. Is there an inverse relation between a poets' poet and an academics' poet?

This essay will 'go back' in two main senses. The first is partly personal. The second concerns ways in which Thomas himself goes back or backtracks. Personally speaking, I have returned to Thomas in that I am revising an annotated edition of his *Poems* and *Last Poems*, which I published in 1973. This task obliges me to consider what has happened since then to Thomas's critical standing, to criticism more generally, and to my own approach; and to ask whether Thomas's poetry is still waiting, like his quietly insistent 'aspens', for readers to catch up. As aspens 'must shake their leaves' over 'all sorts of weather, men, and times', so Thomas's poetry may backtrack to the future.

In March 2004 I did some literal going-back. In the spirit of Thomas's prose book *A Literary Pilgrim in England* (1917), I visited Steep in Hampshire, his home for most of his adult life; Wiltshire where he spent childhood summers and became obsessed with Richard Jefferies; and Dymock in the Forest of Dean where he rented a house near Robert Frost in August 1914. No doubt, like the archaeologists mocked in Thomas's cultural odyssey 'Lob' (1915), I 'thought as there was something to find there'.

Was there? Perhaps three things. First, as on my only previous Thomas pilgrimage (to Steep in 1978 for his centenary), I was reminded that Thomas's landscapes are ultimately symbolic. This is not just to say that place and poem can never be co-extensive, or even to reconfirm F. R Leavis's insight (in *New Bearings in English Poetry*, 1932) that 'the outer scene is accessory to an inner theatre'.[1] Thomas's wind, rain, sun, trees, birds, flowers, houses, roads, seasons, night and day, belong to a metaphysical as well as psychological drama. Second, his metaphysics encompass a meditation on history; and the Wiltshire countryside (which was new to me) still suggests why that county became central to his historical imagination – a faculty in which few modern poets equal him. The first chapter of *Richard Jefferies* (1909) prepares for 'Lob' in evoking 'tumuli and earthworks that make the earth look old', 'Celtic traces', 'untrodden but indelible old roads', 'flint-diggers' cartways . . . and hares' paths lead[ing] over the downs'. Third, any pilgrim on a Thomas path would be moved by the Dymock setting of 'The sun used to shine': the poem that celebrates his friendship with Frost. It was extraordinary to grasp the topographical basis of that precarious Eden where the poets 'walked slowly together', talked of 'men or poetry', and heard 'rumours of the war remote'. Perhaps the question of 'Edward Thomas and Contemporary Poetry' begins here. Besides being a poem about friendship, war, history and memory, 'The sun used to shine' represents poetry as a shared enterprise, as trade mysteries, as tradition. It hands on the conversations it encodes to other poets 'In those fields under the same moon'.

There is always more to decode in Edward Thomas. In going back editorially to his poetry, I realise how much I missed first time round, and will miss again. I can identify with his self-rebukes for failing to notice hidden or half-hidden things like 'summer nests' ('Birds' Nests') or 'the narrow copse / Where now the woodman lops / The last of the willows with his bill' ('First known when lost'). At least the poetry itself is now more widely noticed. Stan Smith, Andrew Motion, Michael Kirkham and others have built on the foundations laid by scholars and critics such as R. George Thomas, H. Coombes and William Cooke. Yet academic attention (not the only kind) remains patchy precisely where the academy might be expected to take note: Thomas's critical ideas and cultural critique, his weighing of tradition and modernity at a pivotal moment. I have lately found myself re-reading him with reference to ecology, war, modernism, and memory. Or perhaps I have been sensing his presence in 'contemporary poetry'.

Where ecology is concerned, criticism has indeed taken time to catch up. Jonathan Bate featured Thomas in his pioneering *Romantic Ecology*

1   F. R. Leavis, *New Bearings in English Poetry* (London: Chatto and Windus, 1932), p. 61.

(1991), but even Bate underestimates Thomas's importance as ecological poet and thinker. His relation to the Romantic poets is a large topic in itself. But insofar as he absorbed elements from all the Romantics, Thomas also synthesises and advances their poetry's ecological implications. He grew up in London amid further leaps of that urban modernisation which had originally brought country and city into new literary juxtapositions. The material circumstances of his attraction to the natural world and rural England were the rise of suburbia and the exodus of labourers from a radically changed rural economy. This led him to explore what modernity might endanger, but neither to ignore 'the dark side of the landscape' nor to reject intellectual modernity. Thomas's reputation has suffered both from the soft streak in English understandings of 'nature poetry' and from hard modernist or Marxist correctives like that of Raymond Williams in *The Country and the City* (1973), where Williams charges Thomas with nostalgic 'fantasy'.[2] While Thomas's prose partly succumbs to conventional tropes, his self-critical instinct ensured that he would see and work through them. Thomas was a theorist as well as practitioner of English pastoral, profoundly knowledgeable about its historical and contemporary incarnations in prose and poetry. As with the Romantics, this tradition – and a testing of it – informs deep strata of his poetry. And he could be as hard as Williams on writers who cry out for both 'a return to Nature and her beneficent simplicity' and 'a return to simplicity in literature'. Reviewing new poetry, he complained: 'These men are trying to write as if there were no such thing as a Tube, Grape Nuts, love of Nature, a Fabian Society' (*Daily Chronicle*, 30 August 1905).[3] Thomas did not especially like 'those wonders of our age', but knew that a serious 'love of Nature' must do more than wish them away. Not to employ urban imagery need not be to ignore the city. Thomas and London (in some respects, his literary matrix) is a neglected topic.

Asked by Walter de la Mare, in 1908, 'to define Nature', Thomas replied:

> I [use] it vulgarly for all that is not man, perhaps because man contemplates it so, as outside himself, and has a sort of belief that Nature is only a house, furniture etc round about him. It is not my belief, and I don't oppose Nature to Man. Quite the contrary. Man seems to me a very little part of nature and the part I enjoy least.

2 Raymond Williams, *The Country and the City* (London: Chatto and Windus, 1973), p. 258.
3 Included in Edna Longley, ed., *A Language Not to be Betrayed: Selected Prose of Edward Thomas* (Manchester: Carcanet, 1981).

But civilisation has estranged us superficially from Nature, and towns make it possible for a man to live as if a millionaire could really produce all the necessities of life – food, drink, clothes, vehicles etc and then a tombstone.[4]

In *In Pursuit of Spring* (1914) Thomas anticipates Rachel Carson's *Silent Spring* when he remarks that W.H. Hudson 'so writes of birds [in *Adventures among Birds*, 1913] that if ever, in spite of his practical work, his warnings and indignant scorn, they should cease to exist, and should leave us to ourselves on a benighted planet, we should have to learn from him what birds were'.[5] Thomas had already made some suggestions for saving the planet. In *The South Country* (1909), he outlines attitudes to Nature since the Romantic revival, and proposes an ideal 'Nature-study' that would fuse Romantic 'joy' with science – in effect, an ecological model: 'Knowledge aids joy by discipline . . . by showing us in animals, in plants . . . what life is, how our own is related to theirs, showing us, in fact, our position, responsibilities and debts among the other inhabitants of the earth'.[6] 'Earth' will be a prominent word in Thomas's poetry, and he takes a long historical, or eco-historical, view of our situation as its inhabitants: 'The eye that sees the things of today, and the ear that hears, the mind that contemplates or dreams, is itself an instrument of antiquity equal to whatever it is called upon to apprehend'.[7] In a climactic stanza of 'The Other', complex psychological and metaphysical conflicts are briefly assuaged when the speaker discovers himself to be 'An old inhabitant of earth'.

Thomas's ability to pull back from human parochialism (without compromising psychic complexity) at once belongs to and challenges the emergent literature of modern selfhood. What he had called, and called for – 'a diminution of man's importance in the landscape' (Preface to *British Country Life in Autumn and Winter*, 1908)[8] – is realised by the ecocentric structures of his poetry: by the 'position' of the 'I'-speaker, of human consciousness or the human figure, relative to other phenomena. The outer scene is not only accessory to an inner theatre: it also calls anthropocentric theatricals into question. Thomas's landscapes strategically diminish man's importance. People 'disappear', trees encroach on

---

4 Edward Thomas, *Selected Letters* (Oxford: Oxford University Press, 1995), p. 51.
5 Edward Thomas, *In Pursuit of Spring* (London: Thomas Nelson, 1914), p. 245.
6 Edward Thomas, *The South Country* (London: J. M. Dent, 1909), p. 144.
7 Thomas, *The South Country*, pp. 151–2.
8 Included in Longley, ed., *A Language Not to be Betrayed*.

dwellings; in 'The Mill-Water' Nature reclaims ground 'Where once men had a work-place and a home'. The amnesiac speaker of 'The Word' has forgotten 'names of the mighty men / That fought and lost or won in the old wars' but can recall 'a pure thrush word'. 'The Mountain Chapel' ends chillingly: 'When Gods were young, / This wind was old'.

Thomas's poetry seems dialectically poised in relation to the now-developing 'ecocritical' field. On the one hand, he is toughly anti-humanist, sometimes misanthropic ('the part I enjoy least'), in accepting that humanity might be surplus to the earth's requirements. On the other, he accepts that consciousness entails responsibilities: a later thrush poem contrasts the bird's song, empty of memory, with his own. Thomas moves between these poles in his images of how man and Nature have mutually constituted one another, as in the evolution of language. Here he is a deep cultural ecologist too. Again, the darkest direction of Thomas's symbolism – a projection from the condition of rural England and conditions in France – forebodes what is now termed 'environmental apocalypse'; yet his poetry also constructively probes that key ecological concept 'home'. 'The Green Roads' sets up these dialectics as a riddle:

> The green roads that end in the forest
> Are strewn with white goose feathers this June,
>
> Like marks left behind by some one gone to the forest
> To show his track. But he has never come back.
>
> Down each green road a cottage looks at the forest.
> Round one the nettle towers; two are bathed in flowers.
>
> An old man along the green road to the forest
> Strays from one, from another a child alone.
>
> In the thicket bordering the forest,
> All day long a thrush twiddles his song.
>
> It is old, but the trees are young in the forest,
> All but one like a castle keep, in the middle deep.
>
> That oak saw the ages pass in the forest:
> They were a host, but their memories are lost,

For the tree is dead: all things forget the forest
Excepting perhaps me, when now I see

The old man, the child, the goose feathers at the edge of the forest,
And hear all day long the thrush repeat his song.

Here the human actors (poet-speaker, old man, child) and the dwellings assigned the ability to 'look' co-habit with nettles, flowers, trees, geese and thrush. Mortality links man and Nature, or situates man in Nature. But there is also a partial standoff between them. The forest, like Thomas's 'old' wind, is associated with a power that engulfs historical record. The roads and feathers draw the eye towards the forest, its symbolism also mediated by the ear (by intricate refrain, including an unsettling mix of same rhyme and internal rhyme), and towards the oblivion that the dead oak figures. 'Middle deep' is an ambiguously reflexive phrase at the heart of the poem, since 'deep' could be as much noun as adjective. 'The Green Roads' incorporates a portrait of the 'green' artist. Once again poet and thrush are juxtaposed, as species perhaps, in a way that revises a Romantic trope. The poem enquires of itself whether it parallels the thrush's repetitive 'twiddle', or whether it evinces a finer capacity to see, hear and remember. The last couplet, an extended refrain that 'repeats' what the poem has 'seen', intensifies this enquiry. And, like the ending of 'Aspens', it implies that Thomas notices what other poets miss.

Thomas wrote 'The Green Roads' in June 1916, the month in which he applied for a commission in the Royal Artillery. It belongs, as does 'The sun used to shine', to the last phase of his poetry, departure to France being on the horizon. This is one reason why his forest-symbolism is taking on new tones of earthly valediction and apocalyptic foreboding. In 'Lights Out', 'the nettle towers' will be recast as 'the tall forest towers'. Thomas has been better appreciated as a 'war poet' since William Cooke, in *Edward Thomas: A Critical Biography* (1970), argued that the 'whole perspective . . . needs to be changed', and that Frost identified the 'true origin of Thomas's poetry' when he said it 'ought to be called Roads to France'.[9] Perhaps other 'origins', such as events in his unconscious and Frost's stimulus, also turned Thomas from prose writer into poet at the age of thirty-six. But the fact that he wrote his first poems in December

9 William Cooke, *Edward Thomas: A Critical Biography* (London: Faber and Faber, 1970), p. 212; p. 242.

1914, and that 'a long series of moods & thoughts' led him to enlist in July 1915,[10] attaches him to the small group of poets for whom the Great War was a perverse muse. Reading Thomas as a war poet has helped to change the view that 'Great War poetry' is synonymous with trench poetry. He can be called a poet of the home front, if 'home front' is construed as a disturbing oxymoron. His poetry takes the shock of the war's epistemological upheaval: green roads becoming roads to France, ploughmen 'dead in battle', the cross-roads in 'Aspens' turning 'to a ghostly room', the dead 'that never / More than half hidden lie' in 'Two Houses'. If 'France' partly stands for England in trench poetry, 'England' partly stands for France in Thomas's poetry.

But to call Thomas a war poet, or even to note his influence on later war-pastoral, is not quite enough. It's not just that his attitude to the war was so complicated – neither for nor against – or that he writes different kinds of 'war poem': war poetry itself remains a fuzzy critical category, hovering somewhere between aesthetics and politics. Thanks to his track record as critic and reviewer, Thomas was the poet best placed to adumbrate an aesthetic of war poetry, to resist the first wave of patriotic verse, to scan possible models (he nominated Coleridge's 'Fears in Solitude' because 'a large part of it is humble'), and to recognise that English poetry was implicated in the upheaval. He ended a largely scathing review-article 'War Poetry' by praising Hardy, and by prophesying: 'I should . . . expect the work of other real poets to improve as the war advances, perhaps after it is over, as they understand it and themselves more completely' (*Poetry and Drama*, 2, 8, December 1914).[11]

It can be equally said of Thomas, Charles Hamilton Sorley, Wilfred Owen, Isaac Rosenberg, Siegfried Sassoon and Ivor Gurney that out of the quarrel with Rupert Brooke they made war poetry. But, given Thomas's interests, he was the least likely to let Brooke appropriate 'England'. He conceived *This England* (1915), an anthology of poetry and prose into which he inserted two of his own poems, to counter the patriotic anthologies that starred Brooke's sonnets and spearheaded the cultural war effort. Thomas's preface explains that he has 'excluded professedly patriotic writing because it is generally bad'; and that he wants to 'remind others, as I did myself continually, of some of the echoes called up by the name of England'. 'Echoes' from the anthology itself get into 'Lob', as in the lines:

10 Edward Thomas, *Letters from Edward Thomas to Gordon Bottomley*, ed. R. George Thomas (London: Oxford University Press, 1968), p. 253.
11 Included in Longley, ed., *A Language Not to be Betrayed*.

'This is tall Tom that bore / The logs in, and with Shakespeare in the hall / Once talked, when icicles hung by the wall'. Thomas's quest for 'Englishness' (his preface calls this Shakespearean song 'most English') sometimes troubles critics, if not poets. Yet *This England* subversively breaks up Britain by 'never aiming at what a committee from Great Britain and Ireland might call complete'. Similarly, by shrinking his horizon to England or its local constituents, Thomas opened up the horizons of the English lyric. And just as his construction of England was conditioned by his Welsh hinterland and influenced by the Irish revival, so his posterity spans these islands.

The connection between *This England* and Thomas's origins as a poet suggests that the war precipitated a strange recall of English literature, especially poetry, as an infinitely subtle form of cultural defence. Folklore and Anon., as well as Chaucer and Shakespeare, are sewn into 'Lob'. Thomas's literary patriotism is not in the spirit of E. B. Osborn's anthology *The Muse in Arms* (1917). When the poem insists that 'Lob' 'lives yet', the target is not Germany but all who 'grind men's bones for bread'. 'Lives yet' also implies that the war has made English literature matter so vitally as to fire Thomas's own inspiration. His poetry's allusive links with the Romantic poets, English pastoral, and poet-contemporaries are part of the picture.

There are paradoxes here. The first is that Thomas the prose-writer struggled against bookishness, yet his poetry – invisibly packed with other poetry – makes his reading a constituent of new vision. The second is that Thomas's echoing allusiveness bypasses theorists of modernism, who may either need more obvious signposts or believe that 'nature poetry' invariably 'returns to simplicity'. The third is that Thomas's English version of poetic tradition, his enquiry as to whether it might be 'Worn new' (to quote 'Words'), is rarely compared with Yeats's Irish and Eliot's American versions. After all, 'Lob' could be read as a pre-emptive strike against *The Waste Land*, and Thomas's mixed reaction to Ezra Pound's early poetry included the prescient remark: 'If he is not careful he will take to meaning what he says instead of saying what he means' (review of Pound's *Exultations*, 1909).[12] Finally, despite Thomas's closeness to Frost, and his poetry's intertextual ramifications, he can be left slightly isolated in his period. For instance, he and Wilfred Owen are not consistently brought into aesthetic proximity – one result of the continuing tendency to read

12 Included in Longley, ed., *A Language Not to be Betrayed*.

Great War poetry thematically, or as the sum of its parts. It's a fallacy to think that, because Thomas and Owen never met, we cannot configure their roles in remaking the English lyric under extreme pressure.

Of all Great War poets Thomas and Owen were the most 'concerned with poetry', even if Thomas was fifteen years ahead of Owen with respect to arguments about poetry that had begun in the 1890s. The common ground on which they meet is the Romantic legacy combined with the aftermath of aestheticism. This shapes their different responses to Keats, for instance (Owen possessed Thomas's short book on Keats). It also brings them into the orbit of Symbolism. Before he wrote poetry, Thomas's reviews and critical works conducted a running quarrel with the 1890s and with Symbolist doctrines. Yet the quarrel was simultaneously a quarrel with himself: a quarrel that underlies his poems and sometimes surfaces, as in the dialectical structure of his miniature *ars poetica*, 'The Watchers':

> By the ford at the town's edge
> Horse and carter rest:
> The carter smokes on the bridge
> Watching the water press in swathes about his horse's chest.
>
> From the inn one watches, too,
> In the room for visitors
> That has no fire, but a view
> And many cases of stuffed fish, vermin, and kingfishers.

The antithesis here condenses key passages in Thomas's criticism, which often contrasts writing responsive to the pulse of life and language with a claustrophobic art of spectatorial distance, 'stuffed' images and 'dictionary words'. *Maurice Maeterlinck* (1911) contains his most sustained critique of symbolism.[13] Thomas dismisses a poem as 'a catalogue of symbols that have no more literary value than words in a dictionary'; and, despite his admiration for Yeats, he says of Yeats's essay 'The Symbolism of Poetry': 'when he comes to give examples of potent symbolism he finds them chiefly in writers like Burns who did not know the word'. He also queries Yeats's 'dead or merely private' symbolism in parts of *The Wind Among the Reeds*. Thomas's point is, first, that symbolism should derive from widely

---

13   Edward Thomas, *Maurice Maeterlinck* (London: Methuen 1911), pp. 18–34.

recognisable sources; second, that it should be mediated by the whole poetic fabric. He speaks of words supporting one another so that 'each word is living its intensest life'. This is what enables poems to become 'regions of the earth . . . separated from the rest and made independent'. There is finally little difference between Thomas's and Yeats's approaches to symbolism. Their poems depend in theory on symbol and poem being coterminous; in practice, on a nexus of image, syntax and rhythm (the counterpointed stanzas of 'The Watchers'). Significantly, both poets saw Imagism as a truncation, rather than purgation, of form. This may represent a refusal to cut ties finally with Romanticism; and, in Thomas's case, with English pastoral, which he pulls towards the condition of symbol.

To align Thomas with Yeats and symbolism (in its wider sense) is one way of situating his poetry in the modern movement. But it's less a matter of giving him modernist credentials than of promoting a less restrictive account of poetry in English between 1900 and 1922. Michael Roberts should have included Frost and Thomas in the *Faber Book of Modern Verse* (1936). Yeats himself, as in his contemporaneous *Oxford Book of Modern Verse*, mostly sits outside the academic narrative predicated on Eliot and Pound. In fact, some critics have persuasively 'modernised' Thomas by stressing the instabilities of his text and context, his self-estrangement and social alienation, his mingled desire and failure to recreate Romantic unities. In *Structure and Dissolution in English Writing, 1910–1920* (1999) Stuart Sillars refers Thomas's poem 'Old Man' to poststructuralist 'dissolution of self and dissolution of language in relation to objects'.[14] 'Old Man', which begins: 'Old Man, or Lad's-love – in the name there's nothing / To one that knows not Lad's-love, or Old Man', certainly denies any straightforward correspondence between word and thing. Puzzling over this plant's contradictory names and their relation to 'the thing it is', the speaker says: 'At least, what that is clings not to the names'. The poem famously ends: 'Only an avenue, dark, nameless, without end'.

Yet, if the gap between word and thing exposes a cognitive fissure, it also marks an ecological space where humanity and earth may associate and negotiate. Words acquire shades, language evolves by naming the world, and poetry internalises that evolution by allowing words to live their 'intensest life'. Thomas's dark forests and avenues symbolise prospects of cognitive nihilism as well as human absence. But he would have been surprised by the notion of some 'language poets' that you

14 Stuart Sillars, *Structure and Dissolution in English Writing, 1910–1920* (London: Palgrave Macmillan, 1999), p. 178.

liberate words by isolating them rather than by entering the evolving field of their historical, social and literary being to set them 'Fixed and free / In a rhyme' ('Words'). 'Rain' is another poem of dark symbolism:

> Rain, midnight rain, nothing but the wild rain
> On this bleak hut, and solitude, and me
> Remembering again that I shall die
> And neither hear the rain nor give it thanks
> For washing me cleaner than I have been
> Since I was born into this solitude ...

This soliloquy connects internal and external dissolutions, including death in war: 'Myriads of broken reeds all still and stiff'. Yet the poem's structures, like those of Yeats's 'Second Coming', do not fall apart. Refrain and assonance effect an ominous coherence. That Thomas gives seeming blank verse such intensity is one of his distinctive formal innovations.

'Remembering again that I shall die' situates 'Rain' in a present tense not just haunted, but constituted, by memory. The speaker seems to be remembering 'remembering'. The problem of memory pervades Thomas's poetry: 'They were a host, but their memories are lost', 'all things forget the forest'. Thomas grasps memory's slipperiness: that it is inextricable from forgetting and loss, that some forgetting is salutary, some a dark avenue. Other poems besides 'Old Man' are overtly constructed as efforts to remember, 'recall', 'call back', or equate the acts of writing and remembering. The self-image of 'The sun used to shine' (written from inside the war that proleptically haunts it) is 'memory's sand'. Thomas's syntactical inversions serve his interpenetrations of present and past. They take us into 'the middle deep'. The quester in 'Lob' says: 'And whether Alton, not Manningford, it was / My memory could not decide, because / There was both Alton Barnes and Alton Priors'.

Thomas knew that, considered as memory, literature or poetry belongs to an unstable series of transformations. At the end of 'Women He Liked', which traces a history of human negotiation with landscape, 'the name alone survives, Bob's Lane'. In *Richard Jefferies* Thomas says more positively: 'the things are forgotten, and it is an aspect of them, a recreation of them, a finer development of them, which endures in the written words'.[15] But 'what that is' will only endure if words themselves prove memorable. This may be why Thomas, like Yeats, reinvigorates traditional forms

---

15 Edward Thomas, *Richard Jefferies: His Life and Work* (London: Hutchinson, 1909), p. 298.

such as couplet and quatrain, and listens for the folk-ghost – surely present in 'The Green Roads'.

A late starter, like a prodigy, illuminates particular capacities of poetry. Besides their literary recall, Thomas's poems rework many passages from his own prose, and from years and layers of note-taking. Thus they carry with them their creative origins as a synaptic spark between short-term and long-term memory. Such memory-work partly belongs to the psychotherapeutic aspect of Thomas's poetry, which bridges Romantic and modern versions of subjectivity. Thomas was briefly a patient of Godwin Baynes who later became Carl Jung's main conduit in England. When he began to write poetry, one way in which stored-up memory emerged was as unresolved conflicts. Thomas's poetry relates to his neurotic past, or a past in which his neurosis was less controllable, as analyst to patient. His poems dramatise both roles. As in 'Rain', this structure sometimes crosses over to the cultural and literary meanings of 'going back to Edward Thomas' or forward from him. The prose passage behind 'Rain' includes the depressive sentence: 'Memory, the last chord of the lute, is broken'.[16] Thomas warns that there is such a thing as cultural breakdown or Alzheimer's, environmental collapse or apocalypse. Poetry, too, is an endangered habitat, like the 'lost homes' of which words are traces. So it matters that the quester does not give up, despite the confusing Manningfords and Altons. And if Edward Thomas's poetry is a kind of memory bank, or reconnects poetry with its own mnemonic origins, what it ultimately wants us to remember is poetry.

16 Edward Thomas, *The Icknield Way* (London: Constable, 1913), p. 282.

Edward Thomas in 1899.

I Cannot Tell: Edward Thomas's Uncertainties

JEM POSTER

Two publishing events of 1917, both appearing vastly more significant in retrospect than they could possibly have done at the time: in June of that year, *The Egoist* brought out T. S. Eliot's first collection, *Prufrock and Other Observations*, while October saw the publication by Selwyn and Blount of the first commercial edition of Edward Thomas's poems.

It's possible to interpret the alignment of those two events as evidence of a watershed in English-language poetry. On one side of the notional divide stands Eliot, American-born representative of a cosmopolitan urbanism, of careful obscurity and a knowing intellectualism – features which will subsequently come to be seen as diagnostic of literary modernism; on the other stands the displaced Welshman with his passionate interest in the rural, the parochial and the traditional. On this analysis, Eliot in 1917 represents the future and Thomas the past, a view reinforced by the fact that *Prufrock* laid the foundation for a literary career spanning the best part of the following half-century, while by the time his *Poems* appeared Thomas was already dead, victim of a war which itself seemed to mark a rift between old ways and new.

It's a tempting formulation but, like most neatly antithetical constructs, it doesn't stand up to close scrutiny. It's not only that it ignores Eliot's backward gaze, his famous preoccupation with a cultural history which, as he explains in 'Tradition and the Individual Talent', needs to be intimately understood by any modern poet worthy of the name; equally importantly, it overlooks crucial features of Thomas's writing, features suggestive of a strong affinity with his modernist contemporaries. I'm thinking in particular of the variform indeterminacies of the poetry – of the equivocations, hesitancies, questions and qualifications which reflect not merely Thomas's personal psychology but, more broadly, the concerns of the age.

In his 1985 biography, *Edward Thomas: A Portrait*, R. George Thomas highlights the debilitating neurasthenia against which Thomas struggled throughout his adult life, and it's not difficult to see the connection between the poet's condition and the patterns of his discourse. The obsessive weighing of alternatives, the uncommitted occupation of liminal

vantage points and the resistance to unambiguously progressive move-
ment are widely-recognised symptoms of depression; they are also, in
transmuted form, key features of Thomas's poetry. Robert Frost's slippery
and often misunderstood 'The Road Not Taken' was said by Frost himself
to be based on Thomas's vacillations during the two poets' regular walks
together through the countryside: 'No matter which road you take,'
Frost remembered saying to his friend, 'you'll always sigh, and wish
you'd taken another.' Frost's most recent biographer, Jay Parini, invokes
in this context 'the image of Thomas stuck at a crossroads, uncertain
about which branch to follow';[1] and although the image subtly misrepre-
sents Frost's poem – which dwells on regret rather than paralysis – there's
no doubt that Thomas's life and work were both deeply informed by
his consciousness of choice and dilemma.

But such matters need to be seen in their cultural context. Every
historical period might be described as an age of uncertainty for those
who live through it, but commentators tend to agree that the years from
1890 to 1930 – the period conventionally regarded as the age of European
modernism – were marked by an unusually acute sense of disturbance,
readily traceable in the artistic productions of the time. If we treat
Thomas's anxious deliberations as a purely personal matter, or examine
in isolation the elaborate indeterminacies of his poetry, we're likely to
miss significant correspondences – most notably with the poetry of
Eliot, who speaks, in accents not so very far removed from Thomas's own,
about matters the British poet would have recognised only too well. The
insistent questions, the elegant evasions, the self-conscious acknowledge-
ment of moral and verbal inadequacy, the explicit awareness of life as
offering scope 'for a hundred indecisions / And for a hundred visions
and revisions' – all of these seemed to contemporary readers to mark the
young American poet, together with his troubled, world-weary alter ego,
J. Alfred Prufrock, as representative of his time. Once we begin to register
the correspondences, it becomes clear that Thomas must be regarded as
similarly, if perhaps less knowingly, representative.

Approached from this angle, Thomas's poetry can be seen to exemplify
the near-paradox which lies at the heart of modernism itself: the vacilla-
tions and liminalities which might logically be associated with a failure
of impetus are actually a source of extraordinary artistic energy. This
is because, whatever else they may reflect, modernism's ambiguities are

1 Jay Parini, *Robert Frost: A Life* (London: Pimlico, 2001), p. 153.

bound up with a heightened awareness of plurality – of the richness of a multi-faceted world and the variety of ways in which that world can be interpreted. In this context, equivocation seems less a nervous mannerism than a necessary strategy, less a form of inhibition than the measured response to a perceived problem. It's the problem articulated by Virginia Woolf in the first novel of her maturity, *Jacob's Room*: the 'difficulty', as she sees it, is that 'we must choose. Never was there a harsher necessity! or one which entails greater pain, more certain disaster; for wherever I seat myself, I die in exile.'[2] The complexities of Woolf's style arose in part from her struggle to circumvent that difficulty; close reading suggests that a similar struggle helped to determine the patterns of Thomas's poetry.

I want to turn first to 'But these things also', a poem brief enough to allow quotation in full, and significant enough to merit it:

> But these things also are Spring's –
> On banks by the roadside the grass
> Long-dead that is greyer now
> Than all the Winter it was;
>
> The shell of a little snail bleached
> In the grass: chip of flint, and mite
> Of chalk; and the small birds' dung
> In splashes of purest white:
>
> All the white things a man mistakes
> For earliest violets
> Who seeks through Winter's ruins
> Something to pay Winter's debts,
>
> While the North blows, and starling flocks
> By chattering on and on
> Keep their spirits up in the mist,
> And Spring's here, Winter's not gone.

With the arresting opening line, Thomas establishes the equivocatory dynamic which governs the poem as a whole. 'But' and 'also' gesture out beyond the frame of the text to a vision of spring which, though

---

2 Virginia Woolf, *Jacob's Room*, ed. Sue Roe (Harmondsworth: Penguin, 1992), p. 57.

unarticulated, is nevertheless defined by implication as significantly different from that at the centre of the poem. What is privileged here is the intimate, the small-scale, the humble: closing in tightly on 'chip' and 'mite', the poet raises the possibility that the marginalised and unspecified alternative is an altogether more expansive view of spring.

I don't reject that possibility, but I want to bring into play a second reading, not inconsistent with the first: shell, flint, chalk and dung are not merely examples of unregarded littleness, but emblems of ambiguity. If, as we're explicitly told, they belong to spring, they also belong to winter: misleadingly mimicking spring's less equivocal manifestations – the violets – they simultaneously evoke and deny the arrival of the new season. The liminal position of the hopeful, deluded seeker parallels that of the speaker in 'March', a poem whose oscillatory phrasing insists on the unresolved tension at a similar point of transition: '. . . the wind was lost, / And yet 'twas cold, and though I knew that Spring / Would come again, I knew it had not come'. Both poems' conclusions pointedly withhold resolution. 'March' ends with a deferred half-promise communicated through the paradoxical agency of a speaking silence – 'a silence / Saying that Spring returns, perhaps tomorrow' – while the closing line of 'But these things also' leaves us trembling between contradictory alternatives.

Winter or Spring? We're not obliged to choose between the two; indeed, to put the matter more strongly, we're obliged not to choose. When, towards the end of To the Lighthouse, James finds himself confronted by the stark actuality of the tower, he sees that this doesn't simply cancel out the softer image he has carried with him through the years, but has to be accommodated alongside it: 'the other was also the lighthouse. For nothing was simply one thing. The other was the lighthouse too'.[3] For Thomas, as for Woolf, truth is more nearly approached through an interplay of alternative possibilities than through any monolithic statement. The equivocations of 'The Unknown Bird' are characteristic, indicative not of culpable vagueness on the poet's part but of the scrupulousness of his attempt to balance the antithetical suggestions of the bird's song:

> Sad more than joyful it was, if I must say
> That it was one or other, but if sad
> 'Twas sad only with joy too, too far off
> For me to taste it.

3 Virginia Woolf, To the Lighthouse, ed. Stella McNichol and Hermione Lee (Harmondsworth: Penguin, 1992), p. 202.

That last phrase points us towards a second, related source of indeterminacy in Thomas's poetry: again and again the poems pattern out an unfulfilled quest for a truth that lies beyond firm apprehension, and still further beyond clear definition. The bird's call seems 'far-off –/ As if a cock crowed past the edge of the world', and the speaker, now doubly distanced from the experience by the passage of time, seems repeatedly to approach his unseen quarry only to find that it has eluded him. He may have the call notes 'clear by heart', but the rendering of those notes ('La-la-la') tantalises the reader with its lack of specificity and recalls the earlier, more explicit frustration: 'I alone could hear him | Though many listened . . . | Nor could I ever make another hear.'

The uncertainties generated by partial or suspect recollection produce further complications. Even a simple matter of chronology raises questions – 'Was it but four years | Ago? or five?' – while a more complex interrogation of memory towards the close of the poem sets up tremors of doubt that resonate backward through the text:

> But I cannot tell
> If truly never anything but fair
> The days were when he sang, as now they seem.

'I cannot tell . . .'. By positioning that crucial phrase at the line's end, Thomas emphasises its inherent ambiguity: although our reading of the sentence as a whole must privilege the idea that the speaker is unable to *determine* the truth of things, it's difficult to exclude the demonstrably relevant secondary suggestion that he's unable to *articulate* that truth.

The unreliability of memory re-emerges as a dominant theme in 'The Word':

> There are so many things I have forgot,
> That once were much to me, or that were not,
> All lost, as is a childless woman's child
> And its child's children, in the undefiled
> Abyss of what can never be again.

That undistinguished opening couplet hardly prepares us for the delicacy of what follows as Thomas goes on to explore an absence characterised first as loss and then, through a subtly parenthesised similative sleight, as something even more extreme: the childless woman's child is – and

Thomas's phrasing pushes us inexorably towards the paradox – a non-existent entity, whose imagined, impossible offspring lead the mind down a recessive vista of nothingness.

As the poem progresses we're likely to become increasingly aware of the complexity of its argument. A superficial reading might register only the primary structure of that argument – in brief, that the speaker has lost track of many details of his past life and learning, but that there is one detail which, as a result of recurrent promptings, he is unable to forget. The argument appears to turn on the phrase 'But lesser things there are, remembered yet . . .', but the turn introduces not the clear-cut memory that might validate the statement, but a series of further indeterminacies:

> One name that I have not –
> Though 'tis an empty thingless name – forgot
> Never can die because Spring after Spring
> Some thrushes learn to say it as they sing.
> There is always one at midday saying it clear
> And tart   the name, only the name I hear.

'One name that I have not': the sentence continues, of course, beyond the parenthesis, but the phrase is held long enough in suspension to develop its own negative resonance, suggesting a meaning directly antithetical to the overt thrust of the sentence as a whole. And before we reach the other side of the parenthesis, Thomas destabilises us still further: a thingless name – a signifier with nothing to signify – is an impossibility of the same order as the childless woman's child in the first part of the poem. 'Only the name' echoes 'Adlestrop', but whereas, in that poem, the phrase opens a window onto a world of specific detail ('willows, willow-herb and grass, / And meadowsweet, and haycocks dry'), 'The Word' uses it to baffle us with meaningful indefinition. 'Clear and tart' recalls 'clear by heart' in 'The Unknown Bird' and functions in a similar way, with the speaker invoking a clarity which the text itself refutes.

Indefinition is, in fact, the subject of the poem. It's appropriate that Thomas should use the elusive, evocative scent of flowers and the slippery approximations of simile ('the elder scent / That is like food . . ./ . . . the wild rose scent that is like memory') as means of approaching his subject; and inevitable that the name or word he circles so obsessively throughout the second half of the poem should remain unspoken by him at its conclusion:

This name suddenly is cried out to me
From somewhere in the bushes by a bird
Over and over again, a pure thrush word.

The word's purity depends both upon the absence of any correlative in the material world – its 'thinglessness' – and its distance from human language. It's another example of the 'undefiled', a sound so absolutely unsullied by meaning, as we conventionally understand the term, that it can find no place either on human lips or on the printed page.

Nowhere does Thomas grapple more compellingly with the problem of naming the unnameable than in 'Old Man', arguably the finest and most richly complex of all his poems. Its opening insists, partly through emphatic repetition, on the importance of names:

Old Man, or Lad's-love, – in the name there's nothing
To one that knows not Lad's-love, or Old Man,
The hoar-green feathery herb, almost a tree,
Growing with rosemary and lavender.
Even to one that knows it well, the names
Half decorate, half perplex, the thing it is:
At least, what that is clings not to the names
In spite of time. And yet I like the names.

Even at the most basic level, nomenclature is revealed as problematic. Old Man, one of several popular names for *Artemisia abrotanum*, provides an obviously ambiguous title; and even as the speaker broaches his subject, the equivocations begin. It's not simply that the plant has more than one name, but that the names, suggestive of age on the one hand and youth on the other, pull in opposing directions. In what sense can either or both of these antithetical terms be said to define the plant itself?

The names in this instance are not exactly 'thingless', but the speaker identifies a troubling disjunction between name and thing. If you don't already know the plant, he suggests, the names convey nothing, while even if you do know it, they are still woefully inadequate. The equivocation of 'half decorate, half perplex' is more deeply destabilising than it might initially appear: these aren't the neatly balanced oppositions of (for example) 'half illuminate, half obscure', but a pair of alternatives which *both* imply frustration in the quest for meaning. Decoration seduces the eye and mind with surface detail, impeding the approach to a meaningful centre, while 'perplex', though primarily indicative of the disturbance set up by the interplay of signifier and signified, also hints at the speaker's bafflement as he attempts to close on his subject. 'I . . . try / Once more to think what it is I am remembering, / Always in vain.' The sense of frustration is palpable, recalling the despairing cry at the close of 'The Glory': 'I cannot bite the day to the core.'

The final stanza of 'Old Man' is – again one is driven to speak paradoxically – a masterly articulation of the inarticulable:

> I have mislaid the key. I sniff the spray
> And think of nothing; I see and I hear nothing;
> Yet seem, too, to be listening, lying in wait
> For what I should, yet never can, remember:
> No garden appears, no path, no hoar-green bush
> Of Lad's-love, or Old Man, no child beside,
> Neither father nor mother, nor any playmate;
> Only an avenue, dark, nameless, without end.

To interpret this negative consummation simply as a failure of apprehension would be to miss its deeper significance. It's not – or not merely – that the speaker is unable to lay hold of anything, but that nothingness itself has been revealed as the true focus of his contemplation. One thinks in this connection of Wordsworth's 'blank desertion' in the aftermath of his Patterdale adventure in the first book of The Prelude – of the 'darkness' in which he finds 'no familiar shapes / Of hourly objects, images of trees / Of sea or sky, no colours of green fields'. Like his predecessor, Thomas has been vouchsafed a glimpse of a formless emptiness which can be conceptually approached only through a series of negations.

Thomas's life and work are unusually resistant to conclusive summary. If we highlight the uncertainties that inform both, we must also register the determination with which Thomas followed his profession as a writer, as well as the soldierly resolution he appears to have discovered in himself in the period between his enlistment and his death. And I think, too, that the conclusion of 'Old Man' shows the poet pressing beyond the acknowledged uncertainties of life and language to a place of sombre, incontrovertible stillness; to a place where the divided spirit might find itself – to borrow a resonant phrase from Frost's 'Directive' – 'whole again beyond confusion'.

The Teenage Poet and the Edward Thomasy Poem

GUY CUTHBERTSON

Anyone forming an adjective from a writer's name has a number of suffixes to choose from: 'ian' is stately and solid; 'esque' is continental and flashy; 'ic' is cold and classical; 'like' is a little lax; 'ish' is ambiguous (remember Jonathan Miller's joke about being 'Jew-*ish*').[1] In 1972, W. H. Auden sent Cyril Connolly an old poem called 'Rain', describing it as 'the Edward Thomasy poem I can't recall writing'.[2] The 'y' suffix is jokey and friendly (Thomas created 'Frosty' out of his friend Robert Frost);[3] and in 'Thomasy' there is something of the schoolboy's nickname, a 'Smithy, the Bounder of Greyfriars'. In fact, Thomas had a considerable influence on the schoolboy Auden, and Gavin Ewart has said of Thomas's poems that 'they are very accessible to adolescents'.[4] Thomas's poetry is not adolescent, but it appeals to adolescents, and his influence on many of the poets of the twentieth century might be explained by the fact that poets took to him at an age when they were finding the style and subject-matter that would characterise their mature work. Auden and, say, Philip Larkin are evidence of how if you give Thomas to a poet at an impressionable age then, to some extent at least, he will be a Thomasy poet for life.

In this book, a number of the poets reveal that they have liked Thomas's poetry since their teens. Jeremy Hooker was moved by Thomas's poems when he discovered them at 'the age of seventeen or eighteen'. Helen Farish, who was born in 1962, begins by noting that 'My school girl's handwriting tells me on the title page of my copy of Thomas's *Selected Poems* that it's been in my possession since 19th December 1979'. Robert Wells is an exception because he was given Thomas's poems 'a few weeks

---

1 A *Beyond the Fringe* joke: 'I'm not really a Jew. Just Jew-*ish*'. See, for instance, Ned Sherrin, ed., *The Oxford Dictionary of Humorous Quotations* (Oxford: Oxford University Press, 1996), p. 77.

2 W. H. Auden, *Juvenilia: Poems 1922–1928*, ed. Katherine Bucknell (London: Faber and Faber, 1994), p. 110.

3 In 1915, Edward Thomas told John Freeman that 'since the first take off they haven't been Frosty very much or so I imagine'. Edward Thomas, *Selected Letters*, ed. R. George Thomas (Oxford: Oxford University Press, 1995), p. 106.

4 Ewart in Anne Harvey, ed., *Elected Friends: Poems for and about Edward Thomas* (London: Enitharmon, 1991), p. 135.

short of my fourteenth birthday' but 'didn't care for the poems at first' (although he warmed to them later). In some cases, the poets acknowledge Thomas's influence on their juvenilia. Tom Paulin describes reading Thomas's work while at Annadale Grammar School: 'It was the time I started to try and write poetry and prose, a very uncertain beginning, but it would have been even more uncertain if I hadn't read Thomas's poetry in my teens'. The poets of one's teenage years have a power that persists: David Harsent 'first read "Rain" when I was sixteen or seventeen' and, returning to it later in life, 'I was intrigued to find that I still had the poem by heart'. Robert Crawford says that 'a small number of his poems have pleasantly haunted me ever since school when our Welsh English teacher, Margaret Vickers, taught us the two Thomases'. Schools and schoolteachers are frequently recalled. Patrick McGuinness 'came across "Adlestrop" for the first time in school', and enjoyed it, as did James Nash, who has 'been aware of the poetry of Edward Thomas ever since I was at secondary school', where 'Adlestrop' was 'the first of his poems that I came across'. In addition, Bernard O'Donoghue points out that Thomas was popular amongst undergraduates at Lincoln, Thomas's college at Oxford.

Thomas wrote some poetry as an undergraduate, but he was barely a teenage poet,[5] and when he started to write the poetry of his *Collected Poems*, he was middle-aged. In fact, adolescence doesn't feature a great deal in Thomas's poetry, despite his having, during the previous two years, written about his own teens in 'How I Began' (1913), *The Happy-Go-Lucky Morgans* (1913), *The Childhood of Edward Thomas* (1938) and an unpublished 'Fiction', and written a book on Keats (1916).[6] Even the example of Thomas's juvenilia in R. George Thomas's edition of Thomas's poetry is a poem about an old woman, to be compared, as Thomas says, with 'Simon Lee, the Old Huntsman'.[7] Thomas is accessible to adolescents because he is not difficult, but also because, like Keats's, his work possesses characteristics that appeal to, or reflect, adolescence. For instance, there

---

5 Jon Stallworthy doesn't include a Thomas poem in his anthology of great poets' juvenilia, and ends his introduction by saying that 'it seems likely that Edward Thomas wrote his first at thirty-six'. Jon Stallworthy, ed., *First Lines: Poems Written in Youth, from Herbert to Heaney* (Manchester: Carcanet, 1987), p. 13.

6 Eleanor Farjeon edited Edward Thomas, *The Green Roads: Poems for Young Readers* (London: Bodley Head, 1965). There are four poems by Edward Thomas in Edward Blishen, ed., *The Oxford Book of Poetry for Children* (Oxford: Oxford University Press, 1963).

7 Some juvenilia is included at the back of R. George Thomas's edition of *The Collected Poems of Edward Thomas* (Oxford: Clarendon Press, 1978), p. 454. 'Headington Hill is steep' is on p. 458.

is the combination of beauty with decay, celebration with morbidity. In this sense, as well as others, Thomas is like A. E. Housman, on whom Auden commented that, to his generation, 'no other English poet seemed so perfectly to express the sensibility of a male adolescent'.[8] When David Harsent first read Thomas's 'Rain' at sixteen or seventeen, he found in it 'a sweet nihilism'. Gavin Ewart, in his poem 'Edward Thomas', notes that as a teenager he was attracted to Thomas because in the teens 'adolescent *à quoi bon?* | is mixed with what's romantic' (ll. 9–10). He goes on to say that

> The sadness and the wistfulness,
> the 'Lights Out' feeling, chimed
> well with our awkward, young distress.
> The whole thing was well-timed.
> (ll. 17–20)[9]

'Straightforward, nostalgic, wistful, they are very accessible to adolescents', said Ewart, who discovered Thomas's poems at the age of sixteen.[10] Thomas also shares with teenagers an inclination towards introspection, worrying about his identity and future, and it is combined with a feeling of, even love of, isolation – he was quite aware of his similarity to Hamlet.

Indeed, it was the subject matter of the poetry, rather than the style, that most appealed to Auden. The usual argument is that poets have picked up not what Thomas has to say but the way he says it; not what he describes but the way he describes. For instance, in a little book called *Twentieth-Century English Poetry: An Introduction* (1978), Anthony Thwaite says

> Thomas's special achievement in his poems was the rare one of speaking with an unforced, unrhetorical voice which is at the same time memorable in its timbre and cadences. Rhythmically, he is one of the subtlest poets in English; his language (with the exception of a handful of rather awkward archaisms and whimsies) is precise, evocative and haunting. His most characteristic subject-matter – the whole sense of rural England – was endangered when he wrote and is rapidly being engulfed now; only such a poet as

8   W. H. Auden, *Forewords and Afterwords*, ed. Edward Mendelson (London: Faber and Faber, 1973), p.332. For Housman's influence on Thomas, see Guy Cuthbertson, '"Bredon Hill" and "Adlestrop"', *The Housman Society Journal*, xxx (2004), pp. 163–6.
9   Ewart in Harvey, *Elected Friends*, p. 100.
10 Ewart in Harvey, *Elected Friends*, p. 135.

his namesake, R. S. Thomas in rural Wales, can nowadays come unselfconsciously close to such concerns.

Thwaite adds that Edward Thomas's poems 'are quite centrally part of an English tradition that continues today' but Thomas's contribution was his voice: 'The materials are different but the manner is pervasive'.[11] For the critics and poets who have promoted it, this English tradition, or English line, is frequently a tradition in which style, far more than subject-matter, links the poets together and distinguishes them from modernism. Yet Auden's early poetry, in particular, doesn't quite fit with this line of argument.

Auden's 'Rain' is Edward Thomasy because of its subject-matter (and its title) more than anything else: Thomas's interest in rain is well-known. Auden's 'Rain' is similar to Thomas's poem called 'Rain', and it is even closer to Thomas's 'It rains'.[12] Thomasy poems often involve rain, not least Alun Lewis's 'All Day It Has Rained', written in 1940. Admittedly, Auden's juvenilia also includes a poem called 'Woods in Rain', which was accidentally and wonderfully published under the name 'W. H. Arden', and that poem is W. H. Daviesy rather than Thomasy, but Auden's 'Rain' is just one of many Edward Thomasy poems in Katherine Bucknell's edition of Auden's *Juvenilia: Poems 1922–1928*. Bucknell's notes often mention Thomas, and, as she points out, Auden owned two copies of the 1920 edition of Thomas's *Collected Poems*, published by Selwyn and Blount – in one copy Auden wrote out, at the back, his poem about Edward Thomas, 'To E. T.', an especially Edward Thomasy poem; the other copy is, Bucknell says, 'battered and well-annotated in Auden's hand', and carries the date June 1924.[13]

Auden had decided to become a poet in March 1922. He discovered Edward Thomas's poetry in 1924, when he was seventeen. Right at the end of his life, in a poem called 'A Thanksgiving', probably written in May 1973, Auden wrote that 'when I started to verse, / I presently sat at the feet of / *Hardy* and *Thomas* and *Frost*' (ll.4–6).[14] 'There could not be better guides for a beginner' was A. L. Rowse's comment on these lines.[15] So Auden was

11 Anthony Thwaite, *Twentieth-Century English Poetry: An Introduction* (London: Heinemann, 1978), p. 38.
12 Thomas's poems are taken from *The Collected Poems*, ed. R. George Thomas (London: Faber and Faber, 2004).
13 Bucknell, ed., *Juvenilia*, by Auden, p. 100.
14 W. H. Auden, *Collected Poems*, ed. Edward Mendelson (London: Faber and Faber, 1991), p. 891.
15 A. L. Rowse, *The Poet Auden: A Personal Memoir* (London: Methuen, 1987), p. 134.

the first major poet to be influenced by Thomas's poetry, unless one counts Thomas Hardy, who might have borrowed the encounter in 'Out in the dark over the snow' for 'The Fallow Deer at the Lonely House', which was published in 1922.[16] It is possible that Auden was introduced to Thomas's poetry by Michael Davidson, the homosexual journalist who was close friends with Auden in 1923 and 1924. Davidson and Auden exchanged many letters about poetry, discussing Auden's poems but also the poetry of, among others, Edward Thomas.

It should be noted that *Lads: Love Poetry of the Trenches* (1989), Martin Taylor's anthology of homo-erotic war poetry,[17] includes three poems by Edward Thomas: some of Thomas's poems, 'The sun used to shine' for instance, offer a subject-matter that is congenial to the homosexual reader, the homosexual poet, and, most of all, the homosexual teenager. Edward Mendelson has noted that Auden discusses his own homosexuality in 'a poem he wrote probably when he was eighteen, in 1925, in the voice of Edward Thomas'.[18] Perhaps any adolescent might be drawn to Thomas's work by the hints of sex in poems such as 'The Chalk Pit', 'Tonight' and 'Lovers'.

The poems Auden wrote in 1924 and 1925 are especially Edward Thomasy. But during his years at Christ Church, Auden tried to put Edward Thomas to one side. Later, in 'Letter to Lord Byron' in 1936, Auden said that he 'forsook' Thomas and moved on to modernism:

> A raw provincial, my good taste was tardy,
>   And Edward Thomas I as yet preferred;
> I was still listening to Thomas Hardy
>   Putting divinity about a bird;
>   But Eliot spoke the still unspoken word;
> For gasworks and dried tubers I forsook
> The clock at Grantchester, the English rook.[19]

16 See Edna Longley's essay. Elsewhere, she has said that there is 'an interesting resemblance' between the two poems, and suggests that Hardy 'may have been influenced by the younger poet'. Edward Thomas, *Poems and Last Poems*, ed. Edna Longley (London: Collins, 1973), pp. 379–80. Andrew Motion is more convinced in *Interrupted Lives*, and suggests that Hardy and Thomas would have become friends if Thomas had survived the war. Andrew Motion, ed., *Interrupted Lives in Literature* (London: National Portrait Gallery, 2004), p. 46.

17 Martin Taylor, *Lads: Love Poetry of the Trenches* (London: Duckworth, 1989).

18 Edward Mendelson, *Early Auden* (London: Faber and Faber, 1981), p. 29.

19 W. H. Auden, *The English Auden: Poems, Essays and Dramatic Writings 1927–1939*, ed. Edward Mendelson (London: Faber and Faber, 1986), p. 195.

Hardy and Thomas 'were both defeated by Eliot at the battle of Oxford in 1926'.[20] Nevertheless, the gasworks should not be seen as the opposite, and the replacement, of Thomas's subject-matter: first, because Auden wrote about the gasworks and similar places in Edward Thomasy poems; second, because Auden's gasworks, and his disused industrial sites, were pre-empted by Thomas's disused work-places and decaying buildings. Auden's heavily-annotated copy of Thomas's *Collected Poems* bears a bookplate announcing that it was a prize presented by Gresham's School, Holt: 'W. H. Auden / Eccles Science Prize (Chemistry) / June 1924'.[21] Now, Thomas might not often be associated with Science or Chemistry, or Eccles for that matter, but Auden's interest in industrial England and the machinery of science was connected to his interest in the poetry of Edward Thomas (perhaps this is a valuable connection, if Thomas's association with the rural South Country puts some people off Thomas's poetry). Before Eliot, Thomas showed Auden that he could, and how he could, write about the gasworks, mines and machinery that Auden is still frequently associated with, and which Auden was so attracted to when he was a young boy on holidays in Yorkshire and Wales, or at home near Birmingham. 'We lived at Solihull, a village then; / Those at the gasworks were my favourite men', he says in 'Letter to Lord Byron'.[22]

It is worth looking closely at the poem that Auden seems to have been recalling when he wrote those two lines in 'Letter to Lord Byron' – a poem called 'By the Gasworks, Solihull', written in June 1924, which begins with that 'men/then' rhyme:

> This spot is loved by all wild things since men
> Left some old drain-pipes here; all the weeds then
> Had their way with them, until cow parsley,
> That the flies seem to love, stands five feet high
> At least; nettle and dock grow up together,
> And to the wren of all places, this is dear
> To pour his joy into; he always sings
> His loveliest among these broken things.[23]

Here we have those characteristics of Auden's juvenilia that Peter Porter has noted: 'The country metaphors / (That almanac birdsong, / Those

20 Auden in Mendelson, *Early Auden*, p. 28.
21 Bucknell, ed., *Juvenilia*, by Auden, p. 100.
22 Auden, *The English Auden*, p. 191.
23 Auden, *Juvenilia*, ed. Bucknell, p. 55.

Edward Thomas spores)' ('About Auden's Juvenilia', ll. 9–11).[24] This is possibly the first Edward Thomasy poem by W. H. Auden. It is quite a good poem, although one which is clearly, and heavily, indebted to Thomas's 'Tall Nettles'. Both poems are eight lines long; Thomas says 'Tall nettles cover up', Auden says 'nettle and dock grow up' and the cow parsley is five feet high; Auden describes 'This spot', Thomas describes 'This corner'; Auden describes old and broken things, Thomas describes rusty worn out things. But the poem also shows how Auden, even when he was seventeen, was keen and able to be different from Thomas. It is a poem that shows a young poet developing his own style and his own subject-matter, even if both were influenced by another poet. Auden's poem is not quite in the style of 'Tall Nettles': Auden's poem, about broken things, is more broken, more difficult; Thomas's poem is all ease and uses a simpler rhyme pattern. Auden is also somehow more knowing, detached, urbane (more Audenesque).

Auden's poem is also more urban. Solihull, in the Forest of Arden, was a village then, but it was also an ordinary suburb of Birmingham. Nonetheless, 'Tall Nettles' is a poem about disused machinery – the machinery of industry even. Auden describes 'some old drain-pipes', Thomas describes the rusty harrow, the plough, the roller. Auden's mines and disused industrial sites are related to 'Tall Nettles', and also, for instance, Thomas's 'The Barn', about the old barn that is now full of holes and covered in grass, 'The Chalk Pit', about 'a silent place that once rang loud' (l. 55), where no-one has dug chalk for a century, and 'The Mill-Water', about the old mill 'Where once men had a work-place and a home' (l. 32). Auden's favourite Thomas poems (poems that he marked in his copy of Thomas's *Collected Poems*, and also imitated) included those that portray disused buildings – poems such as 'The Mill-Water'. As Katherine Bucknell notes, Auden's 'The Mill', written in 1924, 'draws closely on Thomas's "The Mill-Water"',[25] and her note at the foot of Auden's 'The Sawmill', from May 1925, says that 'The influence of Thomas persists' – one could be more specific and say that the influence of 'The Mill-Water' persists.[26]

The neglected buildings and tools of industrial England might actually call to mind the world of the teenager. There is the Keatsian love of beautiful things, the optimism of youth, but also the melancholy and the

---

24 Peter Porter, *Dragons in their Pleasant Palaces* (Oxford: Oxford University Press, 1997), p. 4.
25 Bucknell, ed., *Juvenilia*, by Auden, p. 37.
26 Bucknell, ed., *Juvenilia*, by Auden, p. 93.

thoughts of death. The celebration goes hand-in-hand with the sense of decay: 'he always sings / His loveliest among these broken things'. Both of these sides are also captured by the rain that recurs in Thomas's poetry, such as 'Tall Nettles', and in Auden's. In 'Tall Nettles' Thomas refers to 'the sweetness of a shower' (l. 8) but it is associated with loss, while in 'Rain' the rain reminds Thomas that 'I shall die' (l. 3) but death is something he loves. Similarly, 'Tall Nettles' and 'By the Gasworks, Solihull' capture the mess and disorder of adolescence (one could even suggest that the corner of the farmyard in 'Tall Nettles' is the rustic equivalent of the teenager's bedroom). Moreover, poems like 'The Barn' and 'The Mill-Water', and Auden's 'By the Gasworks, Solihull' and 'The Pumping Engine, Cashwell', are about how the appearance of a place will change dramatically over time, which would seem to be rather relevant to adolescence, when one moves from childhood into adulthood. In the first stanza of 'The Barn', Thomas emphasises that the elm has grown up: 'then it was young. Now it is old' (l. 3). In 'By the Gasworks, Solihull', Auden notes that 'nettle and dock grow up together' (l. 5).

The border might also capture this time of transition, and just as the derelict industrial sites are there in Thomas's poetry, so too is the border, which has often been identified in Auden's work. Edward Mendelson notes that a frontier was first used by Auden in 1927: 'In Zagreb, in July, he opened a sonnet in the tones of Edward Thomas: "On the frontier at dawn getting down / Hot eyes were soothed with swallows".'[27] Thomas's poetry includes borders, though they are not between countries – Adlestrop is on the border between two counties, Oxfordshire and Gloucestershire; that border is a border that holds back neither bird-song nor trains. Thomas's borders are more humble: an inn stood 'on the border of a waste' ('Up in the Wind', l. 36); a road 'has a border new / Of purple hue / Inside the border of bright thin grass' ('After Rain', ll. 5–7). One frequent border is the point where the forest meets 'the sum / Of what's not forest' ('The Other', ll. 6–7). 'The Other' begins with the three-word sentence 'The forest ended' – he explains that 'I had come / To an end of forest' (ll. 4–5). 'I have come to the borders of sleep, / The unfathomable deep / Forest' is the start of one of Thomas's best-known poems, 'Lights Out'. There is, too, for instance, 'the thicket bordering the forest' in 'The Green Roads' (l. 9).

Gates and doorways are also frequently encountered in Thomas's work. In 'Over the Hills', the horizon, like the hedge, is a border:

27 Mendelson, *Early Auden*, p. 31.

Often and often it came back again
To mind, the day I passed the horizon ridge
To a new country, the path I had to find
By half-gaps that were stiles once in the hedge,
The pack of scarlet clouds running across
The harvest evening that seemed endless then
And after, and the inn where all were kind,
All were strangers. I did not know my loss
Till one day twelve months later suddenly
I leaned upon my spade and saw it all,
Though far beyond the sky-line.
(ll. 1–11)

The poem clearly influenced Auden's 'The Hidden Lane (Near Selbrigg, March 1925)', where 'I walked a little way until / I found a gate to lean upon' (ll. 13–14), and the road 'ran on till lost to view / Behind a shoulder of the hill' (ll. 18–19).[28] Mendelson argues that the frontier, the border between countries, wasn't used until 1927, but the teenage Auden produced a number of Thomasy poems in which gates, hedges and stone walls feature prominently, and these borders must be at least partly due to Thomas. 'The Mill (Hempstead)', of April 1925, begins: 'All features of the wood are known to me / For I have latched the gate which borders it'.[29] In 'It was upon', a poem similar to 'Over the Hills', Thomas does for once describe his teenage days, 'a score years' before he wrote the poem at the age of thirty-eight, and the stile before 'The earth outspread, / Like meadows of the future' does seem to represent that stage in his life:

It was upon a July evening.
At a stile I stood, looking along a path
Over the country by a second Spring
Drenched perfect green again. 'The lattermath
Will be a fine one.' So the stranger said,
A wandering man. Albeit I stood at rest
Flushed with desire I was. The earth outspread,
Like meadows of the future, I possessed.

And as an unaccomplished prophecy
The stranger's words, after the interval

28 Bucknell, ed., *Juvenilia*, by Auden, p. 86.
29 Bucknell, ed., *Juvenilia*, by Auden, p. 87.

Of a score years, when those fields are by me
Never to be recrossed, now I recall,
This July eve, and question, wondering,
What of the lattermath to this hoar Spring?

Auden's mature poetry is less Thomasy, but one could still identify Thomasy elements, not least because Auden was always interested in adolescence, and his opponents, such as Orwell and Leavis, condemned his poetry as the work of an undergraduate or even a schoolboy. The border is still there in his later work, most famously of all in 1935's 'Night Mail': 'This is the Night Mail crossing the Border, / Bringing the cheque and the postal order' (ll. 1–2).[30] More specifically, the border in 'Lights Out' seems to have contributed to a poem that Auden wrote several years after the juvenilia and the defeat of Thomas by Eliot at the battle of Oxford in 1926. In 'A Communist to Others', first published in September 1932, Auden wrote: 'We know the terrifying brink / From which in dreams you nightly shrink' (ll. 11–12).[31] This brings to mind Thomas's description of sleep in 'Lights Out', where he rhymes 'brink' with not 'shrink' but 'sink':

> Many a road and track
> That since the dawn's first crack
> Up to the forest brink
> Deceived the travellers,
> Suddenly now blurs,
> And in they sink.
> (ll. 7–12)

Similarly, Philip Larkin's earlier poetry is more Thomasy, and Audenesque, than his later work. Auden's 'A Communist to Others' was rewritten for *Look, Stranger!* in 1936, and *Look, Stranger!* is the Auden collection that, more than any other, attracted and influenced Larkin. In April 1941, while he was an eighteen-year-old undergraduate at Oxford, Larkin wrote a foreword to a collection of his called 'title poems 1941', in which he noted 'traces of the Auden manner' and said that 'towards the end the poems are to be judged solely by comparison with the Auden of "Look, Stranger!"': 'Auden's ease and vividness were the qualities I most wished

---

30 Auden, *Collected Poems*, p. 131. In *The English Auden*, they are the third and fourth lines of the poem.
31 Auden, *The English Auden*, p. 121.

to gain'.[32] When, a few weeks later, in a letter written on 7 and 8 May 1941, Philip Larkin told Jim Sutton that 'I've bought a half-crown edition of the Poems of Edward Thomas', and said that they are 'Bloody nice, really [. . .] his verse is really fairly modern', Larkin also added that 'You remember Auden liked him'.[33] Larkin discovered Thomas long before he discovered Hardy (and Larkin argued that 'I don't think Hardy, as a poet, is a poet for young people').[34]

Larkin's enthusiastic discovery of Thomas was repeated later in the decade by a first-year undergraduate called Marie in his story called 'Michaelmas Term at St Bride's': Marie arrives 'in high spirits, carrying a copy of *Oxford*, by Edward Thomas' and she says that 'It's marvellous!' (Thomas's book is practically a minor character in the story).[35] Thomas's *Oxford* (1903) also seems to have had an influence on Larkin's Oxford novel, *Jill* (1946), but it was Thomas's poems that had the most significant impact on Larkin. Thomas's poetry can be detected in the poetry that Larkin wrote as an undergraduate. To some extent, the influence might have come through Auden: for example, Stephen Regan argues that 'Hardy and Edward Thomas are echoed in "Out in the lane I pause"',[36] and even though that title might suggest Thomas's 'Out in the dark over the snow', Larkin wrote the Audenesque 'Out in the lane I pause' at Christmas 1940 before he had bought Thomas's poems, and later in life Larkin suggested that he hadn't read Thomas before 1941.[37] Thomas's influence is clearer in poems

---

32 Philip Larkin, *Collected Poems*, ed. Anthony Thwaite (London: Marvell Press and Faber and Faber, 1988), p. xix.

33 Hull, Brynmor Jones Library, Hull University Archives, The Larkin-Sutton Letters, MS DP/174/2/22, f. 13r. Larkin might have remembered Thomas and 'Letter to Lord Byron' in early 1941 because Alun Lewis's 'All Day It Has Rained' was printed in the January 1941 issue of *Horizon*. Larkin read and admired *Horizon* when he was as an undergraduate (so on 7 April 1942, he mentioned the Year's Poetry in *Horizon*' in a letter to Norman Iles). The January 1941 issue of *Horizon* also contained a review by Lewis of *The Trumpet and Other Poems*, a Faber and Faber selection of forty-five poems by Thomas, sold at 2s 6d – this was the 'half-crown edition of the Poems of Edward Thomas' that Larkin mentioned to Sutton.

34 Philip Larkin, *Required Writing* (London: Faber and Faber, 1983), p. 175.

35 Philip Larkin, *Trouble at Willow Gables and Other Fictions*, ed. James Booth (London: Faber and Faber, 2002), p. 158. Also see Guy Cuthbertson, 'Back to the Oxford Country', *Oxford Magazine*, 219 (Fourth Week, Michaelmas Term 2003), pp. 8–9. Stephen Cooper has noted Thomas's 'pervasive influence' on both 'Michaelmas Term at St Bride's' and its predecessor, 'Trouble at Willow Gables'. Stephen Cooper, *Philip Larkin: Subversive Writer* (Brighton: Sussex Academic Press, 2004), p. 31.

36 Stephen Regan, *Philip Larkin* (Basingstoke: Macmillan, 1992), p. 71.

37 In January 1974, Larkin said that 'I do like Thomas and always have, since 1941'. Philip Larkin, *Selected Letters*, ed. Anthony Thwaite (London: Faber and Faber, 1992), p. 501.

written in the months after he bought Thomas's poems. To take one example, the poem 'Blind through the shouting sun', written in the first half of 1942, contains this central stanza:

> The hedge's eager hands stretch green towards me
> And I am free
> To snap a spray, twist it, gaily or cruelly[38]

In 'Old Man', Thomas's daughter 'plucks a feather from the door-side bush' (l. 11), and is seen 'snipping the tips and shrivelling / The shreds' (ll. 13–14), and then Thomas says: 'I, too, often shrivel the grey shreds, [. . .] I sniff the spray' (l. 26; l. 32).

Over a period of three and a half years after May 1941, Larkin wrote *The North Ship* (1945), and in several places that collection is very similar to the subject-matter and vocabulary of the poetry of Edward Thomas.[39] For instance, Thomas's 'Will you come?', with its lines 'the night / Has a moon, / Full and bright' (ll. 9–11) could lie behind Larkin's 'The moon is full tonight', which begins 'The moon is full tonight / And hurts the eyes, / It is so definite and bright'.[40] 'This was your place of birth, this daytime palace' contains lines that echo Thomas's 'The long small room', regarding which Peter Levi commented that 'We had to wait for Larkin for any more poems like that'.[41] Thomas's poem ends:

> One thing remains the same – this my right hand
>
> Crawling crab-like over the clean white page,
> Resting awhile each morning on the pillow,
> Then once more starting to crawl on towards age.
> The hundred last leaves stream upon the willow.
> (ll. 12–16)

At the centre of Larkin's poem, there are these lines:

38 Philip Larkin, *Early Poems and Juvenilia*, ed. A. T. Tolley (London: Faber and Faber, 2005), p. 184. The poem is not in *Collected Poems*.

39 More was said on this in a paper called '"Really fairly modern": Edward Thomas and *The North Ship*', which I gave on 30 June 2002 at 'Larkin in Context: The Second Hull International Conference on the Work of Philip Larkin', University of Hull (28–30 June 2002).

40 Larkin, *Collected Poems*, p. 274.

41 Peter Levi, 'Notes on Edward Thomas', *The Art of Edward Thomas*, ed. Jonathan Barker (Bridgend: Poetry Wales Press, 1987), p. 29.

To puzzle out the name, or with a hand
Resting a second on a random page –

The clouds cast moving shadows on the land
(ll. 6–8)[42]

That last line matches the detached statement at the end of 'The long
small room', but it is probably echoing the start of another Thomas
poem, 'Song [2]': 'The clouds that are so light / Beautiful, swift and
bright, / Cast shadows on field and park' (ll. 1–3).

In fact, in March 1947, not long after *The North Ship* was published,
Kingsley Amis announced to Larkin that 'I have just bought Ed. Thomas's
poems' and 'Some of them are very like you' – he added that '*This is
intended as a comp. limb meant*'.[43] Nonetheless, what Larkin called 'Thomas's
meditative, fitful wandering line'[44] is hardly found in *The North Ship* or
Larkin's other poems of the period. Larkin's later poetry, with which
he moved into the English line, is closer to Thomas's distinctive conversa-
tional and personal voice. Edna Longley has identified Thomas's influence
on Larkin's later work, as well as 'a significant coincidence and continuity
of effort', and in January 1974 Larkin admitted that 'Longley has certainly
noticed something no one else has, if she's right – and I do like Thomas
and always have, since 1941'.[45] Equally, Auden is supposed to have
replaced Thomas with Eliot in 1926, but Thomas still lingered. Even in the
summer of 1927, Auden and Cecil Day Lewis included Thomas in their
'extremely short' list of 'the poets whom we had little hope of ever
equalling'.[46] In 'A Thanksgiving', written towards the end of his life, Auden
thanks the poets who influenced him, including Thomas: 'without You
I couldn't have managed / even my weakest of lines' (ll. 29–30).[47]

42 Larkin, *Collected Poems*, p. 265.
43 Kingsley Amis, *The Letters of Kingsley Amis*, ed. Zachary Leader (London: HarperCollins,
    2000), p. 127.
44 Philip Larkin, 'Keeping Up with the Graveses' (15 May 1959), *Further Requirements*
    (London: Faber and Faber), p. 206.
45 Larkin is referring to Longley's essay called 'Larkin, Edward Thomas and the Tradition',
    Phoenix, 11–12 (Autumn-Winter 1973–74), pp. 63–9. Philip Larkin, *Selected Letters*, ed.
    Anthony Thwaite (London: Faber and Faber, 1992), p. 501. Longley later developed the
    essay into '"Any-angled Light": Philip Larkin and Edward Thomas' in Edna Longley,
    Poetry in the Wars (Newcastle: Bloodaxe, 1986). She says: 'I am less concerned with
    any possible "influence" of Thomas on Larkin than with a significant coincidence and
    continuity of effort'. Longley, *Poetry in the Wars*, p. 116.
46 C. Day Lewis, *The Buried Day* (London: Chatto and Windus, 1960), p. 178.
47 Auden, *Collected Poems*, p. 892.

Manuscript of 'Roads', in the Bodleian Library, Oxford (MS. Don. d. 28, f. 22r).

'The shape of the sentences':
Edward Thomas's tracks in contemporary poetry

LUCY NEWLYN

> Tell them how
> You walked and how you saw, and how your pen
>   Did nothing more than that,
> And, when it stopped, what you were gazing at.
> (Glyn Maxwell, 'Letters to Edward Thomas')

Several motifs and images from Edward Thomas's writing are repeatedly evoked in contemporary poetry: rain, nettles, place-names, disused buildings; the bitter scent of 'Old Man'; the train stopping in the middle of nowhere. But none of these has been as productive of associations and allusions as the path or road, and its accompanying figure of the walker.[1] With or without his accoutrements – knapsack, map, walking-stick, notebook – Thomas is chiefly remembered as a wayfarer whose identity was linked with the open road.

Even in his lifetime, Thomas the walker achieved an iconic status. Gordon Bottomley likened him, in a poem of 1907, to Matthew Arnold's 'Gypsy-Scholar',[2] and Clifford Bax and Herbert Farjeon wrote a light-hearted picaresque poem about him in 1913, called 'Walking Tom'. Frost saw him as a 'traveller' pausing at a crossroads in his poem 'The Road Not Taken', and in a later poem, 'Iris by Night', Thomas and Frost are figured as 'one another's guide.'[3]

Further tributes published after Thomas's death picked up the walking motif. The Welsh bard Gwili immortalised Edward Eastaway as a wanderer amongst the caves and castles of his 'mother Wales'.[4] Helen Thomas remembers walking with him as one of the happiest experiences of their

---

1 For the significance of footpaths in English literature, see Kim Taplin, *The English Path* (Sudbury: Perry Green Press, 2000).

2 Anne Harvey, ed., *Elected Friends: Poems for and about Edward Thomas* (London: Enitharmon, 1991), p. 15.

3 Robert Frost, *The Poetry of Robert Frost*, ed. Edward Connery Lathem (London: Jonathan Cape, 1971).

4 *Elected Friends*, ed. Harvey, p. 24.

married life; but she associates his solitary walks with a darker, more desperate side of his temperament: he would often 'walk and walk far into the night', she recalls, and 'come home, worn out with deadly fatigue.'[5] Eleanor Farjeon fondly evokes him as a walking companion – chiefly in *The Last Four Years*, but also in a selection for children, *The Green Roads*. He was, she says, 'wonderful to walk with, and talk with, and not to talk with. And when he was alone . . . he walked with *himself.*'[6] Numerous twentieth-century poets, including Sylvia Townsend Warner, Alun Lewis, and Elizabeth Jennings, identified with Thomas through the action of walking. Indeed, it seems that Thomas the pilgrim has become an object of pilgrimage[7]: Anne Harvey's collection, *Elected Friends*, contains no fewer than nine poems describing the climb to his memorial stone in Steep, which bears the apposite inscription, 'and I rose up and knew that I was tired, and continued my journey'.

Walking was an antidote for the depression that periodically gripped this 'somewhat sharply unhappy man.'[8] As a 'doomed hack'[9] obliged to live near London, but moving from one rented accommodation to another around the 'Home' counties, Thomas sensed that he had lost his Welsh roots, that he had 'no particular home'.[10] He once described himself as 'one of those modern people who belong nowhere.'[11] There is a feeling of *displacement* in his writing – a restlessness, or spiritual malaise – expressed through the figure and action of walking. It is well-caught in a short story of his, 'The Pilgrim', in which he imagines meeting a young man seeking to be 'born again'. Thomas links this dissatisfied, driven figure with himself, surmising that he is 'perhaps a poet of a kind, who made a living out of prose.'[12] The spiritual associations of journeys were never far from his mind, even in his most minutely topographical writing. *The Icknield Way* touches on the symbolism of roads, 'with their beginnings

5   Helen Thomas, *As It Was* (London: Faber and Faber, 1971), p. 47.

6   Eleanor Farjeon, *Edward Thomas: The Last Four Years* (Oxford: Oxford University Press, 1958), p. 6; p. 232.

7   Guy Cuthbertson has written about literary pilgrimages in his doctoral thesis, *The Literary Geography in Edward Thomas's Work* (Oxford, 2004); and he alludes to the importance of pilgrimage above, in the introduction to this book.

8   John Powell Ward, *The English Line: Poetry of the Un-poetic from Wordsworth to Larkin* (London: Macmillan, 1991), p. 142.

9   A phrase used by Thomas to describe Mr Torrance, a character (partly self-portrait) in *The Happy-Go-Lucky-Morgans* (London: Duckworth, 1913), p. 127.

10 From a passage by Thoreau, quoted in *Horae Solitariae* (London: Duckworth, 1902), pp. 7–8.

11 Edward Thomas, *The South Country* (London: Dent, 1909) p. 10.

12 Edward Thomas, *The Ship of Swallows*, ed. Jeremy Hooker (London: Enitharmon, 2005), p. 82.

and ends always in immortal darkness'[13]; and in *The South Country* he echoes Whitman by evoking 'the endless pale road, before and behind, which the soul has to travel.'[14]

Thomas loved 'The Scholar Gypsy', with its evocation of wandering as an escape from the 'strange disease of modern life' (l. 203).[15] But walking was not an escape for Thomas, so much as a vocation: 'For him working and walking went together. His long legs and his hawk's eyes were part of his stock-in-trade'.[16] Earning his living by writing country books, he walked numerous roads in Kent and Surrey, Wiltshire and Hampshire, often describing them in minute detail. During his life-time he was seen chiefly as a freelance writer who knew the south of England like the back of his hand. Eleanor Farjeon remembers him using large maps, and 'finding his way up hill and down dale by the contour-shading where no footpaths were marked'[17]: a skill that came in handy when he was a map-reading instructor during the war. By all accounts, though, he did not always use a map in his pre-war walks, preferring to 'saunter'.[18] *The Icknield Way* follows a careful itinerary; but in *The South Country*, a book he associated with freedom, he comments on the pleasure of being 'guided by the hills or the sun or a stream.'[19]

Thomas's prose-style was shaped by the rhythm, experience, and literature of walking. From very early on, he understood how a relaxed walking pace can stimulate the thinking process. 'His gait when walking was easy, never hurried,'[20] like his style. He saw analogies between the movement of roads and the way thoughts branch sideways, or pause to take in random and fleeting associations, without losing their sense of direction. As David Gervais observes, 'His most typical way of looking at nature is by walking deeper and deeper into it, through a searching that is itself a metaphor for thought.'[21]

Thomas's taste in prose reflected his habits as a walker. He identified

---

13 Edward Thomas, *The Icknield Way* (London: Constable, 1913), p. vii.
14 Thomas, *The South Country*, p. 79.
15 Matthew Arnold, *The Complete Poems*, ed. Kenneth Allott; second edition by Miriam Allott (Harlow: Longman, 1987), p. 366.
16 Eleanor Farjeon, 'Walking with Edward Thomas'; *The Last Four Years* (Stroud: Sutton, 1997), p. 278.
17 Ibid.
18 See Lucy Newlyn, '"Having no particular home": Edward Thomas and sauntering', *Dymock Poets and Friends*, 5 (2006).
19 Thomas, *The South Country*, p. 11.
20 Eleanor Farjeon, 'Walking with Edward Thomas', p. 278.
21 David Gervais, *Literary Englands* (Cambridge: Cambridge University Press, 1993), p. 46.

with previous walkers (Iolo Morganwg, Hazlitt, Borrow), and with a line of peripatetic writing that included Richard Jefferies, as well as Whitman and Thoreau. He described his predecessors closely, noticing their mannerisms in walking and writing: Jefferies, for instance, 'taking long strides, or swinging his arms with a good stick', was 'always a walker, moving about and taking notes. . . . [His writings] resemble the record of an actual walk, and of whatever is seen and thought in the course of a walk.' [22] Jefferies was an important model for pedestrian style, but there were others. Imitating the Romantic familiar essayists, Thomas trained his sentences to follow an easy, meandering pattern, accommodating obstacles and pauses, as well as distractions *en route*.[23] This ambulatory motion enabled him 'by taking a series of turns to the left or a series to the right, to take much beauty by surprise.'[24]

For Thomas, walking and talking had much in common, in books as in life. Both were traditionally seen as levelling activities – walking, because it is a means of travel everyone can afford; and talking, because it is a more immediate and universal mode of communication than writing. Both provided analogies for digressive style; and were linked in the English dissenting tradition, where road-travel is associated with plain speech, hardship, and the quest for spiritual truth. In this genre, encounters with travellers on the open road are important staging-posts in the journey towards self-discovery; and they often use reported speech. *Pilgrim's Progress*, 'full of plain English country wayfaring,'[25] belongs to this tradition, as does Cobbett's *Rural Rides* and Hazlitt's 'On Going a Journey' – works that Thomas admired, and mentioned frequently.

As his writing matured, Thomas explored the connections between wayfaring, speech, and prose-style. Plain speech is frequently used or evoked in his accounts of the daily occupations of country life, and chance encounters while travelling. In *The Icknield Way*, he incorporates the lives and language of England's 'vital commoners'[26] into the places he describes – recording his conversations with people he met on his journeys. *In Pursuit of Spring*, written during 1913, celebrates his affinities with Wordsworth and Coleridge. Describing his pilgrimage to Nether

22 Edward Thomas, *Richard Jefferies: His Life and Work* (London: Hutchinson, 1909), p. 78.
23 See Lucy Newlyn, 'Hazlitt and Edward Thomas on Walking', *Essays in Criticism*, lvi, 2 (April 2006).
24 Thomas, *The South Country*, p. 11.
25 Thomas, *The Icknield Way*, p. 7.
26 The phrase occurs in his anthology, *This England* (1915), where it is used as the heading for a section of excerpts.

Stowey in Somerset, the birth-place of *Lyrical Ballads*, Thomas implies his allegiance to the radical agenda of that volume: its concern with 'incidents and situations from common life',[27] and with people who lived on the open road. Wordsworth's identification with vagrants and travellers chimed with a lifelong interest of his own, in tramps and gypsies.

Thomas's emergence as a poet could not have taken place without his experience as a writer of pedestrian prose. But the catalyst for this transformation, when it eventually came, was his friendship with Robert Frost, who shared his interests in walking, talking, and style. Thomas did not come under Frost's influence until 1914. In the lead-up to this decisive year, he thought a great deal about style – his own and others' – and especially about the relationship between speech-patterns and writing. He had always written for the 'common reader', and although he started his career using an artificial register (influenced chiefly by Walter Pater), he increasingly favoured conversational language. In his critical works, too, he expressed a preference for natural speech cadences. He admired the 'effortless, and in places almost slipshod' style of Jefferies's *The Gamekeeper*, noting that 'the breath of elaboration might have made it less rustic'; and he praised Jefferies's last essays, when he was 'dictating, not writing', because 'there is no long-sought *mot propre* intruding upon the sentences that are like speech . . . nothing ornate, nothing luxurious, the eye is quiet.'[28] In many places, as Edna Longley has shown, Thomas anticipates Frost's credo: 'We must write with the ear or the speaking voice. We must imagine the speaking voice.'[29]

As early as his student days, Thomas had shown an interest in the similarities between prose and poetry, seeing the potential for a cross-over which in due course proved relevant to his own career. As his emphasis on the importance of speech-rhythms grew, so too did his interest in the poetics of prose. Like Wordsworth, he saw no *essential* difference between prose and poetry, only a difference in quality. He found poetic ingredients in the vernacular, just as he admired verse dealing with humdrum or 'prosaic' subject-matter. In *Maurice Maeterlinck* he observed that 'Anything, however small, may make a poem: nothing, however

27 Preface to *Lyrical Ballads* (1800); William Wordsworth, *Selected Prose*, ed. John O. Hayden (Harmondsworth: Penguin, 1988), p. 281.

28 *Richard Jefferies*, p. 125; p. 151.

29 Robert Frost, *Selected Letters of Robert Frost*, ed. Lawrance Thompson (London: Jonathan Cape, 1965), p. 427. Edna Longley, in her introduction to *A Language not to be Betrayed* (Manchester: Carcanet, 1981), charts the progress of Thomas's prose style in detail; and both she and Andrew Motion have observed his anticipations of Frost.

great, is certain to,'[30] and he would later refer to his own poems as 'quintessences of the best part of his prose books.'[31] It seems that he was 'on the look-out for the poet who could release his own poetry'[32] when he read *North of Boston*, met its author, and struck up the most important friendship of his life.

'1914 was our year' Frost later recalled: 'I never had, I never shall have such a year of friendship.'[33] Both poets experienced something akin to the collaborative excitement of Wordsworth and Coleridge in 1798, as they explored their common interests and enthusiasms – including the pleasures of walking and talking. Four retrospective poems of friendship, as well as Thomas's essay 'This England', grew out of walks taken in each other's company at this time.[34] The memory of walking together became a metaphor for their easy, harmonious interchange of ideas. Thomas's 'The sun used to shine' especially 'says more than any other what walking with Edward Thomas could be when the two are in perfect accord, as these two were . . . when the silences fell easily on speech and thought.'[35] The actual conversations of the friends while walking are, in the nature of things, irrecoverable. But Thomas recalled that they 'turned from men or poetry / To rumours of the war remote' (ll. 8–9); and it is likely that they touched repeatedly on the crucial question of speech-cadences in writing.

What Frost awakened in Thomas was nothing more nor less than what Thomas awakened in Frost: confirmation of the poetic possibilities of prose. In *North of Boston*, Frost's collection of blank-verse eclogues, which he reviewed three times in 1914, Thomas discovered aesthetic allegiances that closely corresponded to his own.[36] Frost used colloquial language to tell powerful, simple stories. His roots went back into *Lyrical Ballads*, finding poetic materials in rural life and the dignity of labour. His register was that of the familiar walking-talking companion, in touch with the Protestant traditions of proverb and parable. He sometimes attempted a

30 Edward Thomas, *Maurice Maeterlinck* (London: Methuen, 1911), p. 28.
31 Letter to John Freeman; see John Moore, *The Life and Letters of Edward Thomas* (London: Heinemann, 1939), p. 326.
32 John Lucas, *Starting to Explain: Essays on Twentieth-Century British and Irish Poetry* (Nottingham: Trent Books, 2003), p. 65.
33 Frost, *Selected Letters*, p. 220.
34 Possibly Frost's 'The Road Not Taken'; certainly his later 'Iris by Night'; and Thomas's 'The sun used to shine' and 'A Dream'.
35 Farjeon, 'Walking with Edward Thomas', p. 283.
36 All quotations from the reviews of *North of Boston* refer to *Elected Friends: Robert Frost and Edward Thomas to One Another*, ed. Matthew Spencer (New York: Handsel Books, 2003), pp. 16–25.

redaction of actual speech, at other times a characterisation of 'common speech'; but what interested him most was the mannerisms that dramatise the speaking voice. Thomas observed that Frost's medium was distinguishable from prose in one important respect: it was 'closer knit and more intimate than the finest prose is except in its finest passages'. Reading Frost was, for Thomas, like reading the best passages of his own prose, translated into blank verse; and the final sentence of his review sounds the quiet note of recognition: 'It is poetry because it is better than prose.'

Thomas's development of a 'pedestrian' prose style – one that explored the three-way connection between walking, talking, and sentence structure – was fully developed by the time he met Frost. But the stimulus of his friend's ideas caused him to think about how this style could be adapted to the writing of verse; and in particular how he could make poetic use of the convergence between a walking pace and a talking rhythm. Frost persuaded him that his gift for poetry lay hidden in his most recent prose (*In Pursuit of Spring* was published in 1914); and strengthened his love of the vernacular. Through encouragement and example, the American poet enabled the English one to 'transform traditional metres by feeding them the roughage of speech.'[37] Under Frost's guidance, Thomas made his first experiments in writing poetry. He began by revisiting passages of recent prose and translating them into verse; then later gathered confidence to start from scratch. 'I am trying to get rid of the last rags of rhetoric and formality which left my prose so often with a dead rhythm only', he wrote in December 1914.[38]

As a walker, Thomas was interested in how journeys are shaped by starting out and coming to an end; and how roads themselves seem to 'go', like those who travel on them.[39] His pilgrimage books convey the sense of long journeys by using the rhythms of the day – the sun's rising and setting – to give each segment of the journey a sense of completion. In poetry, he achieved his effects more tersely. Just as Hardy rose to the challenge of collapsing plots suitable for novels into ballads of three or four stanzas, so Thomas created miniature journeys. Their symbolic resonances are not spelt out, any more than in the Bunyan-esque moments of his prose; and he never wrote anything with quite the proverbial force of Frost's 'The Road Not Taken'. But poems like 'The Signpost', 'The Path', 'Over the Hills', 'Roads', and 'Lights Out' belong to a parabolic tradition

37 Edna Longley, *Poetry in the Wars* (Newcastle upon Tyne: Bloodaxe, 1986) p. 26.
38 Farjeon, *The Last Four Years*, p. 110.
39 Thomas, *The Icknield Way*, p. 2.

of wayfaring. 'A walk to Thomas was like a quest', writes David Gervais: 'Paths gave him a metaphor for knowing.'[40]

A devotion to the local and the particular is one of the many things Thomas's prose had in common with the poetry of Wordsworth and Clare. He shared with them a preference for the humble details of rustic life; and for what he called 'the commonwealth of things.'[41] In his topographical books, he used realistic notation and inventories to catch fleeting impressions of the nearby, the accidental and the ordinary, instead of trying for grand prospects and picturesque compositions. He liked rain, because it 'keeps the eyes down so they see one-by-one the little things of the wayside';[42] and he preferred walking to cycling, for the same reason. When he took up verse, his skill in using images he had 'happened on' in the course of a walk bore fruit in poems like 'But these things also' and 'Tall Nettles', which have become touchstones of his gift for cherishing little-regarded things. Essential to this gift is what Jeremy Hooker calls his 'clear prose sense', his use of details noted in passing by the road-side. His poetry shows the wayfarer's respect for the ground, and for things noticed at ground level: the 'firm soaked road' of 'Interval' (l. 5); the paths 'dinted with hobnails' and 'overprinted' in 'November Sky' (ll. 5–6); 'the road's dust / And the dusty thought / Of passers-by' in 'Two Houses' (ll. 10–12). 'He knew the unselfconscious poetry that lurks in unpromising places', U. A. Fanthorpe writes.

Thomas's training in the observation and selection of images, while moving along roads, had already, by 1914, evolved into a prose style that corresponded with the six 'essentials of all great poetry' as defined by the Imagists.[43] As Frost pointed out, it needed only an understanding of prosody and lineation to translate this into the distilled images and sounds of verse. Thomas had a natural, un-taught musicality, which came from his love of ballads, folk songs, and English poetry. But he had to *learn* how to rough up the regular metres. One of his loveliest lyrics about walking begins, 'Early one morning in May I set out, / And nobody I knew was about'. Listening to the first line, we expect the second to follow the same metrical pattern: 'And nobody knew that I was about'. The ghost-line

---

40 Gervais, *Literary Englands*, p. 59.

41 Thomas, *The South Country*, p. 26.

42 Thomas, *The South Country*, p. 214.

43 Andrew Motion quotes from Amy Lowell's anthology *Some Imagist Poets* (1915) and discusses Thomas's affinities with the Imagist movement in *The Poetry of Edward Thomas* (London: Routledge and Kegan Paul, 1980), p. 3.

shadows the actual one, like a musical accompaniment to a snatch of speech. It is the missed beat that quickens the verse into a living rhythm.

In reading Thomas's prose, we undergo an experience akin to that of a walker, responding not just to the train of visual impressions he captures on the page, but to the illusion he creates – through rhythm and syntax – of moving along. His best prose is closely in touch with the pace of walking, and there is already a connection between the beat of a syllable and the tread of a foot on the ground. (The metrical term 'foot' is commonly taken to refer to the movement of the foot in beating time.) In his poetry, Thomas took this aspect of pedestrian writing further. He understood how variations in the number of feet in a poetic line can suggest the irregularities that occur in a walking rhythm – hesitations analogous to the ones that occur in informal speech. 'Interval' is a key word in his writing, which often pauses, like a traveller – or gives us pause, like a road.

Thomas was peculiarly alive to the pleasure of thinking as one walks, and to the way a thought moves in a sentence, as a person moves along a road. 'I feel the shape of the sentences & alter continually with some unseen end in view,' he wrote to Eleanor Farjeon, while composing his autobiography.[44] Poetry gave him an opportunity not afforded by prose, for experimenting with the shape of sentences on the page, so as to create a subtle visual complement to sound-patterns. He knew Thoreau's poem, 'The old Marlborough road' (from the essay, 'Walking'), which imitates the shape of the road it describes. His own poem 'Words' is similarly shaped, moving down the page somewhat like a long thin path. This is his only experiment of the kind; but in many poems he uses punctuation to navigate a path-like progress.

The fluidity of Thomas's writing (especially his handling of line-endings) has some affinities with free verse. But, like Frost, he believed that rhyme and metre were crucial: 'the accent of sense' was 'only lovely when thrown and drawn and *displayed* across spaces of the footed line.'[45] (Note Frost's analogy between the visual and the acoustic, as well as the key word, 'footed', with its literal connotations.) Especially important was Thomas's use of stanza breaks and mid-line caesurae, as here in 'The sun used to shine', where the paired activities of walking and talking come together in a rhyme:

44 Farjeon, *The Last Four Years*, p. 51.
45 Frost, *Selected Letters*, p. 140.

The sun used to shine while we two walked
Slowly together, paused and started
Again, and sometimes mused, sometimes talked
As either pleased, and cheerfully parted

Each night.   (ll. 1–5)

The easy rapport of Thomas's friendship with Frost is caught in the steady rhythm and pace of this sentence, which pauses lightly at the end of each line, and more heavily at varying intervals within lines, unexpectedly crossing a stanza break before coming to a close. Words are carefully positioned so as to bring sound and sense together: 'paused' comes appropriately after a comma; 'started | Again' is broken across a line; and 'parted' ends the stanza – but not the sentence, which is picked up anew in the next verse. Sustained enjambment suggests a companionable continuity, through many interruptions. In the alternating rhyme scheme, masculine and feminine line-endings are interleaved, conveying a rising-falling motion suggestive of voices in conversation. We *hear* all this, if the poem is read aloud. But it helps to see the shape of the sentences on the page, because the line endings are like stage directions, indicating the semi-pauses within each sub-clause. They suggest the momentary lulls that are part of companionable walking and talking.

There is a measured, internal quietness in Thomas's poetry, which often takes it closer to thought than to speech; but speech-rhythms are important to the way that thoughts are explored through a kind of voicing. Frost's emphasis on the importance of sentences, rather than syllables or metre, struck a chord with this prose-writer turned poet: 'A sentence is a sound in itself on which other sounds called words may be strung.'[46] So, too, did his friend's views on syntax: 'The living part of a poem is the intonation entangled somehow in the syntax, idiom and meaning of a sentence.'[47] With his long experience of writing about roads, and of walking while talking, Thomas saw how to 'entangle' the speaking voice in the syntax of his sentences, so as to create an audio-visual record of his unfolding thoughts.

Although Thomas is an accessible writer, there is a pressure towards difficulty in his verse, often revealed to us in its path-like structure, which

46 Frost, *Selected Letters*, p. 110.
47 Frost, *Selected Letters*, p. 107.

74

has proved formative. Take this sentence, in which the word 'now' is positioned like a signpost:

> Many years since, Bob Hayward died, and now
> None passes there because the mist and the rain
> Out of the elms have turned the lane to slough
> And gloom, the name alone survives, Bob's Lane. (ll. 13–16)

'Now' introduces a long dependent clause that unfolds over three further lines till the word 'gloom', branching out into a sub-clause introduced by the word 'because'. It's easy to miss the parenthesis at a first reading; and if this happens, we end up following a path that peters out into nothing. Only by re-tracing our steps and *voicing* the sentence do we find a way through. The process enacted in this sentence is remarkably like a walk that ends in a clearing – one of Thomas's favourite experiences. But it also resembles a conversation, moving towards clarity. The kind of conversation he had with Frost, perhaps, on one of their walks.

Donald Davie made Thomas out to be anti-intellectual, observing that his vocabulary 'lacks nearly all the English words that stand for disciplined conceptual thinking about the things that preoccupied him most.'[48] But it is Thomas's syntax, not his vocabulary, which carries the freight of complex patterns of thought. The involutions of his sentences are often at odds with a beguiling use of mostly single-syllable words – as in the lines 'and now I might / As happy be as earth is beautiful', from his poem 'October' (ll. 12–13). We are teased, here, into almost hearing the colloquial 'I might as well be happy, since earth is beautiful'; and this helps us to see that a potential happiness is being compared to an actual beauty. But we must pause for a moment, to un-tease the sentence, before continuing on our path.

Frost, Thomas said, showed 'absolute fidelity to the postures which the voice assumes in the *most expressive intimate speech*'.[49] It was this expressive intimacy that Thomas also achieved, by showing that when preoccupied by an emotion, mood, or idea, straightforward grammatical constructions are suspended, and thoughts are articulated through a mannered syntax. The 'postures' in his verse are not excrescences, left over from the days when he wrote artificial prose; they are variations in sentence structure that dramatise obstructions in the course of thinking. The frequent

48 Donald Davie, 'Lessons in Honesty', *The Times Literary Supplement*, 4001 (23 November 1979), p. 22.
49 John Moore, *The Life and Letters of Edward Thomas*, p. 328.

alternation between complex and straightforward syntax creates an effect similar to that of moving along uneven ground. This is perhaps what Derek Walcott means when he observes that the lie of the land has a shaping influence on 'the formal and informal prose / of Edward Thomas's poems' ('Homage to Edward Thomas', ll. 6–7).[50]

Inversions are a common feature of Thomas's style, whether he is using a demotic register, as in 'Women he liked, did shovel-bearded Bob' ('Bob's Lane', l. 1), or an abstract one: 'And fortunate my search was then / While what I sought, nevertheless, / That I was seeking, I did not guess.' ('The Other', ll. 88–90). So too is what Edna Longley has called the 'complicating resistance' of clauses that begin 'Even', 'At least', 'And yet'.[51] John Powell Ward observes how much weight Thomas places on 'seemingly innocent parts of grammar', like conjunctions and qualifications.[52] These small connective words play an important part, he says, in enacting 'the movement of mind itself'.[53]

The 'movement of mind' is a very good phrase to describe what lies at the centre of Thomas's poetry; just as 'the work of knowing' describes well what lies at the heart of Frost's.[54] Many of Thomas's poems move tentatively, coaxing what Leavis called 'a shy intuition on the edge of consciousness'[55] into the open, and accompanying it as it advances. Sometimes his sentences will interrupt or double back on themselves, pausing in the midst of perplexing modifiers before gently pressing on. Question marks, as David Gervais observes, are 'positive signs in his poetry; they give his thought a shape of its own, in a subtle, winding syntax.'[56] Negation and demurral are favourite devices, enabling the direction of a thought to be checked even as it is starting out. The opening line of 'But these things also' suggests an interrupted altercation – a fragment of conversation, overheard. Jem Poster imitates this opening in his poem 'Again', which in a very Thomas-like way keeps going back on itself while moving forward.

The equivocations in Thomas's syntax are associated by poets and

50 *Elected Friends*, ed. Harvey, p. 51.
51 Longley, *Poetry in the Wars*, p. 43.
52 Ward, *The English Line*, p. 11.
53 Ward, *The English Line*, p. 139.
54 See Richard Poirier, *Robert Frost: The Work of Knowing* (Oxford: Oxford University Press, 1979).
55 F. R. Leavis, *New Bearings in English Poetry* (Harmondsworth: Penguin, 1932; repr. 1963), p. 61.
56 Gervais, *Literary Englands*, p. 46.

critics with modesty, understatement, what Jonty Driver calls 'the good Anglican habit of not being too certain about anything, except maybe uncertainty itself'. But this hesitancy and elusiveness are not symptomatic of the 'blurred or indefinite' ideas condemned by Imagists.[57] Instead, they are indicative of the absolute clarity with which Thomas leaves a speaking thought-trail on the page. Jamie McKendrick observes that 'few other lyric poets offer such an unerring sense of the poem as a means, often by indirections, to "find directions out", as though the poem itself was a compass, or a "path, winding like silver"'. Thomas's use of interruptions, negatives, conditionals, adds to the sense that he is hunting for the most precise words he can find. He speaks his thoughts – as Frost puts it, 'making the sentences talk to each other as two or more speakers do in a drama'[58] – to test out their fidelity to the truth. This Jamesian or Proustian fastidiousness is felt most strongly in his inverted sentences: 'What I desired I knew not, but whate'er my choice / Vain it must be, I knew' ('Melancholy', ll. 6–7). The complex entanglement of this sentence is of a piece with Thomas's rigorous candour, and it bears a significant relation to the Protestant tradition of plain speech.

If feeling 'the shape of the sentences' is what Thomas did in writing his poems, it is also what others do in reading or imitating them. Contemporary poets do not so much 'inherit' Thomas's syntax, as inhabit it. When describing its pervasive influence on their writing, they draw on analogies dear to both Thomas and Frost. The metaphor of a 'line' is often used to connote the tradition Thomas is part of. John Powell Ward uses it, for instance, in his book *The English Line: Poetry of the Un-poetic from Wordsworth to Larkin* (1991). The metaphor works by associating three different ideas: the writerly 'line' which a poet sets down on the page; the territorial 'line', or path, which a person walks across the land; and the 'line' of influence that can be traced (or paced) from one poet, or generation of poets, to another. In the context of Frost's and Thomas's joint influence on contemporary poetry, the word 'line' takes on associations with walking and talking that are specific to the way these two poets thought about the sound and shape of sentences. Tom Paulin's phrase 'Walking a Line' alludes to Frost's poem 'Mending Wall',[59] and brings some of these associations together.

Frost used another 'line' analogy, just as famous as the one in 'Mending

57 See Andrew Motion, *The Poetry of Edward Thomas*, p. 3.
58 Frost, *Selected Letters*, p. 427.
59 Frost, 'Mending Wall', l. 13.

Wall', when he outlined his 'two or three cardinal principles' of poetry in a much-mentioned letter of February 1914. Likening a sentence to a line on which 'sounds called words are strung', he extends this metaphor into a simile: 'You may string words together without a sentence-sound to string them on just as you may tie clothes together by the sleeves and stretch them without a clothes line between the trees, but – it is bad for the clothes.'[60] This homespun analogy for the act of writing takes us to the heart of the poetic credo Frost shared with Thomas. The 'line' as understood by these two writers is not just a line of print. It is the shape and sound of a sentence.

Several contemporary poets place themselves in a 'line' descending from Frost and Thomas, treating the confluence of these two poets as a generative moment in literary history, when poetry opened itself up to the creative possibilities of the vernacular. Andrew Motion, Tom Paulin, and Michael Schmidt differ on the relative importance of Thomas and Frost, but agree in identifying what their joint legacy has been. In his 'Letters to Edward Thomas' Glyn Maxwell imagines Frost 'flying around the world on a fine line | That starts in you, or grows out from the days | You passed together'. Both Frost and Thomas trod a 'fine line' between prose and poetry, and the metaphor calls up associations between walking, talking, and sentence structure that emerged in conversation between the two friends. Robert Crawford, too, uses the metaphor of a 'line' which starts in a conversation: 'Frost helped shape a line of quietly conversational yet also ambitious verse which is sometimes thought of in terms of "Englishness", but which is heard in Irish poetry also'. His own poem, 'E.T.', slips into Scottish vernacular to claim kinship with the 'to-and-fro' correspondence between Thomas and Frost, which he mentions as a touchstone of the deft informality he admires. (His title is a good example of the walking-talking association that often creeps in, when describing Frost and Thomas.)

All these connotations of the word 'line' are suggestive, as ways of thinking about the way poets feel the shape of sentences. When we catch Thomas's resonances in contemporary writing, we are listening both to the way poets have experienced his thought patterns unfolding, and to the way their own thought patterns have been shaped by his. Poets are moving, metaphorically and performatively, in his path, or line.

The Thomas-like nuances of a poet's syntax are often transitory and

---

60 To John T. Bartlett, 22 February 1914; Frost, *Selected Letters*, pp. 110–14.

unconscious, especially when he is not the subject-matter of the poem in question. They become more noticeable in tributes, parodies, and imitations. In the section of his poem 'Letters to Edward Thomas' beginning 'Poem to Mr Thomas and Mr Frost', Glyn Maxwell catches what Frost would call the 'accent' of Thomas exactly. He is responsive to the shape of Thomas's long spooling sentences, where the clarity of what emerges is all the stronger for the tentative path taken.

David Constantine is alluding to the clarity in Thomas's writing when he adds the following to his list of reasons for valuing and identifying with him: 'Because he found his way there in the end. Because he wrote his way towards it, feeling, he said, "the shape of the sentences and altering continually with some unseen end in view."' His prose-tribute works through imitation: enacting Thomas's exploratory, investigative movement towards an unseen goal, and using the conjunction 'because' to keep the thought on track through numerous branching lines of association: 'Because he could walk and talk with a companion, pausing to listen, pausing to make a thing more clear, because as they walked the most important things came clear, at walking pace, with many pauses, they had true conversation and some vital things came clear.' The insistent rhythm – irregular at first, but increasingly iambic – conveys the sense that thoughts and words are pressing onwards, in unison with steps; that something urgent and important is unfolding, as it does when one is thinking aloud while walking with a friend.

Charles Tomlinson observes of Thomas's 'The Path', that 'It is the energy of the poem's syntax that impresses, by creating a distinctive path of its own'. The comment provides a gloss on his own poem about a path, 'Old Man, or Lad's-Love', a touching tribute to Thomas, and to his daughter Myfanwy. It is a poem about the importance of place, and poetic origins; about Tomlinson's own place in a line of poets; and about poetry's powers of regeneration. In the last sentence, sixteen lines long, Tomlinson suggests that there is an unbroken line connecting his poem with the parent poem from which it has grown. Everything in the sentence reminds one of a path. Reading the poem aloud, it takes practice, and careful breath-control, to do full justice to the steady unravelling of associative thought; to the way the sentence wanders while moving forward; and to the increasing line-lengths, as the poem nears conclusion. It begins in free verse; but as the path moves gently westward, the full rhymes enter ('Myfanwy', 'see', 'me'); ending with a feminine rhyme so as to soften the closure. This is very nearly a 'concrete poem', especially if one follows the contours of its line-endings down the right hand side. But the Thomas-like syntax – the 'living flow of contradiction unforeseen' – does most of the work.

'Some poets are for ever linked / with special times and places', Gavin Ewart says, in his poem 'Edward Thomas' (ll. 1–2).[61] It's a comment especially apposite for Thomas, whose writing is deeply rooted in the 'South Country' he made his own. But his paths and roads also lead elsewhere: to Wales, 'the place of origin for all Thomases' ('Old Man, or Lad's-Love', l. 26); and to his ultimate destination in France. As much as the winding syntax of his writing, the motif of the path or road is his hall-mark; and its traces are everywhere apparent in his reception and afterlife. 'With their beginnings and ends always in immortal darkness', roads have been especially significant in the representation of his death.

When Frost observed that Thomas's first collection of poems 'ought to be called Roads to France', he was thinking of 'Roads', with its sombre line, 'Now all roads lead to France' (l. 53).[62] Thomas did not single-handedly patent the road as a symbol of war-time England. But there is an important connection between the local roads he named and described in his prose, and the metaphorical roads in his poems, many of them composed after he enlisted. It's as though the war itself somehow crystallised the regional significance of roads, into a symbol of England which could be transplanted elsewhere.

During the war, trenches were often named after streets in England, to remind soldiers of home. Roads served as points of anchorage for memories. After the war, when Helen Thomas visited Ivor Gurney in his mental asylum, she took with her 'Edward's well-used ordnance maps of Gloucestershire where we often walked'. She and Gurney spent time tracing with their fingers 'the lanes and byways and villages' he knew by heart, which she and Edward had also explored. Through this act of shared map-reading, something of pre-war England was recovered for Gurney – as though he was being re-rooted to the land. 'He trod, in a way we who were sane could not emulate, the lanes and fields he knew and loved so well, his guide being his finger tracing the way on the map'.[63]

The war is often present in the way that Thomas is linked with roads, and even the roads of his prose are coloured by wartime associations. P. J. Kavanagh switches very quickly from a picture of Thomas 'Walking

61 *Elected Friends*, ed. Harvey, p. 100.
62 Letter to Edward Garnett, 29 April 1917; Frost, *Selected Letters*, p. 217.
63 Helen Thomas, *Under Storm's Wing* (Manchester: Carcanet, 1988), p. 241.

in England, haversack sagging, emptied of lies' to the avenue 'dark, nameless, without end' that foreshadows his death in France ('Edward Thomas in Heaven', ll. 2–4). This same image from 'Old Man' is evoked by Leslie Norris, to describe the path 'Coming from nowhere, moving into nowhere' that features in Laurence Whistler's memorial window at Eastbury – a path that chills this observer with its resemblance to 'That sullen lane leading you out of sight / In darkening France, the road taken.'[64]

Thomas's return from the Front is imagined by a number of contemporary poets – including Seamus Heaney, who transposes Thomas from his usual setting in the Home Counties, and 'sets him walking' on the Lagans road, near his own childhood home in rural County Derry. Heaney is haunted by Thomas the walker-soldier, hearing his 'step / On the grass-crowned road, the whip of daisy heads / On the toes of boots' before seeing 'his long-legged self', as in the war-time photos: 'in his khaki tunic' ('Edward Thomas on the Lagans Road', ll. 1–3; 12–13). This is the ghost of Thomas, returning from the dead, like a kind of *genius loci*, to take possession of the quiet country lanes he walked before the war. But if so, he is a 'compound ghost'; for Heaney is also remembering a local boy, demobbed after fighting 'with Monty in the desert' (l. 16). Nowhere is Thomas so much remembered, in connection with both world wars, as in contemporary Irish poetry.[65]

The haunting image of the nameless avenue in 'Old Man' has all the qualities of a Jungian archetype; but its association with trenches, and with a backward gaze which is peculiarly Thomas-like, establish it as a symbol both of the Great War and of 'modern memory'.[66] A hint of 'Old Man' can sometimes be detected in the recurring metaphor of a path, at the end of which someone stands, remembering or reconstructing, and down which an untranslatable experience vanishes into nothing. The poem has acquired a talismanic status: pre-figuring Thomas's death, but enabling a collective-unconscious recall of him, on home ground. To echo it is to engage in a form of restitution, akin to Helen Thomas's act of re-tracing old footpaths with Ivor Gurney.

The scent of 'Old Man', like the scent of Proust's madeleine, lingers in the mind, and comes to be associated with the writer himself, or with

---

64 'A Glass Window, in Memory of Edward Thomas, at Eastbury Church', l. 14; ll. 17–18; *Elected Friends* compiled by Anne Harvey, p. 54.

65 See the poems by Michael Longley, collected at the end of this volume.

66 See Paul Fussell, *The Great War and Modern Memory* (Oxford: Oxford University Press, 1975).

his sensibility. Derek Walcott's phrase, 'The subtle scent of Edward Thomas' ('Homage to Edward Thomas', l. 8), suggests the pervasiveness of Thomas's influence, its unmistakable quality and power. Scents of many kinds drift in and out of the poems in this collection, sometimes connoting the process of actively remembering. There is a quiet deliberation in Clive Wilmer's gesture – 'Gently I splay the petals, bend and sniff' ('Dog Rose in June', l. 3) – which suggests a need to revisit and restore. But more often, smell signifies the involuntary re-surfacing of a deep-buried memory. 'Thomas steals up on you', John Fuller writes.

Harold Bloom claimed, in *The Anxiety of Influence,* that 'criticism is the art of knowing the hidden roads that go from poem to poem.'[67] It's a sentence Thomas would have enjoyed, not just for the road metaphor, but for the iambic rhythm and internal rhyme. Many 'hidden roads' come to light, as poets discuss their affinities with the great writer who preceded them. And still more will emerge, as readers follow the tracks, meandering all over the map of contemporary poetry, which go back to Thomas:

> So lightly right I can't get away from him,
> Though all the time I know he isn't there.[68]

---

67 Harold Bloom, *The Anxiety of Influence: A Theory of Poetry* (Oxford: Oxford University Press, 1973), p. 96.
68 Robert Crawford, 'E. T.'; see below.

Linocut of Edward Thomas by Robin Guthrie.

Edward Thomas in 1905.

Dannie Abse

In 1977, London Weekend Television intended to broadcast a series of seven programmes called *Friends of John Betjeman* with Betjeman himself, another poet, and Prunella Scales. For the pilot programme I was invited because Betjeman wished to recite Thomas's 'Adlestrop' and thought it would be amusing if I followed with 'Not Adlestrop'.

Over lunch, Betjeman asked me my opinion of 'Adlestrop'. I confessed it was not my favourite Thomas poem: it did not completely eschew Georgian inversions or a poetic vocabulary. I liked Thomas best when he displayed not only his deep love of the English countryside but also his quiet desperation, his melancholy, his yearning for something lost which cannot be quite named or entirely recovered.

But there was much to admire in 'Adlestrop' of course. I liked the conversational tone with which it begins: 'Yes, I remember, Adlestrop', as if the poet is answering a companion before continuing (sub vocal?) thought. I admire also the economy of the poem, the way for instance Thomas evokes the feeling of silence around and about the railway platform by simply remarking 'Someone cleared his throat'. And one has the feeling the poem was written out of direct experience.

Some of these qualities I tried for in 'Not Adlestrop' – the conversational tone, the narrative of seemingly true experience – in this case of human behaviour – and the economy of statement. In addition, I found I could not in my intertextual references avoid humour.

'I like the ambiguity of June heat', said Betjeman.

ADLESTROP

Yes, I remember Adlestrop –
The name, because one afternoon
Of heat the express-train drew up there
Unwontedly. It was late June.

The steam hissed. Someone cleared his throat.
No one left and no one came
On the bare platform. What I saw
Was Adlestrop – only the name

And willows, willow-herb, and grass,
And meadowsweet, and haycocks dry,
No whit less still and lonely fair
Than the high cloudlets in the sky.

And for that minute a blackbird sang
Close by, and round him, mistier,
Farther and farther, all the birds
Of Oxfordshire and Gloucestershire.

Edward Thomas

NOT ADLESTROP

Not Adlestrop, no – besides, the name
hardly matters. Nor did I languish in June heat.
Simply, I stood, too early, on the empty platform,
and the wrong train came in slowly, surprised, stopped.
Directly facing me, from a window,
a very, *very* pretty girl leaned out.

      When I, all instinct,
stared at her, she, all instinct, inclined her head away
as if she'd divined the much married life in me,
or as if she might spot, up platform,
some unlikely familiar.

For my part, under the clock, I continued
my scrutiny with unmitigated pleasure.
And she knew it, she certainly knew it, and would not
glance at me in the silence of not Adlestrop.

      Only when the train heaved noisily, only
when it jolted, when it slid away, only *then*,
daring and secure, she smiled back at my smile,
and I, daring and secure, waved back at her waving.
And so it was, all the way down the hurrying platform
as the train gathered atrocious speed
towards Oxfordshire or Gloucestershire.

Dannie Abse
from *A Small Desperation* (London: Hutchinson, 1968),
and *New and Collected Poems* (London: Hutchinson, 2003)

Carmen Bugan

I wrote 'Yearning' after spending a month by the River Esk in Scotland when everything growing or staying seemingly still on the ancient landscape told me that I don't belong to the land and the land does not belong to me. Many years ago I was separated from my native land and I suppose the violence of that separation gave me the wanderer's mind, which imagines, nostalgically, a place to belong to, to grow old in. In 'Yearning' the 'promised land' is Michigan, where my family was exiled to. The landscape I am describing is the grounds of Hawthornden Castle in Scotland. Imagining what it would be like to grow old in that landscape – going forward in time – and remembering, or rather re-inventing *Birlad*, my childhood river, caused the yearning in the poem. But, as in Thomas, for whom the nostalgia in his poem 'House and Man' is occasioned by the magpie perched on top of the tree in two times (present and past), the yearning here is occasioned by the details which I describe.

Not until it was pointed out to me did I see similar imagery and a similar sense of nostalgic contemplation of the future in 'Yearning' and 'Old Man'. The speaker in Thomas's poem says:

> And I can only wonder how much hereafter
> She will remember, with that bitter scent,
> Of garden rows, and ancient damson-trees
> Topping a hedge, a bent path to a door,
> A low thick bush beside the door, and me
> Forbidding her to pick.

I am not able to acknowledge a direct debt to Edward Thomas for my poem, since I came to his work too recently for his sadness and his sense of home to wash through me, but I am grateful, now just as a reader, to find that he has something for me in his poems – this Jungian nostalgia. As he says 'in the name there's nothing / To one that knows not' what the names 'Half decorate, half perplex', so I am glad that with such different lives and origins, the imagination makes emotions from the plants which grow outside the door and makes poems out of forgetting them.

YEARNING

I want to know one plot of land slowly –
The way in which wrinkles begin to mould
A loved face into the scowl of its soul –
For I believe one needs a place
Or the permanence of longtime love.

I would notice the slow knotting of trees,
How they shrivel like the skin on old hands,
The rotting of pines, the white mushroom growing
In the bruise the ivy cut in the graying bark, a new
Yellow mushroom, a snail among nettles and ferns.

Climbing through the roots of fallen rhododendron
I would cling to the wet earth and crawl to the place
Where the rain made a face in the face of the rock:
And learn that it took years of the rain and stone
Working with each other.

I would watch the butterflies in the ravine
Knocked sideways by the river current,
And I'd know the times for poppies and phlox
Wild pansies and sweet mint, the honeysuckle leaning in
From hedges, the day when the dog rose blooms.

I would learn the rhythm of the river by seasons,
I wouldn't imagine a river for when I will settle
Or reinvent, nostalgically, the river of my childhood.

But in the promised land
The silver maple digs its roots under the porch,
And moles dig our crops out of the earth.

Carmen Bugan

Polly Clark

I took 'There was a time' as the inspiration for my poem, and also kept the length and the idea of looking back on one's life. What began to interest me as I thought about Thomas's poem was looking back on a life from a point of distance, and I took this further in my poem, separating the life entirely from the individual. The sea as a life began to emerge in my poem: its vastness, incomprehensibility, and the sense of it being inescapable even as you leave it all gave shape to my poem. The speaker in my poem is less focused on the young part of their life being wasted than on the dissonant relationship between a person's sense of themselves and their actual life. My poem would not have come about without my having read Thomas's and what I hope is that the two poems complement each other, both in their shape and in their notion of what it is to understand a life.

THERE WAS A TIME

There was a time when this poor frame was whole
And I had youth and never another care,
Or none that should have troubled a strong soul.
Yet, except sometimes in a frosty air
When my heels hammered out a melody
From pavements of a city left behind,
I never would acknowledge my own glee
Because it was less mighty than my mind
Had dreamed of. Since I could not boast of strength
Great as I wished, weakness was all my boast.
I sought yet hated pity till at length
I earned it. Oh, too heavy was the cost.
But now that there is something I could use
My youth and strength for, I deny the age,
The care and weakness that I know – refuse
To admit I am unworthy of the wage
Paid to a man who gives up eyes and breath
For what can neither ask nor heed his death.

Edward Thomas

MY LIFE, THE SEA

There was a time when I was empty
and my life was ravenous: it lapped at me
though I had nothing to give it.
It yowled in the rolling rooms I inhabited,
it pawed the lovers who followed me there
to see what they were made of, recoiling
when it found them full of gold and blood.
I was weak and I lied to my life.
It sobbed at the shore as I left, its face ugly,
its breath sour. It swore to drink itself to death.
I opened my mouth to the sky and the sun.
I was free as a ghost. I stopped speaking.
I hid myself in crowds and a new language.
Sometimes phones would ring when I passed them.
Sometimes letters would reach me, torn into pieces.
I never spoke of my life and it did not find me,
except at night when I rolled wide awake
and it slept in my arms like a beautiful fish.

Polly Clark
from *Take Me With You* (Tarset: Bloodaxe, 2005)

1 v i 6   Anethull

Tall nettles cover up, as they have done
These many years, the rusty harrow, the plough
Long worn out, & the roller made of stone!
Only the elm-butt tops the nettles now.

This corner of the farmyard I like most:
As well as any bloom upon a flower
I like the dust on the nettles, never lost
Except to prove the sweetness of a shower

By the ford at the town's edge
Horse & carter rest:
The carter smokes on the bridge,
Watching the water press in swathes about
                    his horse's chest.

From the inn one watches, too,
In the room for visitors
That has no fire but a view
And many cares of stuffed fish, vermin, &
                    kingfishers.

Manuscript of 'Tall Nettles' and 'By the ford at the town's edge', in the Bodleian Library, Oxford (MS. Don. d. 28, f. 41r).

Gillian Clarke

Why, strolling in the garden on a fine evening, crushing an aromatic herb between my fingers, do I think of university, summer and being young? It brings a smell of cut grass, a park bench, a book, and revising for a literature exam. The feeling evaporates, forgotten till the next time. I don't pause to analyse it.

We're tired and pleased with ourselves after a day's gardening. We admire our mown grass, the neat ruffles of vegetables in clean, weeded soil. We notice, again, the nettles rising from a disused compost heap. We ought to dig them up and barrow away the compost, now a mound of black soil. Stands of nettles are left untouched in far corners for the butterflies, but not here. We talk about tidying up, but never get round to it. We don't ask ourselves why.

Poetry is subversive. Our living experience is spoken by all the poets living and dead whose words have touched us. The nettles are protected by a spell as powerful as the enchanted thicket in the fairy story, the words of a long dead poet. Poets change the way we see and experience the world. One favourite poet or another has spoken for almost all the great and small moments of my life. They have layered the world with metaphor, given it voice, sung it alive.

We look closer and see that the nettles, which we would have cleared weeks back, are weighed down with the newly hatched caterpillars of peacock butterflies. Weeks earlier, before hatching, they would have been invisible. We would have swept them away were it not for words heard in the deep and secret place of the subconscious mind, a poem first read in summer long ago, and read so many times since that I know it by heart:

TALL NETTLES

Tall nettles cover up, as they have done
These many springs, the rusty harrow, the plough
Long worn out, and the roller made of stone:
Only the elm butt tops the nettles now.

This corner of the farmyard I like most:
As well as any bloom upon a flower
I like the dust on the nettles, never lost
Except to prove the sweetness of a shower.

Edward Thomas

NETTLES
for Edward Thomas

No old machinery, no tangled chains
of a harrow locked in rust and rising grasses,
nor the fallen stones of ancient habitation
where nettles feed on what we leave behind.
Nothing but a careless compost heap
warmed to a simmer of sickly pungency,
lawn clippings we never moved, but meant to,

and can't, now, because nettles have moved in,
and it's your human words inhabit this.
And, closer, look! The stems lean with the weight,
the young of peacock butterflies, just hatched,
their glittering black spines and spots of pearl.
And I want to say to the dead, look what a poet sings
to life: the bite of nettles, caterpillars, wings.

Gillian Clarke

David Constantine

Why? Because.

Because in a photograph taken before he was killed at Arras he has the decency my grandfather has in a photograph taken before *he* was killed at Guillemont. Because each left a widow and three children, two girls and a boy.

Because I was born with him under the sign of the Fishes, only a day apart. Because those born under Pisces love the rain, and they incline to melancholia and depression.

Because his wife was Helen. Because mine is. Because in one of our rows she threw a pot of Lad's Love (or Old Man) at me, I was unharmed, she helped me plant it by the door. Because his Helen in her writings calls him David. Because her last letter to him was on his body when he was killed. Because one Remembrance Sunday, when I had given a talk about him, a gentleman came up and shook me by the hand and said: 'My name is Edward Thomas.'

Because I was put on to him by a friend. Because I found him in that blue Faber edition on Durham market, and read him in our first home, under the castle, by the fire, in a very cold winter, on my own. Because I read that book at a sitting, poem by poem, all the way through and felt as I had not felt since reading Lawrence and Graves ten years before: I love this man, I can learn from him. Because when I left Durham he was my leaving present, in the good OUP edition with the variants. Because my friends there signed it. And so I give him to people I love, to people I feel he might help.

Because he was a walker. Because he could walk for miles with a companion, neither speaking, both at ease. Because he could walk and talk with a companion, pausing to listen, pausing to make a thing more clear, because as they walked the most important things came clear, at walking pace, with many pauses, they had true conversation and some vital things came clear. Because, out walking, he saw, as Graves and Lawrence, Wordsworth, Coleridge and Clare all did, 'solemnities not easy to withstand'. Because coming down off the Malverns with Robert Frost he witnessed the making of a rainbow out of moonlight and dew, because this watery phenomenon encircled them, because they stood in it, they were ringed around 'in a relation of elected friends'. Because Frost lived to remember the event.

Because he lived for a while on the Cowley Road, which is an Oxford road I like. Because he was at High Beech in Epping, where Clare was confined and fled from, home.

Because he woke up often with the blues all around his bed. Because when it was bad he dug the garden or went out walking in the wind and the rain. Because he struggled. Because he was a long time finding how to say it. Because at Dunwich he saw the skulls roll out of the graveyard and over the crumbling cliff. Because he was in love there, and suffering.

Because I had a friend who always put things my way that he thought might help. Because he particularly relished the placing of the commas in line 12 of 'Lob' – 'they could not find it, by digging, anywhere'. Because he would say aloud with pleasure 'Women he liked, did shovel-bearded Bob . . . but he / Loved horses.' Because that friend is dead and all the things he put my way did help.

Because he found his way there in the end. Because he wrote his way towards it, feeling, as he said, 'the shape of the sentences and altering continually with some unseen end in view'.

Because of the team's head brass and the lovers going into the wood; because of the rain, the soft rain after a day of planting in the garden, exactly right; the black rain of his misery, his loss of love and faith; because of the celandines, the green roads, the path along the parapet, the parleying starlings, the chalk-pit, the dust on nettles and the thrushes singing their hearts out in the gap before the dark; because of the woman high up at The White Horse in the wind; because of the soldiers and the poor lying out at night in the cold under the owls. And because of the hand – this above all, perhaps – the hand 'crawling crab-like over the clean white page', brave hand of a writer trying to make a living for himself and his family, and the hand of a poet coming into his own, into the making of 144 poems late in his life, just before the end. Because of every one of those twelve dozen poems.

Robert Crawford

Left, Right

I am writing this without my copy of Edward Thomas's poems. I don't need it, because a small number of his poems have pleasantly haunted me ever since school when our Welsh English teacher, Margaret Vickers, taught us the two Thomases in attractively incongruous succession. Edward Thomas loved England and is often associated with kinds of Englishness, but Mrs Vickers was not daft when she linked him with Wales. The Welsh names in his family show how much Wales mattered to him, and the use of the phrase 'English words' in his poem 'Words' may hint at an awareness that there are good words for poetry in other languages too, not least those which carry 'some sweetness / From Wales.'

Still, it is for his idiomatically featherlight English that I love Thomas most: he lets lines move with a consummate ease so close to speech, yet so sound and sounded as poetry. At the same time, this very closeness to the grain of language makes him a poet of international appeal. Shortly after Guy Cuthbertson (whom I remember as a student of mine at St Andrews University) asked me, on Turl Street, if I might write something about Thomas, I found by chance in the secondhand section of a St Louis bookstore a copy of the 2003 Handsel Press New York edition of the letters and poems addressed by Thomas and Frost to each other, collected under the title *Elected Friends*. There are moments when Frost and Thomas seem like left and right hemispheres of one brain. Though Thomas dreamed of a life in America, only Frost physically crossed the Atlantic. There is a Wordsworthian line of American poetry in America that runs though Frost to Mary Oliver; surely the mapreading, intently observant Thomas is also part of that line with its principled attention to achieving a true, intense focus on ecological (including human) details which are found to have a resonance far beyond themselves. Similarly, Frost helped shape a line of quietly conversational yet also ambitious verse which is sometimes thought of in terms of 'Englishness', but which is heard in Irish poetry also. The more exposed girderwork, the proclaimed constructedness of some Scottish poetry goes in another direction; still, in their different ways, both Norman MacCaig and the Kathleen Jamie of *The Tree House* might be aligned revealingly with Thomas.

Thomas, rare exemplar of the poet as sympathetic and demanding friend, and true if too typical example of the strolling poet who marched off and was killed in action, may also stand in other company. His hushed then chirrupy 'Adlestrop' is illuminated not just by Imagist poetry, but also beside the silence and music of that little poem by the Mandelstam of *Stone*, which speaks of a fruit falling in the centre of a forest. Like 'Adlestrop' Mandelstam's poem zeroes in on pinpoint co-ordinates, then follows what ripples away in all directions. Where Thomas harkens to birdsong, Mandelstam listens to the music of silence. Though Thomas is long gone, his best poetry does not seem or sound long gone. It is meticulously immediate, and sends out a ripple that never stops, a resonance that quietly crosses oceans and continents. For that I honour him.

Edward and Merfyn Thomas at Ammanford in 1900.

E. T.
'somehow someday I shall be here again'

When we met by chance on the Turl, were you aware
Yon door opposite was exactly the dark door where
Your man Edward Thomas, before he became a poet,
Nipped out of the world and into Lincoln College?
Odd we met and spoke about him there.

Odd, too, in St Louis, seeing in the Left Bank bookstore
That book of his to-and-fro with Robert Frost.
I bought it on impulse – his finest writing
So lightly right I can't get away from him,
Though all the time I know he isn't there.

Robert Crawford

Manuscript of 'Words', in the Bodleian Library, Oxford (MS. Don. d. 28, f. 2r).

Kevin Crossley-Holland

The hill road wet with rain
In the sun would not gleam
Like a winding stream
If we trod it not again.
('Roads')

Edward Thomas's simple words have brought me close to tears, like Carl Nielsen's ecstatic 'Springtime in Funen' and Samuel Palmer's 'The Bright Cloud'.

I've played many variations on the theme that Britain is a land of layers (our language, landscape, laws, coinage and so on), and likewise on the necessity of revisiting the past if we are not to lose it. Words once so black that they were almost green can soon fade to silver dust, to absences.

'Notes on a Field-Map' is based on an 1842 tithe-map of Walsham-le-Willows in Suffolk, and of course it begs questions about time and memory, renewal, the power of names, and above all about the lives of the individuals who lived on this land. In other pieces, I've stepped inside time and kept company with a Viking Orcadian girl in her grave, a medieval Welsh monk, John Constable, eleven U.S. airmen . . .

These were all matters of moment to Edward Thomas, and I care deeply for his poems, so often leading from the actual to the numinous, so attentive and gentle and unshowy, their learning so lightly worn. I was a small boy when I met him first, inside my parents' well-thumbed copy of *The Icknield Way* – the prehistoric trackway passing through the Chiltern hillside village where I grew up, linking it to chalky high East Anglia, where I live now.

Our road: a winding flint-blue creek.
Ploughed fields a stiff, flashing sea.
The clouds are dun and purple mud,
Creeks and pulks awash with sky.

NOTES ON A FIELD-MAP

Corrugated and clouded,
many acres foxed,
face up in every season.

rookwing to mushroom

The Little Ouse still oozes
through Gallant's Meadow.
Fenced and throttled.

mushroom to muck

Badwell Hill Meadow.
Here I whistled Tempest
down the generous ride.

muck to chestnut

Bales of wild silk.
And the plump does
up-ending into their warrens.

chestnut to straw

Under light's blinding eye
boundaries, features,
characters all faded.

straw to chert

Here is Bull's Croft,
First Beeches. Second…
Felled. Gone to ground.

chert to pigeonwing

  ome   ado
This was Home Meadow.
Silver dust.

Kevin Crossley-Holland
from *The Language of Yes* (London: Enitharmon, 1996)

Peter Dale

One of the interests for me in Edward Thomas's book on Richard Jefferies is the detail it contains of rural life in the Wiltshire of that period. My family on my mother's side can be traced back to the 1590s in the county, near the rising of the Thames at Ashton Keynes, now gentrified beyond all recognition. Though nothing like the long-distance walker Thomas was, I became interested in seeing the country from the higher land of the Ridgeway as described so attractively in Thomas's book, away from the wet lowland I knew sketchily in childhood. An early version of the first of my three poems, 'The Unknown Flower', came out of this experience. But the final shaping occurred on my reading again *The Last Four Years* by Eleanor Farjeon and on visiting the countryside around Ledbury where Thomas and Frost had so fruitfully met. The poems it glances off, 'The sun used to shine' and 'The Unknown Bird', have been in my head for years. The pseudonym in the last verse plays on British flower names and the fact that Edward Thomas lived at Steep and his pen name was Edward Eastaway.

In his poem 'Haymaking', Thomas describes what he took to be an archetypal scene of farming in the still moments of noon. He draws the poem to a close by suggesting it as a scene 'Immortal in a picture of an old grange.' Just before that, he compares the scene with the work of Cowper, Clare, Crome and Morland. My second poem, 'Archival' does not start from this one but from my daughter's fascination for and study of family history. However, Thomas's poem does illustrate one of its concerns. Such scenes, as with works of visual art, are all named after the creator of each as characteristic of their view of things. Clearly now we have to add to that list of creators the name of Edward Thomas. But the bulk of photography has been different: largely untitled by unknown image-makers. Maybe the camera cannot lie but what does the 'viewfinder' really focus on? An amateur like Julia Margaret Cameron may have her name describe a period photograph of some notable but the mass of the photographic record is unnamed.

Thomas's 'Aspens' has been a lifelong favourite poem of mine. Two friends who love the poem named their firstborn daughter after the poem and tree. A poem to celebrate her birth, it seemed to me, could hardly be done without some glancing reference to either or both. The difficulty was in not letting it be too obvious or literary. It is difficult for a veteran pen-pusher to go on writing poems, let alone poems for a birth, and that is perhaps why 'To Aspen' opens with a well known saying of Logan Pearsall Smith.

THE UNKNOWN FLOWER
For E.T.

More yours than mine this countryside,
the high-ridged backbone to the day.
I keep an eye out all the way,
knowing you took it in your stride.

One, spirit of a time-torn house,
the other, of an ancient earth,
how should we meet by track or hearth
unless the house were ruinous?

Gusts in the broken panes. . . Laid ghost,
though Arras, Agny mark your end,
haunt this high ridge where you are mourned.
— Betony, was that, or wishful guess?

My eye, unlike yours, not so sharp,
but sharing your soft spot for rain
I shelter in this leaky ruin,
trying to fix leaf, colour, shape.

Your stateliest of small flowers?
No whisper. Whatever plant it is,
today has made it in my eyes
another flower that was yours.

'Markway steeplet', its pseudonym:
spectator of the passing spectres,
high above the hectared acres;
this way we meet within a name.

Peter Dale

ARCHIVAL

Another house beside a brook,
a similar beside a lane;
light-scribbled water, furrow line
of leaves beside the path, flint, brick.

So many snaps, such varied groups,
posh-tinted, sepia, black and white;
walls warm with sun or glinting wet:
street parties, weddings, birthdays, trips.

Family faces in unrelated hats,
extraordinary millinery finely poised;
subversive kids not to be posed,
cloth caps, trilbies, on rigid heads.

Some named on margins or the back,
most nameless, taken by a love
that needed no reminders of
what was as known as heartbeat or break.

Smiles, in uneasy swimsuits, girls
all waving at the hidden eye.
Beyond, in glide-and-sideslip air,
the forlorn cries of silent gulls.

Bunting and kids' flag-wagging grins.
Behind, the absent ghost of a son
locked in the eye that framed the scene
where parents gaze back past the lens.

Not Brueghels, not Vermeers, anon.
One face, which face? the love of a life.
Light silvered on a wind-turned leaf.
The focus of the eye unknown.

Peter Dale

TO ASPEN
For Julia and Hamish

They say life is the thing,
though, grey, I prefer books.
I hope the luck will bring
those natural good looks
that you, considering
the mirror's glance, would choose
yourself; behind them, brains
that render books not pains
but pleasures to use.

Your father and my friend,
your mother and his wife,
with absolute love will tend
your being throughout life.
There is no need to send
one wish upon that score.
I hope that you respond
with love, a bungee bond
not felt a chore.

I wish the three of you
this gift safe as the breeze
the aspen whispers to
more softly than other trees:
I wish your parents true
pleasure in all the courses
of your work and leisure;
wish you that shared pleasure.
Though life, in morse, is . . .

Peter Dale

Jane Draycott

The day I came across Henry West's memorial near Reading station, two thoughts came almost immediately to mind: initially, the sound-memory of my own experience of a whirlwind in East Africa, like a swarm of bees and then exactly like an approaching express train; and secondly the indelible visual/structural memory of Thomas's 'Adlestrop', the poet's widening vision radiating from the still compass-heart of the station platform, the abiding moment of full attention which to my imagination when I first read it contained the essence of the South English countryside where I lived as a child. It is perhaps for the extraordinary stillness at the eye of Thomas's landscape that 'Adlestrop' is so well loved, as much as for its visionary closing lines: the bare lucid moment held in focus at the centre of the wider landscape and simultaneously holding it in place, the movement between the vividly present and the imagined elsewhere, all in some way connected to the unmentioned but inescapable image of the rails – or tracks, to use a key Thomas image – receding into the past, disappearing ahead into an unknown future.

IN MEMORY OF HENRY WEST

who lost his life in a whirlwind at the Great Western Railway Station,
Reading, March 1840, aged 24 years

Not expecting the future in so soon, he turned
and looked for the swarm of bees. Down the lines
that had never met and never would now, it came,

the hum of the barely discernible: ribbons of flies
in a sheep down a culvert, the crack of the ice-plate
under a boot, himself in the fog.

The ironwork announced his name, then the flat
hand of the storm pushed him towards the gap.
In the eye of the wind he saw himself, halted forever

in the freezing cattle-wagon of the third class waiting room,
stopped on the table top of a Siberian winter, surrounded
by bears and the icy stares of commuters, and round him

further and further, the dopplers of a thousand 125s,
the high speed sleeper and all the other sleepers going west.

Jane Draycott
from *Prince Rupert's Drop* (Manchester: Carcanet, 1999)

Jonty Driver

One of the questions few teachers of poetry will answer properly is: why are poems divided into lines, and why are lines grouped into stanzas? Yet it is the crucial question, since that is what distinguishes poems from prose. I remember trying to get answers to that question myself at school, and feeling I was being fobbed off when I was told it was merely conventional, or was offered technical information about metre and rhyme, vague things about enjambment and caesura.

What Edward Thomas taught me was how to balance syntax against half-line and line, whether in formal structures or in the flow of blank verse. Partly it was learning how to take breath – as a singer or actor does, or as one pauses in thoughtful conversation to allow one's audience to interrupt with ease. Partly it is what I think of as a very English hesitancy, not sounding so sure of oneself that one seems a know-all or a show-off. It's more than technique, of course; it's a way of thinking aloud, of being honest about what one knows and doesn't know, even about love and despair: the good Anglican habit of not being too certain about anything, except maybe uncertainty itself.

Sometimes when a reader tells me he doesn't understand something I've written, I reply: 'Say it out loud and you will.' Read Edward Thomas aloud, giving due weight to line endings and the ends of stanzas, and you will see that meaning resides in the pauses and silences of a poem as well as in the words themselves.

LINCOLNSHIRE FENLAND

If you take it largely, this land
Has no distinction, though looking close
You see the speckling of the grass by wind,
The waterlights of leaves, old grey horse
Cropping in a ditch. But the long way
From here to that horizon gives the eye
Sky-room. It is often drawn away and up;
When light on the ploughed field shifts, you look
Up at the clouds to verify the shapes
Of all their reaches . . .
                                    The things you see
Explain themselves: the clouds, the leaves, the ditch.
Horizon, wind and light do not – none is seen
Except in change or absence. Yet this light
And that horizon hold their objects, make
Borders to the state of being here, and now –
A scape of verbs, not nouns, since it needs
Conjugation. This is lightscape for the restless,
For refugees and exiles. This is landscape
For settlers, the socially immobile, private
People who watch small beasts in hedgerows,
The speckling grass, the leaves spilling light,
And not the random emphases of wind on clouds.

Jonty Driver
from *So Far: Selected Poems 1960–2004* (Cape Town: Snailpress
and John Catt, 2005)

POEM AGAINST RAIN

All day I have been walking. My view
Of the small part of England that's mine
Has been rained away. There's nothing
That belongs to me in this rotting place,

No house, no memory – even my body
Is losing its battle with age, stumbles
In the slack fat and the hard breathing
For the comfort of home. It is raining

Also the slow collapse of the hills,
And no thunder in the sky or the clay;
And my head is falling too slowly down
For my curses to break this coward,

My body, small feeble brother flesh,
Of his clinging to the closed sky's hand.
The rain marches before. I have lost
All day my private war with the rain.

Jonty Driver

TELLING THE TRUTH
i.m. Edward Thomas

I walk the streets
Of what I once
Thought of as home.
It isn't now.

Old age retreats.
What happened since
Fell out of time:
I don't know how.

The past colludes
To make one say
That grace persists –
It never did.

As stone obtrudes
Through graded clay,
The real insists.
It always did.

What ends our song
Is never known:
The rifle shot
Right through the throat,

The pulse gone wrong,
The cancer grown.
What is, what's not,
Have found us out.

Jonty Driver

U. A. Fanthorpe

Edward Thomas is famously the poet of 'you English words'. The ones he uses to express profound emotion are often monosyllabic, familiar, touchingly commonplace. He knew the unselfconscious poetry that lurks in unpromising places. It is characteristic of Thomas that in his 'Household Poem' to Bronwen the first things he thinks of giving her are place-names, and not the picturesque kind, but awkwardly accurate and stuck-in-the-mud

> Codham, Cockridden, and Childerditch,
> Roses, Pyrgo, and Lapwater,

He has put the word *Gloucestershire* (where I live) out of bounds for the rest of us (apart from Dannie Abse), so I have cheated in my poem by including it in the title. The whole thing is an (unacknowledged) tribute to Thomas; but when I come to look into the matter, a good many of my poems are. He comes naturally, I think, to writers in English, like grass growing. The poem itself concentrates on the there-and-now nature of place-names, and is based on a life-long addiction to Ekwall's *Dictionary of English Place-Names*. It seems to me so extraordinary that they have lasted so long through such vicissitudes of spelling and punctuation. I apologise for the footnote,* but it seems rather hard to expect non-locals to recognise not only the rather obscure places but also their meaning in Old English.

STRONG LANGUAGE IN SOUTH GLOUCESTERSHIRE

Vocabulary of earth, names

Tough and diehard as crypts,
Cathedrals perched on their shoulders.

No committee okayed them.
They happened, like grass.

Written down all anyhow
By cosmopolitan clerks in a hurry.

Ramshackle riddles, their meaning
Deconstructed in aloof universities,

Their proper stresses a password
Known only to cautious locals.

Now, inscribed on steel, they confront drivers,
Looming on roads by the restriction signs,

Unreel their quirks along the prim
Mensuration of Ordnance Survey.

Still hard at it, still proclaiming
Here are Soppa's tinpot two acres,

Something holy, a good place for blackbirds,
Duck farm, bridge over mud,

The strangers' bright city.

U. A. Fanthorpe
from *Consequences* (Calstock: Peterloo Poets, 2000)

* *Various Sodburies; Nympsfield; Ozleworth; Doughton; Slimbridge; Gloucester.*
  These are all places in Gloucestershire.

Helen Farish

My schoolgirl's handwriting tells me on the title page of my copy of Thomas's *Selected Poems* that it's been in my possession since 19th December 1979. I've returned to the volume at various times over the years, but what struck me revisiting the poems this summer was how drawn I felt to poems which previously I'd partially missed, not read closely enough. I found myself reading 'The Manor Farm', 'The Path' and 'The Brook' over and over. What 'The Manor Farm' and 'The Brook' do is take the reader from a physical world given in perfect detail to a world which hovers somewhere on the periphery of the poet's vision, a glimpsed timelessness or wholeness which Thomas evokes so enviably. In 'The Manor Farm' it's a 'season of bliss unchangeable / Awakened from farm and church where it had lain / Safe under tile and thatch for ages since'. In 'The Path', the yearning for the 'bliss unchangeable', in this poem given as 'some legendary, / Or fancied place where men have wished to go / And stay', is thwarted. But the word 'underyawns' which this poem uses to describe the relationship between the road and the wood suggests the darker or more troubling aspect of this longing which permeates so many of the poems: its potential to erode and even engulf the self. Perhaps that's why I admire 'The Brook' so much, how the poem negotiates its way between the world of light (the 'gleam' of the water, a butterfly on a hot stone – 'From aloft / He took the heat of the sun, and from below') and the world of shadows, of otherness (the horseman beneath the heath is raised, then all the dead).

Because of the interweaving of the timelessness and the timed (how spring will return after our own deaths), I've chosen my poem 'Slater Bridge' from *Intimates*. A new poem, 'Custodian', has certain echoes with Thomas's 'The sun used to shine', my favourite of his poems and one which touches me deeply, particularly the line, 'We never disagreed / Which gate to rest on.'

CUSTODIAN
for JS

I charge you with the afterlife of that moment.
Return periodically across your life and see us
(you in your second decade, me my fifth) still paused

at the gate between Snary Beck and Mockerkin How.
See again the white horse on the fell, the light
gilding its tail as and when the wind flickered.

We'd passed Snary Beck, Cogra Moss
was behind us, and I thought the animal's
poise as beautiful as anything on earth.

But it's *our* pause, the instinctive accord of it, and the light
which must also have been flickering in *our* hair,
I now find (shifting my gaze) more beautiful.

Helen Farish

SLATER BRIDGE

Because we sat on the bridge and we'll die

Because the spring after each of our deaths
will lead to a summer of the same
beauty as this

Because in the face of the running water
and the bridge serving centuries
I salute the flag of my love

It is waving there still

Helen Farish
from *Intimates* (London: Jonathan Cape, 2005)

Michael Foley

The chancy wonder of poems is that they arrive unexpectedly and for no obvious reason so it is difficult to identify motivation at the time of writing, much less thirty years later. But in fact I do remember why I remembered Adlestrop. The impulse was a revelation about a certain kind of bad poetry that was (and has remained) common in England. What struck me, suddenly and forcibly, was that these poems were products of the decadence of imagism.

The twentieth century could be defined as the century of imagism but whereas the original imagist movement was a liberating force that attempted to eliminate flabby language by use of the image – defined by Pound as 'that which presents an intellectual and emotional complex in an instant of time' – by the end of the century dull poets had realised that images could be used, not to concentrate intellectual and emotional content, but to avoid it altogether. For many poets, equally fearful of emotion and intellect, imagism was an ingenious way of claiming significance without the difficult business of providing it. And then editors in turn came to accept that poetry must be indirect, suggestive, oblique and that any kind of direct statement was as boorish as headbutting. (In his Imagist manifesto Pound said 'Go in fear of abstractions', not 'Never use abstractions'. And he added a crucial warning, 'never take anything as dogma'.) This in spite of the fact that English poetry from Shakespeare to Larkin abounds in glorious direct statement.

'Adlestrop' seemed an early example of the trend – all suggestion and no delivery. But it was unfair to pick on Thomas who has not only written good poems but good imagist poems (for instance 'The Watchers'). He's had the last laugh though because, while I forget the names of London stations I've used for thirty years, the insignificant little station I've never seen remains firmly lodged in my head. I'm still remembering Adlestrop in a recent poem, 'Imminence'.

I REMEMBER ADLESTROP

Yes, I remember Adlestrop.
Such an innocent vague
Neither-here-nor-there poem
– Yet it started so much crap.

Though Thomas was no rat
His poem began the trend
This impression of *Big Things* going on
Though of course you're not told what.

And that resonant hum in the air
As the frigid final phrase
Falls into its well-judged place.
By God, you think, *there's something there.*

All the vaguely mysterious
Bogusly sonorous
Phoneyly resonant slop!
Oh I remember Adlestrop.

Michael Foley
from *True Life Love Stories* (Belfast: Blackstaff, 1976)

IMMINENCE

In that first city summer of shimmering heat *every* Underground station
was Adlestrop,
Eerily pent . . . and *on every trip*. But especially Finchley Road where, no
whit less fair
Than a rose garden, buddleia burgeoned on waste ground and across the
track I saw
A girl waiting, so sensitive, yearning and disconsolate that I wanted to cry
out:
'I'm the one you seek, merely disguised as a gauche Irish barman. Your
kiss will
Bring forth a prince, gracious and eloquent. Plus, I can open two bottles
at once
With one hand. Be the eighth light tonight in *The Seven Stars*.' Never. There
were
No adventures. Nothing happened. It didn't matter. The true joy was
imminence.
In the corridors of the Underground currents of balmy air, zephyrs from
paradise,
Fondled my hair and on the escalator up to the lurid night a warm breeze
caressed
The face I turned towards advertisements for lingerie and new plays,
guarantors of
An end to the age of concealment, when the flesh and the spirit would
both be revealed.

Michael Foley
from *Autumn Beguiles the Fatalist* (Belfast: Blackstaff, 2006)

Edward Thomas in 1904 (by F. H. Evans). 'Very many thanks for the interesting photographs of me [. . .]. My wife says they are all good in different ways, except the sodden one with bowed head as if preparing for the basin' (26 July 1904).

John Fuller

I find that other poets get very easily into the bloodstream. You can take great draughts of them, out of a reasonable thirst, and before long your heart beats with them, and your fingers have to resist their tricks. Or if you anticipate influence in good time, you can take them in more cautiously, like an inoculation.

Thomas steals up on you. My most full-tilt reading of him occurred back in the 1970s, when I was supervising Andrew Motion for his M.Litt. The best outcome of that encounter was Andrew's fine book on the poet, but I am sure that Thomas also passed afresh into both our vascular systems.

I was conscious in writing the poems in my collection *The Mountain in the Sea* (1975) that a lot of Thomas's techniques and attitudes offered themselves as available: the sense of the passing of things, the moments of closeness and affection that require detachment through fear of loss, the strange mood of being 'content with discontent' (as he put it in his poem 'The Glory'), the moving at the wary circumference of a nostalgic centre.

I originally intended to include something from that collection, but decided instead to go for something new, if only to prove that Thomas has never left my consciousness. The poem is called 'Hendre Fawr', which is the name of a neighbouring farm where we often walk looking for horse mushrooms, *agaricus arvensis*.

I am sure that we have all learned from Thomas (perhaps more intimately than from the modernists) how we can best locate a feeling in a natural thing, even when we are not quite sure what that feeling is. I also chose this poem because it contains another Thomas trademark, the encounter with the agricultural worker who knows the land as the townee never can.

HENDRE FAWR

We plod on the brow of the-field-with-the-stone,
That contour between level passivity
And an offering tilt that greets the sun,
And we expect in the course of things to find
Mushrooms, because indeed they grow there.
They are in their appearances neither shy nor brazen,
Taking their time to shoulder up, one by one,
And looking surprised to find others nearby
Who have, like them, come to as much
Of a corner in the grass as they could find
To show themselves and become companions.

We conclude that we are like them, but in motion,
Circling in a planetary complication
About our idea of some future discovery,
You walking up with an inquisitive stoop,
I in a careless saunter, kicking at thistles.
But we know that the future is only lying in wait
And as little to be trusted as anything unknown.
We have lost the expectation of the ordinary miracle
In the iron prow and sweeping arm of the farmer
Whose watching of weather is a working practice
And the act of ambulation a care of the bounds.

What has already happened was sometimes marvellous,
Like Rowland coming across the grass to us,
Bringing his new neighbours mushrooms in cupped hands,
Their cups the sizeable size of his own cap,
The yield of them as complete as his smile,
And the smell (fern-root, aniseed, leaf-mould,
A whiff of kidney) telling of the ancient ways of the field,
A place that horses once would amble from and pause
And lift their heads and briefly snort, grown old
From bracing shoulders against the long drag of the land,
Yearning down the valley to the barking farm.

John Fuller
(Oxford: *Oxford Poetry Broadsides*, 2005)

Elizabeth Garrett

I suppose any poet one has read with excitement and an enduring need to return to, must in some way be an influence on one's own writing. Yet much of what I admire most in Thomas's poetry – the artless simplicity of utterance and its almost proverbial wisdom; the demotic narrative voice; the inspired connection between word and place and time – I find little evidence of in my own poetry. I think that if I could lift, intact, a single gift from Thomas it would be his selfless art of restitution: the way words, through poetry, bless the things they name, rooting them in the history of the English tongue, long after the things themselves, and their singer, have gone.

It is certain that Thomas's valedictory voice attracted me from the outset, and its concomitant preoccupation with time – the uncompromising simultaneity of past, present and future and its subsumption into an irresistible sense of time as always past (e.g. 'The New House'). If Thomas's voice attracted me initially, it is other more implicit qualities that continue to haunt me, and I have chosen the poem 'Vista', written for my mother, and 'Love in Midlife' as instances of this. Even though our stylistic differences are pronounced, the preoccupations and trajectory of 'Vista' owe a debt to Thomas. A kind of outside-inwardness (or vice-versa) in Thomas's use of the first person – the sense of himself both within and beyond the poems – has fascinated me. In Thomas, this inside-outwardness relates both to a philosophical view of man's place in historic time in general (e.g. 'February Afternoon'), and in particular a personal perception of the poet's place in the history of the English language and its literature ('The Long Small Room', 'Words'). In my own poetry the field of reference tends to be the much 'narrower' one of personal history and individual relations, and it is perhaps for this reason that I am particularly haunted by those poems in which the curiously selfless intimacy of the Thomasian first person is momentarily displaced: reading 'Go now' and 'Old Man' my breath is always taken away by an 'I' directly *owning* its existence as the paradoxical embodiment of loss or absence.

In 'Love in Midlife' the mnemonic ritual of crushing and smelling a herb finds an instant parallel in Thomas's 'Old Man', but the implied redress of loss through the use of the ambiguously impersonal pronoun is distinctly un-Thomasian. The poem is as much a love poem to the self as it is to the beloved Other – the 'sudden thought' and 'wrist' of the closure connecting inescapably with the 'mind' and 'hand' of the opening.

VISTA

Standing, with your back turned, taut at work,
Wearing the day's frosted willow-grey skirt
Like a bell of smoke, while a child went on colouring
Under the spell of the Lakeland-Cumberland arc,
You turned suddenly hearing the doorbell ring.
Turned? No – *spun*, till the skirt flared its carillon
And all the poplar leaves of the world shone
Silver, their green gone in the wind's turning.

And here I am, wise at the open door
Trying to remember what it was I came for,
Struck by a knowledge of beauty years beyond
Anything I had yet come to understand,
Watching you disappear down that corridor
Of brilliant sound, my stolen breath in your hand.

Elizabeth Garrett
from *A Two-Part Invention* (Tarset: Bloodaxe, 1998)

LOVE IN MIDLIFE

And it springs to mind
The way the stray wand
Of lavender offers itself
Unbidden to the casual hand

And the dust-dry grey
Grains concede their integrity
Beneath the worrying thumb
Till that sudden scent like an augury

Comes clear and you're all
One in that moment
Of inspiration, inhaling
The ineffable sense of the whole.

The rest is history's husk,
Spent breath, a worn hassock
Of wishing, and wanting
More than we ever dare ask

Or can give. And the rest
Is nothing beside this
Trust in your sudden thought –
Like finding the buried pulse
Still quick at your quiet wrist.

Elizabeth Garrett
(uncollected; first published in *The Oxford Magazine*)

Edward Thomas at Broughton Gifford.

Jane Griffiths

A number of things came together in writing this poem. When asked to contribute, I went back to my first responses to Edward Thomas, more than fifteen years ago. What struck me most then was – perhaps predictably – the story about his sudden transition from prose to poetry after a conversation with Robert Frost. I was delighted by it, but at the same time rather sceptical about the way the story had become almost better known than the writing. The other thing that greatly attracted me was Thomas's habit of looking at a house or a place as if it were the image of the perfect life – and his own questioning of that response.

More recently, I had been reading Thomas's *Oxford*, and Lucy Newlyn's introduction to her edition of it, which gives a tremendous sense of the claustrophobia of the city. I had also just moved from a small flat in Oxford (not far from Thomas's own lodgings on the Cowley Road) to a house on the Oxfordshire / Gloucestershire borders. (To my great amusement, on my first drive to the local Tesco's, I passed a sign saying 'Adlestrop 1/2': it was something like sighting a unicorn.) I couldn't quite believe in the house: it, too, went on looking like the image of a life even once I was living in it. In the poem, I seem roughly to have equated prose with Oxford, and poetry with a sudden sense of new possibility, but I wanted too to keep a questioning tone, and not merely to perpetuate the myth.

LEGEND HAS IT

it was the answer to a prayer after
years of careful construction on the weights
and pulleys of borrowed syntax, lines

of thought running like the black bands
and fretwork of Victorian gothic
to display a niche, a clause, a window

embrasure capped with periods of perfect
equilibrium and the loadbearing mind
countersunk in its shadow:
                           suddenly the poem

sufficient unto itself as the long minute's
view when a train pauses between stations,
the country one part earth to six parts air

and the white house in its clean timber
frame clear and open as if it stood alone
and unlooked-for. Or so they say.

Jane Griffiths

David Harsent

I first read 'Rain' when I was sixteen or seventeen. It was shown to me by a man who often spoke of suicide, but lacked the necessary push. What I found in it was a sweet nihilism: seductive notions of blameless effacement in '. . . heavy, black rain falling straight from invisible, dark sky to invisible, dark earth . . .' There's a poem called 'By Sennen' in my last collection that I had thought to reprint here for its similar (if somewhat longer) narrative progression but, when I came to read 'Rain' once more, I found myself caught up with topography and location and, eventually, the drift of my own thoughts. I was intrigued to find that I still had the poem by heart and, beginning to say it through in my mind for the first time for a long time, remembered the way that second long sentence shakes out to a doomy, near-erotic yearning. It's not the only poem in which Thomas uses 'and' as a line-ending to provide pause, but here it *gives* pause, as if the speaker – or the 'ghostly double' he mentions elsewhere – after a moment's consideration is, yes, agreeing that the combination of image and meditation must lead the poem to bottom out in darkness.

Manuscript of 'Rain', in the Bodleian Library, Oxford (MS. Don. d. 28, f. 20r).

THE HUT IN QUESTION

Rain, midnight rain, nothing but the wild rain
On this bleak hut, and solitude, and me . . .
Edward Thomas, 'Rain'

And here it is, slap on the co-ordinates,
nothing special of course,
a tar-paper roof (is it?) nailed to sloping slats,
a door that goes flush to the floor, and grates
when you draw it back. Weather-worn, half-hidden by gorse
in full fire, it being that time of year; the window
thick with cobwebs, clarty candyfloss;
a smell of rot; things spongy underfoot.

Being here alone is easiest.
There are songbirds in the sedge
(I think it is) and a wind to clout the reeds, a test
of the place, as are these clouds: a long dark flow
pulling fast and heavy off the ridge . . .
Easiest given what we make of quest,
its self-regard, its fearsome lost-and-found, its need to know
the worst and wear its sorrows like a badge.

Do you get what I mean if I speak of light – half-light –
that seems to swarm: a mass
of particles folding and rolling as if you stood too close
to a screen when the image dies? The edge
of night . . . those forms that catch and hold
just at the brink where it's nearly but not quite.

I see, now, by that light. Rain finally coming in, the day
falling short, adrift in shades of grey,
and nowhere to get to from here, or so I guess,
with distances fading fast,
with the road I travelled by a thinning smudge,
with all that lay between us bagged and sold,

with voices in under the door that are nothing more nor less
than voices of those I loved, or said I did,
with nothing at all to mark
fear or fault, nothing to govern loss,
and limitless memory starting up in the dark.

David Harsent
(uncollected; first published in *Poetry Review*)

Seamus Heaney

'As the team's head brass . . .' is perhaps my favourite poem by Edward Thomas and it was on my mind when I set him walking on the Lagans Road. It may be pitched low, but there's a Homeric plane to Thomas's narrative in this particular case: the dailiness, the dialogue that is integral to the action, the shadowing of the scene in the foreground (ploughman and poet in conversation) by what's going on out of shot (the lovers in the wood, the war in Flanders) – it's all reminiscent of moments in *The Odyssey*, as when the disguised Odysseus is attacked by the dogs on his arrival at the swineherd's hut, or when his own dog Argos beats its tail on the ground in recognition. In each case a big wheel of danger is turning above and beyond the poignant and the ordinary. Thomas here walks into English poetry like a soothsayer, his pastoral lyric takes on a tragic dimension, the close-up naturalism is radiated with mortal consequence. But on the Lagans Road I allow him a last evening of elegiac reverie.

AS THE TEAM'S HEAD BRASS

As the team's head brass flashed out on the turn
The lovers disappeared into the wood.
I sat among the boughs of the fallen elm
That strewed an angle of the fallow, and
Watched the plough narrowing a yellow square
Of charlock. Every time the horses turned
Instead of treading me down, the ploughman leaned
Upon the handles to say or ask a word,
About the weather, next about the war.
Scraping the share he faced towards the wood,
And screwed along the furrow till the brass flashed
Once more.
          The blizzard felled the elm whose crest
I sat in, by a woodpecker's round hole,
The ploughman said. 'When will they take it away?'
'When the war's over.' So the talk began –
One minute and an interval of ten,
A minute more and the same interval.

'Have you been out?' 'No.' 'And don't want to,
               perhaps?'
'If I could only come back again, I should.
I could spare an arm. I shouldn't want to lose
A leg. If I should lose my head, why, so,
I should want nothing more… Have many gone
From here?' 'Yes.' 'Many lost?' 'Yes, a good few.
Only two teams work on the farm this year.
One of my mates is dead. The second day
In France they killed him. It was back in March,
The very night of the blizzard, too. Now if
He had stayed here we should have moved the tree.'
'And I should not have sat here. Everything
Would have been different. For it would have been
Another world.' 'Ay, and a better, though
If we could see all all might seem good.' Then
The lovers came out of the wood again:
The horses started and for the last time
I watched the clods crumble and topple over
After the ploughshare and the stumbling team.

EDWARD THOMAS ON THE LAGANS ROAD

He's not in view but I can hear a step
On the grass-crowned road, the whip of daisy heads
On the toes of boots.

                      Behind the hedge
Eamon Murphy and Teresa Brennan –
Fully clothed, strong-arming each other –
Have sensed him and gone quiet. I keep on watching
As they rise and go.
                  And now the road is empty.
Nothing but air and light between their love-nest
And the bracken hillside where I lie alone.

Utter evening, as it was in the beginning,

Until the remembered come and go of lovers
Brings on his long-legged self on the Lagans Road –
Edward Thomas in his khaki tunic
Like one of the Evans brothers out of Leitrim,
Demobbed, 'not much changed', sandy moustached and freckled
From being, they said, with Monty in the desert.

Seamus Heaney
from *District and Circle* (London: Faber and Faber, 2006)

Cpl. P. E. Thomas 4229.

Geoffrey Hill

I have always loved Edward Thomas's poetry and have a liking for some of his prose. I think he is a truly major minor poet like Wyatt. His influence on me, when I was fourteen or fifteen, was disastrous. I produced several very bad pastiches of his work, none of which I kept. By the age of sixteen I was an aggressive modernist. I bought the little Faber selection, *The Trumpet and Other Poems*, either in Stourbridge, Worcs, or Bromsgrove, Worcs. I was brought up in rural Worcestershire and my earliest aspiration was to do justice to the beauties of my county in the E. T. rather than the A. E. H. mode (if memory serves). My A. E. H. phase was more truly a George Butterworth phase. Aside from school, I was educated, like most of my generation, by the BBC Third Programme and I discovered Butterworth's *Shropshire Lad* settings via the radio. Gurney's music meant a great deal to me (the little I knew) but, to my shame, I could at that time make nothing of his poetry.

I think there is a real body politic element to all these people: Edna Longley probably made me aware of that. Much later in life, in my Bateson Memorial lecture on Gurney and in a published essay on Housman I tried to explain myself along these lines.

The Edward Thomas-Alun Lewis connection is I think vital to the body politic line of thought; but who carries on *effectively* from Lewis? I cannot answer my own question, though the editors of this volume tell me that an answer will be forthcoming in its pages. I await this with interest.

One finds the most surprising connections. Just a few days ago I read a memoir of that admirable poet of World War 2, Drummond Allison (1921–1943). He was 'steeped in Auden' but is recorded as having 'delivered a long and deeply researched paper on the work of the First World War poet, Edward Thomas' to a school society. Perhaps this still survives in the archives of Bishop's Stortford College.

ALL DAY IT HAS RAINED...

All day it has rained, and we on the edge of the moors
Have sprawled in our bell-tents, moody and dull as boors,
Groundsheets and blankets spread on the muddy ground
And from the first grey wakening we have found
No refuge from the skirmishing fine rain
And the wind that made the canvas heave and flap
And the taut wet guy-ropes ravel out and snap.
All day the rain has glided, wave and mist and dream,
Drenching the gorse and heather, a gossamer stream
Too light to stir the acorns that suddenly
Snatched from their cups by the wild south-westerly
Pattered against the tent and our upturned dreaming faces.
And we stretched out, unbuttoning our braces,
Smoking a Woodbine, darning dirty socks,
Reading the Sunday papers – I saw a fox
And mentioned it in the note I scribbled home; –
And we talked of girls, and dropping bombs on Rome,
And thought of the quiet dead and the loud celebrities
Exhorting us to slaughter, and the herded refugees;
– Yet thought softly, morosely of them, as indifferently
As of ourselves or those whom we
For years have loved, and will again
Tomorrow maybe love; but now it is the rain
Possesses us entirely, the twilight and the rain.

And I can remember nothing dearer or more to my heart
Than the children I watched in the woods on Saturday
Shaking down burning chestnuts for the schoolyard's merry play,
Or the shaggy patient dog who followed me
By Sheet and Steep and up the wooded scree
To the Shoulder o' Mutton where Edward Thomas brooded long
On death and beauty – till a bullet stopped his song.

Alun Lewis, 1941

Matthew Hollis

On first appearance, 'The Fielder' is not a poem influenced by Edward Thomas: I must confess that when it was written a few years back I knew shamefully little of his work. But re-reading it now I am struck by its happy neighbourhood to Thomas's poem 'As the team's head brass'. Granted, the form and narrative of the two poems are very different, and even the similarity of setting may be misleading (my poem, in fact, began life as 'The Gardener', unable to attend to the weeds at the back wall). Nevertheless, I think I can detect an influence of tone upon my poem, however unwitting its presence may be.

Is it possible to be influenced by a poem you have yet to read? I believe it is. I believe that good poems enter the culture and colour the climate in which other poems operate. Influence is not always express or direct, sometimes it arrives via an intermediary; rather like the way conversation can move across a crowded room, the chatter that reaches you may be third or fourth hand yet it still carries something of the original. 'The Fielder' may have been one conversation among many in a room in which Thomas's poem may also have been present; there is no evidence that the two poems met, but there are clues and introductions. Auden read Edward Thomas, so did Dylan Thomas and Philip Larkin, so did Seamus Heaney and Michael Longley. All of these were poets I came to before Edward Thomas; all of them touched me as they in turn were probably touched by him. Perhaps a little of Thomas's conversational rhythms, his rich grounding in the earth, his strong gentleness, found their way through these poets to me.

This is not, I hasten to add, to make any claims for my own comparatively modest poem. But it is to suggest that there is such a thing as a community of influence which certain poets generate. It does not constitute a 'school' and is not a manifesto, but is something closer to an accent or intonation, which percolates among peers and is nourishing to subsequent generations. Edward Thomas's poems have generated just such a community and have helped establish him, I believe, as a defining influence upon twentieth-century poetry in English. His poems offer a necessary stillness in a world of bewildering speed.

THE FIELDER
for Kim Walwyn

The day is late, later than the sun.
He tastes the dusk of things and eases down,
and feels the shade set in across the yard.
He never thought there'd be so much undone,
so much in need of planing: the haugh unmown
with its fist of bracken, the splinting of the cattle bar,
the half-attended paddock wall
scribbled with blackthorn and broke-wool.

Perhaps he could have turned the plough for one last till,
be sure, or surer, of where the seeding fell.
But then it's not the ply that counts, but the depth of furrow,
knowing the take was deep and real, knowing the change was made.
And field by field the brown hills harvest yellow.
And few of us will touch the landscape in that way.

Matthew Hollis
from *Groundwater* (Tarset: Bloodaxe, 2004)

Jeremy Hooker

My thinking and feeling about Edward Thomas have undergone changes over nearly fifty years. In one essential respect, however, they have remained the same. At the age of seventeen or eighteen, when I first read his poems, what moved me most was his affectionate perception of little-regarded things, in poems such as 'Tall Nettles' and 'But these things also'. His poetry for me, then, was akin to the poetry implicit in Richard Jefferies's essays, which had opened my eyes to nature when I was a boy.

Above all, it was the things and the life in the things that I valued – ways of seeing that went with melancholy moods but could also awake exhilaration, as in the opening of 'The Glory'. The poems gave a voice to things that I saw and felt in the Hampshire countryside, things that could still be experienced despite all that had changed since Edward Thomas's death.

As time passed, I became conscious of Thomas as a man of paradoxes: the Welshman widely thought of as an essentially 'English' poet; the modern man tortured by self-consciousness who was also 'an old inhabitant of earth'; the nature-lover who became a war poet. The latter fact, in particular, raised questions that troubled me. How could one square his moving self-sacrifice for an England symbolized by a handful of earth with what *he* knew about the politics of the British Empire?

So Edward Thomas became for me a problematic figure. Yet what remained was the life of the poems, and the feeling they awoke for the life in things. Something of all this was at the back of my mind one day in the 80s, when a cloudburst broke upon us as we were driving across country near Arras, where Edward Thomas had been killed. Thinking of his life and the circumstances of his death, I was conscious of irony, but I was aware too of the exhilaration he had felt in wind and rain. I couldn't ignore the irony; but what I felt most was gratitude for the intense livingness he experienced, and expressed.

TOWARDS ARRAS

From Picardy and the land of the Somme
the late summer sky had lowered,
become a roof of dark blue cloud.
And it broke in downpour, shattering
on roadside memorials and regiments of graves,
smoking across the fields,
the mounds and ditches, that already,
after seventy years, look prehistoric.
And as we drove towards Arras,
slowly, against the pounding
and blinding cloudburst,
I thought of Edward Thomas
and how he would have loved
the violence of this passing storm.

Jeremy Hooker
from *Our Lady of Europe* (London: Enitharmon, 1997)

Nigel Jenkins

After a youthful false start in poetry, striking romantic poses and taking windy, ill considered liberties with language, it was time to get back to native ground – the family farm in Gower – and start again, from scratch. Edward Thomas may be perceived as a quintessentially English poet, but – Welsh father, half-Welsh mother, and a frequent visitor to the Swansea–Mumbles–Pontarddulais area, among others – there is no denying both the significance to him of various Welsh influences, and his influence, in turn, on such writers of Wales as Alun Lewis, R. S. Thomas, Leslie Norris and Gillian Clarke. Many of his prose treatments of the country, such as *Beautiful Wales*, I find thin on content and heavy on adjectives, and there are not many Welsh references in his poetry; but he offers a way of reading the landscape – any landscape – that is immensely rewarding to a writer seeking to re-enroot himself. Take these tools, he seems to say, and use them to work your own heart's acre: an unflinchingly observant eye; an archaeologist's sensitivity to 'every swelling of the grass, every wavering line of hedge or path or road'; a social historian's awareness, confronting a deserted house, of how 'In its beds have lain / Youth, love, age and pain'; a sense of continuity with the past, coupled with a counter-sense of discontinuity and disruption; a fascination with the elusive and half glimpsed (those enigmatic lovers dipping into and, later, out of the wood); hesitant and tentative thought processes; an insistence on 'living and social words', and a trust in ungarnished language. Such permissions and encouragements I found useful when I stumbled upon my abandoned ridger; the poem became the first in a sequence about farm life.

THE RIDGER

Capsized, by some nosing cow,
in the headland where last unhitched,
it raises to the solitudes
guide-arm, wing and wheel.

What should slide or spin
locks to the touch; a bolt-head
flakes like mud-slate at the push
of a thumb – fit for the scrapyard
or, prettified with roses, some
suburban lawn. Yet there persist,
in a tuck away from the weather,
pinheads of blue original paint.

To describe is to listen, to enter
into detail with this ground
and this ground's labour; to take
and offer outward continuing fruit.

My palm smoothes the imperfect chill
of rusted iron … I weigh against
the free arm, easing up
the underside share – worms retire,
lice waggle away: it stands
on righted beam, rags of root-lace
draped from the delivered haft.

Maker and middleman emblazon
two cracked plaques: Ransomes, Ipswich;
White Bros, Pontarddulais.
Less patent is the deeper tale
that gathers with the touch of rain
on the spike which was a handle,
the nail bent over for an axle-pin.

Nigel Jenkins
from *Acts of Union, Selected Poems 1974–1989*
(Llandysul: Gomer Press, 1990)

P. J. Kavanagh

In the years before the First World War, perhaps because of an uncon-
scious sense of impending change, there was a vogue for country books,
for celebrations of the unchanging state of rural England. It sometimes
seems that no journey was too slight, no observation too trivial – so long
as it contained observations of apparent permanence, descriptions of
wild flowers, hills, country inns, preferably near London – but it could
generate a fee for some literary man prepared to pad out the requisite
number of pages. Edward Thomas was swept into the trade before he
left Oxford – he called it 'the Norfolk-jacket school of writing' – and his
groans to his friends, his increasing desperation at the treadmill it became,
form the saddest part of his biography.

He is commissioned to take a bicycle ride from London to the
Quantocks and write (in the original edition) a three-hundred-page
book about it. Faced with such a task he takes up the first thirty-three
pages describing his hesitations about setting off. But what do we get?
Word-spinning, space-filling, he gives us an Impressionist London of
shadows and glimmers that is reminiscent of Sickert.

> Once in the intense bright of a jeweller's shop, spangled with
> pearls, diamonds, and gold, a large red hand, cold and not quite
> clean, appeared from within, holding in three fearful, careful
> fingers a brooch of gold and diamonds, which it placed among the
> others, tremulously, lest it should work harm to those dazzling
> cressets . . . [A tramp passes, not making a sound] save the flap of
> rotten leather against feet which he scarcely raised lest the shoes
> should fall off . . . Around this figure, clad in complete hue of
> poverty, the dance of women in violet and black, cinnamon and
> green, tawny and grey, scarlet and slate, and the browns and gold
> browns of animal's fur, wove itself fantastically.

All this is seen under changing light-effects, lovingly detailed skyscapes,
that make the picture of 1913 London, interesting enough in itself, also a
picture of impermanence, insignificance, in the face of the permanence
and indifferent splendour of the natural world. It is surprising that Thomas
did not make his readers uncomfortable. Presumably he did not, or he
would not have received so many commissions to write this sort of book.
Yet he is uncomfortable, as he is in his poems. He looks on English things
impatiently, but also as a lover might look on his beloved for the last

time. He seems always conscious that a world is coming to an end, though he never says so, it is in his tone and it is the tone of his poems; which it has taken us fifty years to hear.

From the introduction to *In Pursuit of Spring* (London: Wildwood House, 1981), republished in *People and Places: A Selection 1975–1987* (Manchester: Carcanet, 1988)

EDWARD THOMAS IN HEAVEN

Edward, with thinning hair and hooded eyes
Walking in England, haversack sagging, emptied of lies,
Snuffing and rubbing Old Man in the palm of your hand
You smelled an avenue, dark, nameless, without end.

In France, supposing the shell that missed
You and sucked your breath out as it passed
Released your soul according to the doctrine
You disbelieved and were brought up in,
From slaughtered fields to Christian purgatory?
(Assuming your working life, the sad history
You sweated through, and marvellous middens of rural stuff
You piled together were not purgatory enough?)
Are you now a changed person, gay and certain?
Your eyes unhooded, bland windows without a curtain?
Then it would not be heaven. It would be mere loss
To be welcomed in by an assured Edward Thomas.
There must be doubt in heaven, to accommodate him
And others we listen for daily, who were human,
Snuffing and puzzling, which is why we listen.
How shall we recognise the ones we love
If next we see them fitting round God's finger like a glove?
While close-by round him, mistier,
Farther and farther, all the birds
Of Oxfordshire and Gloucestershire
And angels of Breconshire and Hereford
Sing for them, and unimaginable Edward?

P. J. Kavanagh
from *Collected Poems* (Manchester: Carcanet, 1992)

Grevel Lindop

The poetry of Edward Thomas has been a formative influence on my own work ever since I first read him properly, in the late 1970s. I'm fascinated by three interconnected features of his poems: his treatment of memory, his sense of the evanescence of personal identity, and above all his scepticism about the adequacy of language. From 'Up in the Wind' and its inn without a signboard, to 'Old Man' with its reflection that 'in the name there's nothing' – a statement that introduces a wealth of reflections on youth and age, drawn precisely from the plant's contradictory names – Thomas is fascinated by the uncertainties of language, and of naming in particular. A philosophical historian might make something of the fact that his first poems appeared in 1916, the same year as Saussure's *Course in General Linguistics*. But Thomas's poems also have magic. Their subtle plainness of language expresses a sense of mystery, impermanence and longing which casts an irresistible spell.

Thomas is probably present in much that I've written, but one poem in particular I owe to being reminded of him, repeatedly, a good many years ago when marking student exam scripts on modern poetry. Amid the repeated tedium of the essays – no better or worse, on average, than those of any other year – the occasional quoted lines from Thomas shone like jewels and somehow, by their light, I found myself mentally transported to a much-loved place of my own, not a typical Thomas location but the summit of Helm Crag in the Lake District. The intense solitude of this spot, which is nonetheless within view of a road and several farms, seemed as immediate as if I were actually there; and without thinking I found myself jotting down this short poem.

ON HELM CRAG

Height, expressed only in scraps of sound
carried up from the valley: a dog barks,
a motorcycle scores an inch of road
silence resumes; and once a child's shout
cutting thinly across the air
engraves its diamond-scratch on the clear lens
of height, through which all things appear
small and perfect, and myself invisible,
merged an instant into crag and valley
as if I too expected whatever they wait for
to happen the moment I am gone from here.

Grevel Lindop
from *Tourists* (Manchester: Carcanet, 1987) and
Selected Poems (Manchester: Carcanet, 2000)

Lachlan Mackinnon

I admire the spiritual integrity of Edward Thomas's poems. I admire the extraordinarily developed technique of his verse. Eccentric and central, he made fugitive emotions permanent.

EDWARD THOMAS

We had lunch at his pub up in the wind.
It never blew. Amazingly
elderly bikers, silver-haired,
some of them leather-trousered, clogged
the car park.
                Much later, in the church,
in the visitors' book
below the memorial windows
(heart-shaking windows: Laurence Whistler)
I found a signature from only
nine years ago. Against it
'Artists' Rifles'. A man who might have known him.
Before that, though, we'd driven
a doubtful road until it vanished.
                      Rubble.
We parked and walked. We found the turning-point
and turned downhill.
               A slippery slope,
just enough roots across it
to stay, to balance.
              Underneath us,
almost vertically underneath us,
the valley, road and tiny houses
opened up like a gulf of distance.
                   Beside the stone,
the memorial stone, a young couple lay,
lazing and sunning by the legend

cut in brass.
                    We sat down breathless.

Born of a day in Lambeth. Died at Arras.

I wondered whether that withdrawn man
would have laughed at this
almost unreachable memorial,
this knotty hillside dedicated to him
because he went from here to seek the death
his poems ached for.

And I loved him, who had stopped wanting love
or anything. Who shouldered what he must.

Lachlan Mackinnon

Glyn Maxwell

Many poems are addressed to people who won't read them. We wish they would, but they won't. I think even more poems are addressed to people who can't read them, because they're gone. We care about that audience more. The fourteen poems in 'Letters to Edward Thomas' are fourteen examples of *writing to one who cannot read it*, whether in the form of a note left on a kitchen table and found untouched (I to V), a Valentine sent to a dead man (X), a Christmas list sent up a chimney (IX) or a poem from me to Edward Thomas (XIV). The writer of the first thirteen is a friend of Thomas's, based on Eleanor Farjeon.

All poems need some sort of pressure to get started: the demand of this series of poems was so urgent as to constitute an order. I had recently developed a deep admiration for Thomas's work; I had long thought Frost about as good as a poet can be. I had just moved to Amherst with a wife and new child, a few doors from one of Frost's houses; New England is where Thomas would have lived if he'd taken Frost up on his offer and left England in 1914. I know a good deal about the First World War, because my father used to take us on tours of the war graves when we were young; my grandfather fought on the Somme. And it was the incomparably beautiful autumn of New England at the time, and an autumnal feeling pervades all our thoughts of the war dead, all our thoughts of poets past.

I used pentameters, their sort of pentameters, soft and conversational, but broke them up with trimeters, just to suggest corners being turned, roads being taken and not taken, weather changing, light going.

And I dedicated the poem to Derek Walcott, because it was he who first introduced me to the power of Edward Thomas, and it was he who set in train the sequence of events that led me to New England in the autumn of 1997.

LETTERS TO EDWARD THOMAS
for Derek Walcott

Dear Edward, just a note to say we're here
And nowhere could be better. And your key
Was where you said it would be, and the air
Is fresh with things you think, while looking kindly
On us intruders. Jenny says let's wait,
You can't be far away, while George of course
Has toppled into every single seat
To find his favourite. Five-to-one it's yours
He'll plump for, but Team Captain of the Cottage
Declares it's not allowed. I've said we're off
On a foraging expedition to the village
And that's where we are now, or soon enough
We shall be. We can't wait to see you, Edward.
We feel as if we have. I mean your home
Was breathing softly when we all invaded,
Not only air but breath, as in the poem
   I treasure that you showed me,
Which clings and flutters in me like a leaf
And falls when I remember how you told me
You couldn't write a poem to save your life!
   Consider that thing done.
Here's just a note to say we've been and gone.

*

Dear Edward, just a note to say your wood
Has summoned us away, as you yourself
Hinted it might. The horde has swooped and fed
And drunk (in George's case three times) your health,
And Rose and Peter wouldn't hear of sleep,
Said it was banished back to Hampstead, swore
No path would go untrodden, and no sheep
Untroubled by us – George said: 'And no door
Of any inns unswung!' and so we're gone
A second time, though you'll have no idea
I wrote a first time. Blame the evening sun

153

For luring us back out. We love it here
And only you are missing. What that does
Is make us lonely. True, for all my chatter.
A beauty-spot will do that. What it has
Is one thing missing. Ask me what's the matter
   Anywhere it's beautiful
And there's your answer. Long before it's dark
You'll hear us creatures rolling up the hill
In twos, to be the last into your Ark,
   Or to be told by you
What things we missed, went by, lost, didn't do.

*

Dear Edward, just a note to say today
The sun came in and scooped them up like eggs,
Our hearts, and set them fourteen miles away
And said now get there on your London legs –
So off we've gone, obedient, though sure
It's nothing but an agency of you,
And so I pin this to the master's door
In sure and certain hope you'll be there too,
With all our hearts at journey's end, in some
Vale of picnic-cloth. Last night we played
The word-games Adam taught to Eve, and some
Eve knew but never told him. Jenny made
A game of 'Where Was Edward?' which I won
By saying you were walking and had paused
To hear two nightingales – and not gone on
Until you'd taught them singing. This had caused
   The rumpus of all time
Amid the birds, which we could hear from here,
One saying, 'Do we teach him how to rhyme?'
And all the rest as far as Gloucestershire
   Going 'Yes, don't you remember?'
George said you'd walked so fast it was November.

*

Dear Mr Thomas, now it's been so long
We lost your first name in the meadow grass
At dusk, when on a road we thought was wrong
We started recognising things. Your house
Then viewed us dimly. But you must excuse
The new meander in my messages,
And blame it on the elderflower juice
That George said would be *choice* with sandwiches
And seems so to have been. We all agree
We shall not leave tomorrow if our host
Insists on his invisibility,
And clears the table round us like a ghost
And seems to comment in the silences.
Rose and Peter have to leave, but George
Declares this week is cancelled, or his is.
Or so we can infer from how he snores.
      I tried to start some games
But after walking longer than we've ever
Who's in the mood for folding up the names
Of ones we know in town? Who cares whose lover
      Really cares for whom?
Our heads are bowed and spinning in the room.

*

Dear Edward, just a note to say I left
A quiverful all weekend, in the hope
You'd sit down at your table. Here we laughed
And lolled for what seemed ages, and sat up
For what seemed scarcely time at all, but only
To see grey dawn arrive and blush to find us
Watching, late enchanted into early.
It's Monday noon and everything's behind us.
Rose and Peter took the six-fifteen,
As George and Jenny meant to. They at last
Boarded the nine o'clock, George in a dream
He started telling as the engine hissed,
Commissioning them for London. So I'm left
Abandoned to restore the place to how

It looked on that bright morning we arrived,
That seems so long ago. Time is so slow
       Without you. Then again
The moment that I shut the door, no doubt
You'll reach the gate and grin and ask me when
My friends are coming. I'll ask you about
       Your poems, as if you'd say,
Knocking the ashes from your favourite clay.

*

To punish you I threw the note away
I wrote you in your kitchen. Now my thanks
Are scribbled among strangers as we sway
Through Hampshire towards town, and the sun blinks
Behind the poplars. Edward Thomas, great
Unknowable, omniscient, your cottage
Waits for you: no sign we ever sat
Around your fire, no trace of pie or porridge,
Nor dreg of George's ale remains. No talks
Of ours will last the time you take to light
Your clay, and your first steps will make our walks
As brief and viewless as a shower at night.
These are our heartfelt thanks. We could have haunted
Many houses where we wouldn't see you.
At yours we thought it likely to be granted
Sight or sound, but it was not to be. You
       Were needed in the field,
By hawk or hedge, who knows, their need was greater
Than ours, who wanted names for things revealed
That we should know by now or may ask later.
       And reason not my need,
Who writes what nobody but she will read.

*

Poem to Mr Thomas and Mr Frost,
Created by a dandelion you passed
As you in talk about a stanza crossed

156

Half Herefordshire, till you sat at last
In silence. I'm the dandelion that saw
Two aspens shake and shed in a quick wind,
And tried to loose her own leaves to the floor
Like they did and did manage in the end,
When they were both long gone in the great storm.
One to the west and one to the east, away
Towards the blood-commander in the dawn
And all his soldiers, pink becoming grey.
And you won't see this, if you live as long
As what you sent me: 'As the team's head-brass'
It starts but isn't titled. If I'm wrong
And your great hands one day are holding these
        Dandelion hairs,
The storm would not have come, the trees have kept
Their ground, and through the hearts of all the shires
Would Mr Thomas and Mr Frost have stepped
        And war like a rough sky
Been overlooked in talk, and blown on by.

*

Poem for Mr Edward Eastaway,
Who lives here care of me, so no one knows
His name is Rumplestiltskin and by day
He rips your verse to pieces in great prose.
By night he turns his prose to poetry
Because a poet told him to who saw
A mighty fine recruit for poverty
And wrote the line that opened his front door.
They have rejected Edward Eastaway
Again: the letter came this afternoon.
One knows precisely what a fool will say
Somehow. We've many stars to the one moon
In our night sky, but all that makes a face
Of that recurring rock is the one sun
It likes, without which it must find its place
To hide behind, or make believe it's gone.
        Edward Eastaway,

157

Whose name that isn't and whose time it ain't,
Who's living here or was just yesterday,
Or in Wales, Wiltshire, Oxfordshire or Kent,
        The rumour's that you crossed
The Channel. Stanza-break, sighs Mr Frost.

*

Dear Father Thomas, every Christmas Eve
Good children of the world are quite as shy
As I am to write *Dear* and then believe
For twenty lines our goodness could be why
It's worth our time. Our faith turns to this thread
That shuttles downward while the mischievous
Need nothing but a coalsack by the bed,
And wake to the same carols. Each of us
Is writing, Edward, asking the great space
Below us what is missing still, what gift
Will make us whole again. We fold and place
Our answers in the chimney and are left
These pink embarrassed authors by the fire.
We all talk tommy-rot we understand.
Somebody coughs, politely to enquire
Did they not kick a ball on No Man's Land
        Two years ago? 'That's so,'
Smiles Peter, adding: 'Not tonight, I fear.'
And I hear George's voice say: 'Cricket, though,
So Edward gets a knock.' But he's not here,
        George, he's where you are,
Restless tonight like all good children are.

*

One dead was sent a Valentine, so both
Were spared their lover's blushes. What I write
Is on its way nowhere, is less than breath,
So might be anything, as nothing might.
It's that there's nothing now that doesn't seem
As if it's where it ended. All the paths

Beyond this word or this become the same:
Thickets, or a handing-down of deaths
As by a school official, not a teacher,
A visiting official by one gate.
Now all the hope there is is in a picture
Of P.E.Thomas gone, because my fate
Is never to foresee, believed or no.
Is to be wrong. These words are packing up
And going. Words I mean you not to know
Don't see why they should move in any step
     I fix them with. So go,
You English words, while he's alive, and blow
Through all of him so Englishmen will know
You loved him and who cares how long ago,
     And hide him from the light
He'll strike and hold until his clay's alight.

*

Dear Edward, when the war was over, you
Were standing where a wood had been, and though
Nothing was left for you to name or view
You waited till new trees had hidden you.
Then you came home and in a forest called
The Times your name was found, and not among
The officers but in a clearing filled
With verses, yours. Then your new name was sung
With all the old. And children leafing through
And old men staring and their daughters stilled
With admiration: all this happened too,
Or had already by the time you pulled
The book I hide this in from your top shelf
And blew its dust away. The year is what,
1930? '60? Please yourself,
But do remember as you smile and sit
     That everything's foreseen
By a good reader, as I think I am
On David's Day of 1917,
Reaching for blotting-paper. Now's the time

To fold the work away
And find me on this bleak or brilliant day.

                              *

Choose me, Sie deutsche Worte. This is the first
Of all the letters you will never read,
Edward. I was shy in my own west
Always, so you never read a word
I sent, but this is written with as clear
A mind as has been opened like a shell.
'Greatly loved in the battery,' writes this dear
Major Lushington, who says you fell
In early morning with some battle won
And all the soldiers dancing. You were loved
In the battery and in the morning sun
Brought out the blessed clay, when something moved
Like cloud perhaps. The Major asked us round
To tell us you knew nothing. That your book
Of Shakespeare's Sonnets that they knelt and found
Was strangely creased and the clay didn't break
            Which Helen gave your son,
And Robert's *North of Boston* in your kit
They gave to me, not needing it. And when
They reached you you were not marked, not hit,
            Breeze blowing in your hair,
Chosen. What had stopped your heart was air.

                              *

Dear Edward, now there's no one at the end
There's nothing I can't say. Some eight or nine
I have by heart. Your farmer-poet friend
Is flying around the world on a fine line
That starts in you, or grows out from the days
You passed together. England is the same,
Cheering to order, set in its new ways
It thinks are immemorial. The Somme
Has trees beside it but some shovelwork

Will bring the dead to light. There's so much more
I want to say, because the quiet is dark,
And when the writing ends I reach a shore
Beyond which it's so cold and that's what changed,
Edward, on that Easter Monday. You
Were land to me, were England unestranged,
Were what I thought it had amounted to,
  But look at the fields now,
Look eyelessly at them, like the dug men
Still nodding out of Flanders. Tell them how
You walked and how you saw, and how your pen
  Did nothing more than that,
And, when it stopped, what you were gazing at.

*

Dear Edward Thomas, Frost died, I was born.
I am a father and you'd like the names
We gave our girl. I'm writing this at dawn
Where Robert lived, in Amherst, and your poems
I keep by his, his housebrick to your tile.
I teach you to my students, and aloud
I wonder what you would have come to. While
I wonder they look out at a white cloud
And so we pass the time. Perhaps I'll guess
Which one will ask me what they always ask:
Whom do I write for? Anybody? Yes,
You. And I'll walk home in the great dusk
Of Massachusetts that extends away
Far west and north, the ways you meant to go
To save your life. A good end to the day,
That's going to be. It's going to be cool, though,
  I see out in the town,
And start to turn the trees to what the world
Comes flocking here to see: eight shades of brown
Men never saw, and ninety-nine of gold,
  More shades than can have names,
Or names to bring them back when the snow comes.

Peter McDonald

I believe that Edward Thomas was a great critical, as well as poetic, intelligence of the twentieth century. The achievement of his poetry cannot be separated from that of his criticism; Thomas was not somehow released into poetry from the bondage of reading in 1914, but his writing of verse then did produce poetry – *real* poetry, with its own 'tremendous life' – from the dense matter of a lifetime's reading, reflection, and judgement. These two things – creation and criticism – are not finally separable, and one is not to be estimated at the expense of the other: like all true poetry, Thomas's is full of, and made possible by, an intelligence at a special, and unsparing, pitch of commitment; as the beneficiaries of this in our reading of the poems, we must not pretend that the intelligence has been over-ridden by poetical genius, as if by magic. If it is accepted that the quality of Thomas's poetry obliges us to take seriously the quality of his criticism, then we must be both cautious and scrupulous in our understanding of the relation between critical thinking and poetic composition in general.

As evidence of Thomas's critical centrality, I would cite a passage from his *Walter Pater* (1913), which says almost all that can be said on the matter of a poet's 'voice' and (that other great cliché of ours) 'personality' in poetry:

> Much good poetry is far from the speech of any men now, or perhaps at any recorded time, dwelling on this earth. There would be no poetry if men could speak all they think and all that they feel. Each great new writer is an astonishment to his own age, if it hears him, by the apparent shrillness and discordancy of the speech he has made in solitude.
>
> . . . The more we know of any man the more singular he will appear. . . . Literature . . . has to make words of such a spirit, and arrange them in such a manner, that they will do all a speaker can do by innumerable gestures and their innumerable shades, by tone and pitch of voice, by speed, by pauses, by all that he is and will become.

Intelligence at this level, expressing itself thus, rebukes our own complacency – as great criticism must do – and it stands as a reproach to those who reserve their wholehearted commitment for the promotion of a bland consensus in poetry and about poetry, of what is reasonable, supposedly accessible, or otherwise familiar and deserving. The consensus, of course, is often a tyranny; and the masters who crave critical promotion of their products are liable now – as ever – to be charlatans and bullies. Against all this, I set Edward Thomas in his entirety; the full round of his creative and critical intellect; the diligence and integrity of his life.

The first line of my poem is taken from Edward Thomas's War Diary. It ends, after the entry for 8 April, the penultimate day of his life, with these notes:

The light of the new moon and every star

And no more singing for the bird …

I never understood quite what was meant by God

The morning chill and clear hurts my skin while it delights my mind.

Neuville in early morning with its flat straight crest with trees and houses – the beauty of this silent empty scene of no inhabitants and hid troops, but don't know why I could have cried and didn't.

WAR DIARY

The light of the new moon and every star
concentrates now in a reflection
of trailing grasses and cow-parsley
from a puddle; clear glass is a mirror
as the night goes up into action
on wet roads, never to return:
the country roads long since taken,
known mile by mile, yard by yard,
and still abandoned. What did I see there?
Who, maybe? Some such question.

Peter McDonald
from *House of Clay* (Manchester: Carcanet, 2007)

Patrick McGuinness

When I think of the Edward Thomas poems I value, I think, like most people, of those in which something about to be lost is seen as for the first time. It's a common sensation, common enough to be a cliché, but it takes an uncommon poet to make that the base note of his work without becoming just a dealer in the small change of loss and regret.

It's not that Thomas's nostalgia is pre-emptive, or that he can only see places or experience feelings when they are infused with a foretaste of their pastness. It's that his most characteristic poems unfold in a kind of triple time: a present moment that slides ahead to its resting place in the past. His poems don't try to escape Time by launching themselves, vertically as it were, up and out of it, cordoning off the lyric instant from Time's annihilating sweep the way lesser poems might. Rather, they are intent on inhabiting the moment across the full range of its tenses: the *is*, the *was* and the *will be*. Thomas follows the grain of the tenses the way a carpenter follows the grain of the wood – Time for him makes a pattern rather than a crisis. This I think is what makes him very different from the poets who merely look or sound like him, and makes him more than the poignant elegist he is often made to seem.

A poem of mine which owes a lot to Thomas is 'Déjà-vu'. Although his vantage-point is not so much *déjà-vu* as *first known when lost*, I don't think I'd have written this small poem unless I'd been reading Thomas on a morning when I was preparing to teach a class on Proust. Both writers are obsessed with tense as the grammatical manifestation both of the way we feel and of the way we contemplate our feelings, and consider experience to be the layering of tenses across perceptions.

Like most people I came across 'Adlestrop' for the first time in school. I remember being taken with that opening 'Yes', enjoying that sense that the poem was not just lying on the page but part of an exchange, if only with itself. Then came that delightful, unexpected, clarification: 'I remember Adlestrop – / The name'. This poem toyed with us, especially after the Nature-and-ennobling-thoughts poetry we'd studied before. It promised us a rooted poem of place, only to set itself in a location that was purely transitional, that was in its way a non-place or even an anti-place: an express train on a bare platform, topped off with a Beckettian 'No one left and no one came'. 'What I saw / Was Adlestrop – only the name', the poem reiterated in the second stanza, before suddenly opening out in the next to take in that list of sights and sounds that tumble over in a train of 'ands'. 'Adlestrop' becomes a poem of space rather than mere place, opening upwards and outwards in ways that amaze me now as much as they did when I first read it.

Thomas is particular about names. There is the startling reversal of the expected in 'The Word' when the speaking voice invokes an 'empty thingless name', as distinct from the usual 'nameless thing', sung by a thrush. Here too, he writes, 'the name, only the name I hear', before expanding in what we might call a Proustian way (the two authors have more than skin-deep similarities) on what it triggers. This 'pure thrush word' as he calls it is *thingless*, but, like *Adlestrop*, it is a point of entry into something expansive and resounding.

One of my poems which replays some of these themes is 'Cwlwm'. The word in Welsh means *knot*, and I wrote it when I was tangled up in learning Welsh, that 'rich and massy' language (as Thomas called it). The further you are from a language, the more connections – paradoxically – you think you can make between its words. In a sense you have to, having no inner access to the new tongue, you map your way through it by often quite eccentric mnemonic paths of correspondence, inversion or association. Thus I was struck by how *cwlwm* meant knot and *cwmwl* meant cloud; *canol* meant centre and *calon* meant heart; *adar* and *aderyn* were bird and birds, and *geiriadur* was a dictionary, where I imagined the words were perched. 'Cwlwm' attempts to describe that feeling a learner has when the new language seems difficult and strange: at first the words tangle and catch and bar your way. Then suddenly, if you persevere, you reach that moment, your first taste of fluency, when you feel you've crossed some kind of a border: it gets less like a climb, breathing gets easier, and all that resistance is converted into momentum. The poem tries to reflect that marvellous but unforced sense of opened vistas that 'Adlestrop' finishes with, or that feeling, in 'The Word', of lift-off as the 'pure thrush word' flies up unconstrained by any *thing* it might connote.

DÉJÀ-VU

Two tenses grappling with one instant, one perception:
forgotten as it happens, recalled before it has begun.

Patrick McGuinness
(Uncollected; first published *The Times Literary Supplement*,
16 June 2006)

CWLWM

Cwlwm was the knot the language had me in,
the tangle-throated names of villages and streets;
I saw double before I learned to see them twice.
Then the roadsigns started to take root,

the place-names lifted off the letters
that composed them as in films the spirit
leaves the body. *Calon* into *canol*,
heart into centre, fluent as a stencil

peeling back to leave itself behind.
Adar, aderyn were the birds Clément
Ader's aeroplane translated – the word's
idea of flight joined coast to coast

in the dangerous, sustaining air.
Now from the *geiriadur* the words take off,
the dictionary empties page by page,
letter by letter, column by column.

Patrick McGuinness
from *The Canals of Mars* (Manchester: Carcanet, 2004)

Welsh words: *cwlwm*: knot; *calon*: heart; *canol*: centre; *adar/aderyn*:
bird/birds; *geiriadur*: dictionary.

Jamie McKendrick

Few other lyric poets offer such an unerring sense of the poem as a means, often by indirections, to 'find directions out', as though the poem itself was a compass, or a 'path, winding like silver'. It's as if Edward Thomas's poems are endowed with the magnetite that's said to help birds navigate over long distances by day and night. Each of his poems is like a miniature quest. Some like 'The Glory' admit defeat in their quest: 'I cannot bite the day to the core.' Yet even that ending arrives with well-earned fatigue after lines of such richness – 'And tread the pale dust pitted with small dark drops' – that they negate any sense of defeat for the reader.

A poem like his 'Beauty' seems trapped in depression until, midway, the poet sees himself as a dark river, 'while / Cross breezes cut the surface to a file' – this beautiful characteristic line is where the poem takes light, and flight. The file, an image for surface turbulence as well as for the craft of poetry, seems to secure the accelerated movement of the poem's last half – mediated, as often, by bird imagery. 'There I find my rest, as through the dusk air / Flies what yet lives in me: Beauty is there.' The poem's movement, which begins with him framing an epitaph for himself 'Here lies …', ends with the discovered reversal 'There . . . flies'.

Similarly in 'Adlestrop' the almost comic pointlessness of a train stop in the middle of nowhere becomes grounded – or whatever the aerial equivalent of that would be – with birdsong:

> Close by, and round him, mistier,
> Farther and farther, all the birds
> Of Oxfordshire and Gloucestershire.

The shift from disorientation to re-orientation is done entirely through sound. ('The steam hissed. Someone cleared his throat'). If it were merely a contrast between the mechanical and human (bad) and the natural and avian (good) the poem would sustain little interest. What it does though, in a visionary way, is link place names, naming and language itself to a wider order. It's this almost epic scale of Thomas's small poems which makes him so irreplaceable.

LOSS

If what you hear is like a field
and the height of a lark above it
then the field has dwindled and the wind
bells on the razor wire around
the verge beyond which nothing
but the pointless din of outer space,
the addled Muzak of the spheres,
gets through to you. Acoustic junk.
The earth itself begins to hum
with the infinitesimal tunnelling
of umpteen holts and vaults and brood halls
and the sky each dawn is lower than
the day before as though wound down
like a press-head on a worm-screw
where once you woke and heard the threads
of birdsong trailed from hedge to hedge
as clear and intricately round
as a palm-bark epic in Telugu.

Jamie McKendrick
from *Sky Nails: Poems 1979–1997* (London: Faber and Faber,
2002) and *The Kiosk on the Brink* (Oxford: Oxford University
Press, 1993)

TINNITUS

The rustle of foil, a tide of pins, a wave
which never breaking
crinkles from the far side of the brink

and inches nearer with its crest
of decibels and wreckage under which
still you catch the cars diminishing, phrase

after phrase of the evening bird
fainter each time but holding out
from a twig upon a tree within a wood.

Jamie McKendrick
from *Sky Nails* (London: Faber and Faber, 2002) and *The
Kiosk on the Brink* (Oxford: Oxford University Press, 1993)

Andrew McNeillie

'Windfalls of war's storm' is Gerard Manley Hopkins's phrase, himself a windfall of life's storm. I'd been brooding on this idea while dwelling on vagrancy, and ideas of sanity, and the kind of 'tramps' we used to see in the back country of our archipelago even when I was a boy in North Wales. One or two my father knew in Galloway were windfalls of the Great War's storm, and so perhaps were some of those we saw in Wales. And I had just that day been reading Ivor Gurney for whom the war's storm wrought such mental havoc. In particular one of my favourite poems by him haunted me again: 'First Time In', the poem you'll remember with the 'Welsh colony':

> Hiding in sandbag ditches, whispering consolatory
> Soft foreign things. Then we were taken in
> To low huts candle-lit, shaded close by slitten
> Oilsheets, and there the boys gave us kind welcome,
> So that we looked out as from the edge of home,
> Sang us Welsh things, and changed all former notions
> To human hopeful things.

The edge of home . . . Then unexpectedly I was invited to contribute to this volume, and the first poem that's here is I suppose obliquely informed by all this. I mean especially Hopkins's phrase and then, out of immediate hearing, the grief I register in Gurney. His phrases 'as from the edge of home', among the Welsh boys, and 'To human hopeful things', seem to me particularly potent in the context of Edward Thomas's tragic life, his terrible enlistment and the song it liberated. Thomas's 'The Trumpet' and 'Roads' are also on the radar here, as more obviously is 'The Thrush'.

The first book I read by Edward Thomas was his life of Richard Jefferies. Jefferies was a peripatetic ruralist, though not I think an Aristotelian. His powers of observation expressed so magically in his prose had deep appeal for Edward Thomas. His struggle to earn a living with his pen also struck a chord. Like Jefferies, Thomas was a man for mooching about the country, if ever there was one. But what was it drove him along the open road? Between escaping from and escaping to lies a fine divide, as fine as any poet's thin partition. Some strain in Thomas's melancholy and sense of doom resided in his fractured identity as a London Welshman. He loved to go to Wales, to visit his relations in Pontarddulais, just north of Swansea, and to explore the country roundabout. In my wild youth I identified with Jefferies and Thomas and others like them (Henry David Thoreau, J. M. Synge). I was twenty-one that morning in May when I stepped out the few miles from Rhydamman to Llandeilo to interview Carey Morris for the *South Wales Guardian*. (They paid me £5.00 a week and penny-a-line.) Morris's vivid recall amazed me, as did the dramatic idea that Thomas had been there before me, in living memory still just alive. My poem's a piece of quick reportage, in rough-and-ready sonnet form. I think of it as a shorthand elegy, to Carey Morris and to the ghost of Edward Thomas as he crossed my path that day. Something of the doom in Thomas's gaze that Morris observed (and deplored), I can see as I write this, in the National Portrait Gallery postcard of him that I keep on the wall above my desk.

IN MEMORIAM:
EDWARD THOMAS (1878–1917)

May my poor tribute touch: the sorrow
in your heart, that drove you to enlist;
the guilt and grief you carried in your breast,
its aftertaste foretasted, in all you saw
and wrote of mortal loss, and waste,
between the eye and the object; joy,
that queer word gay, as when a wide-eyed boy
you first stepped out, a latecomer at last,
on the wild road, foot soldier herald
to the birds and broken ranks of hedge.
Life's storm and war's storm since still sharpen their music,
in deadly earnest. But you stand on here and hold
the ground for us, forever, on the stark page,
singing like a thrush, to cut us to the quick.

Andrew McNeillie
from *Slower* (Manchester: Carcanet, 2006)

IN MEMORIAM:
CAREY MORRIS RA (1882–1968)

In the clutter of his studio
he made what I took to be trench tea,
leaves in the cup, hot water. No, Tommy
knew no such luxury, oh no . . .
But those leaves about my gums and teeth
made me gag as if a whiff of gas still
lingered on the air he breathed, enough to kill
a green recruit like me, or hasten death.

But death spared him then. He was a fighter,
this South Wales Borderer of the Slade
and Newlyn schools, a wheezy raconteur
who told how Edward Thomas would call by,
sit where I sat, with that 'doomed look' he had,
as if already claimed for history.

Andrew McNeillie
from *Slower* (Manchester: Carcanet, 2006)

Esther Morgan

Re-reading Thomas, I have been surprised by just how much he's influenced my work, without me even realising it. The following poem is connected obliquely to 'As the team's head brass' and more generally to that vein in his poetry that presages the loss of a way of life which the First World War accelerated. This sense of decline and fall has been re-activated in my imagination over the last couple of years by the house I've been living in – a sprawling Edwardian place in the Oxfordshire countryside which hasn't been renovated for several decades. I don't own it but have had the good fortune, with my partner, to be its care-taker. Much of the original furniture and fittings, such as the servants' bells, are intact if somewhat battered. It was built for a lifestyle that began to disappear almost as soon as the final brick was laid, and yet a century later I find myself a tenant surrounded by the remnants of that time, mildewed family photographs and all. No wonder that Thomas's poems have struck a renewed chord, particularly their sensitivity to the fragile nature of memory and of what can outlast a life, as in 'Bob's Lane':

> Many years since, Bob Hayward died, and now
> None passes there because the mist and the rain
> Out of the elms have turned the lane to slough
> And gloom, the name alone survives, Bob's Lane.

My poem 'Endurance' is very much in this territory: the title is taken from the name of Shackleton's ship on his ill-fated Antarctic voyage and the poem is an attempt to explore different kinds of survival. Shackleton's exploits secured him and his men an enduring fame, but the lives of the women of that period are far more hidden, their legacy nameless but influential nevertheless.

ENDURANCE

It was the photographer who risked his life,
who dived the expedition wreck
to bring back faces to the light,
their glass transparencies.

On the other side of the world
the women turned in again for winter
storing their sweetness
like the bulbs they wrapped in newspaper
to save them from frost.

Keepers of locked rooms and skeleton keys,
they knew how to put a house to sleep,
layering linen with lavender,
swaddling silver against tarnish,
stowing away.

On nights when breath is visible
I listen to timbers creaking
like a seized ship:
the house rigged in ice and going down.

Esther Morgan
from *The Silence Living in Houses* (Tarset: Bloodaxe, 2005)

Andrew Motion

I wrote this poem after giving a reading up on the Norfolk coast; I mentioned liking Robert Frost in the chat between poems, and at the end someone asked me whether I'd ever met him. No, I said, I hadn't (I was nine years old when Frost died) – but this fellow had, and in circumstances which I borrowed for my poem. It seemed appropriate to use the eclogue form that Frost himself employs in some of his own work, but my intention was to glance sideways as well, at some of the narrative techniques that are shared by Edward Thomas. In his earlier poems ('Up in the Wind', for instance) these tend to be comparatively clear and story-driven, but as his voice finds its true pitch they become more subtle and oblique, and the music more complex. In this respect 'Talk About Robert Frost' reflects only a small part of his output, but its subject (the watchful but precarious position of a person in nature) is one he never ceased to explore.

TALK ABOUT ROBERT FROST

'Did you ever hear Frost read?'

                'At Vassar,
In my final year. Some friends and I
Had gone week-ending in the woods –
Two days of reading, fending for ourselves,
And one wise-owl professor taking charge.
He knew Frost from way back, and so Frost came.
Or blew in, rather, through the cabin door.'

'You must have thought…'

                 'I thought
I'd seen the face of God: the snow-fall hair
All blustered up, the kindly uncle face.
I couldn't tell what trouble he had known
Or where he kept it to remember it.
Or how near death he was, he looked so…
Well, I might say. Blithe is what I mean.'

'And sounded what? Content?'

'I'd say he'd sunk so deep into his past
That now the world was not the place he lived.
But never mind. The sudden early dusk
(I should have mentioned it was winter) closed
The second he stepped in, and left the air
Outside the cabin – with the crowded beech
Stripped leafless, and the branches underlined
By bars of ice – a dense, electric blue.
A sold thing, like silk, and smothering
Except in one place where the boughs swept back
To frame a funnel-view of twenty miles
And show the valley with its orange lights.'

'And he read what?'

'Well-worn, familiar things. It made me think
Of how a baker might pass round the rolls
He'd just pulled from an oven. Warm, like that.'

'You mean you'd heard it all before?'

'I mean that while he read a storm brewed up
From nothing, and its passage through the woods
Became a way to us. Town lights disappeared;
Clouds, as white and perfect in their roundness
As a child's idea of weather, swelled and joined;
And you could hear it drawing close: the sky
Began to creak with flakes collecting for the land
As anxiously as footsteps pressing into snow itself.'

'Did Frost pull up?'

                              'He never heard. But there
Behind him in the window – there it was.'

'And you?'

                              'We kept our circle as we had to do,
All watching him, he thought, all keeping step
While he trod backwards through his own old snow,
And came and went through sundry other trees,
But drifting off, in fact – half out to meet the storm
And revel in the thrill of it, half inwards
To ourselves and taking cover where we could.'

'Like him, in fact.'

                              'You could say that. Like him;
Except – I told you – he had no idea. Or none
Until the weather reached us. Then he knew.'

Andrew Motion

THE SUN USED TO SHINE

The sun used to shine while we two walked
Slowly together, paused and started
Again, and sometimes mused, sometimes talked
As either pleased, and cheerfully parted

Each night. We never disagreed
Which gate to rest on. The to be
And the late past we gave small heed.
We turned from men or poetry

To rumours of the war remote
Only till both stood disinclined
For aught but the yellow flavorous coat
Of an apple wasps had undermined;

Or a sentry of dark betonies,
The stateliest of small flowers on earth,
At the forest verge; or crocuses
Pale purple as if they had their birth

In sunless Hades fields. The war
Came back to mind with moonrise
Which soldiers in the east afar
Beheld then. Nevertheless, our eyes

Could as well imagine the Crusades
Or Caesar's battles. Everything
To faintness like those rumours fades –
Like the brook's water glittering

Under the moonlight – like those walks
Now – like us two that took them, and
The fallen apples, all the talks
And silences – like memory's sand

When the tide covers it late or soon,
And other men through other flowers
In those fields under the same moon
Go talking and have easy hours.

Edward Thomas

Paul Muldoon

In 'The Killdeer', from Moy Sand and Gravel, I was hoping against hope that the spirit of Edward Thomas might have been breathing down my neck as I wrote it. I'm certain that I was conscious of the amazing combination of tact and tactility of which he was capable in a short poem like 'Thaw', in which he allows for that wonderful argument from nature of the 'speculating rooks' seeing 'what we below could not see, Winter pass'. I'm certain, too, that I was thinking of the word-play on 'speculating' both in the sense of 'contemplating' and 'the action or practice of buying and selling goods, land, stocks and shares etc. in order to profit by the rise and fall in the market value' (OED), a doubly acute observation of the rooks in their 'high nests', when I attempted a similar play on the 'beech' as the root of book. The 'clutching' in 'The Killdeer' is used much in the way 'speculating' is used in 'Thaw' — that's to say in the sense of grasping at, or grappling with, an idea. The structure of 'The Killdeer' is precisely the same as another of my favourite Edward Thomas poems, 'Tall Nettles', with two four line stanzas rhyming abab. Yet again, I was hoping that the eye for detail Thomas brings to 'the dust on the nettles, never lost / Except to prove the sweetness of a shower' might be translated, however crudely, into the image of the 'four pear-shaped eggs / with their pointed ends touching,' an image borrowed, as it happens, from the Encyclopaedia Britannica.

THE KILLDEER

Why was he trying to clear
a space in the forest of beech
by turning beech posts and, by beech pegs,
fitting each to each?

For the reason at which the killdeer
seems to be clutching
when she lays her four pear-shaped eggs
with the pointed ends touching.

Paul Muldoon
from *Moy Sand and Gravel* (London: Faber and Faber, 2002)

James Nash

I have been aware of the poetry of Edward Thomas ever since I was at secondary school over forty years ago. 'Adlestrop' was the first of his poems that I came across; how quintessentially English it seemed in its evocation of countryside, its lingering regret, and its elegiac quality. I discovered with interest that he was born in London to Welsh parents, just as I was born in Greater London, to a father from South Wales. Other poems came my way over time; 'The Owl', for example, with 'the bird's voice / Speaking for all who lay under the stars'. Then 'When First', where in the fifth stanza, Thomas declares,

> Perhaps
> I may love other hills yet more
> Than this: the future and the maps
> Hide something I was waiting for.

and 'October', where I see a typical Thomas equivocation in its final four lines,

> But if this be not happiness, who knows?
> Some day I shall think this a happy day,
> And this mood by the name of melancholy
> Shall no more blackened and obscured be.

I have always loved the lucidity and simple language to be found in Wordsworth; I take equal delight in these qualities in the poetry of Thomas, qualities which Robert Frost was very quick to recognise in his friend's work. Such simplicity of diction employed to describe equivocal feelings, the mysteries of being, and the sense, perhaps, of being lost in something much larger than oneself, make for exquisite lyrical poetry. My two poems contain more natural description than one might expect from such a resolute townie as myself, together with some other things I recognise as being rather Thomas-like. It is as if his world view has seeped into my consciousness, and the consciousness of many of us, who are writing in a clear poetic tradition, almost a hundred years after his death. I recognise something of his feeling for nature in 'Aubade' and something of his wondering spirit, if not his poetic form, in 'Vespers'.

AUBADE

Waking slowly, I look
through the window
at the silver sky and fields of frost,
reflections of each other,
where nothing moves,
where lines of wall and hedge converge,
and at their corners
large trees see out the final,
chilly disciplines of their watch.
I carefully clasp my mug of tea,
as if it holds your heartbeat,
your dreaming breath.

A dog barks on a nearby farm,
the sky becomes the faintest blue,
and cattle move stiffly
out of a frozen enchantment.
The machinery of morning is starting up,
and I stand there, considering,
trying
to trace
your sleeping outline in the hills.

James Nash
from *Deadly Sensitive* (Leeds: Grassroots Press, 1999)

VESPERS

It is night, the world is still,
only the wind-chime in the crab-apple tree,
carried on the same warm cheek of air
as mock orange scent, stirs.

And I take time out of time,
a shadow in the doorway,
feeling I see it all, though probably too close
to see the whole, which may be chaos.

The stars, tangled like a kite string of brilliants
are fixed amongst the leaves, yet steer a lurching journey
through cold canyons of space and time,
on invisible tracks, alone.

Are they touched by the love that I am somehow filled with?
For it may be the memory of not having love
which catches in the branches of the crab-apple tree,
as the distant stars are caught, and chimes.

James Nash
from *Coma Songs* (Leeds: Grassroots Press, 2003)

Lucy Newlyn

Thomas's sense of the humanness of place is something he shared with Hardy, and also with Wordsworth, whose 'Poems on the Naming of Places' are composed in a hybrid genre, somewhere between inscription and epitaph. Much of Thomas's loco-descriptive prose is haunted by the presence of past writers: they inhabit his style, just as they once inhabited the places he describes. Place-names fascinated him. He found in them something akin to folklore's power of preserving communal memory orally. In his poems, local people are associated with places long after their lives come to an end. 'Bob's Lane' honours 'shovel-bearded' Bob, who once planted an avenue of elms. The lane is disused; the man is long dead; but still the name lives on:

> Many years since, Bob Hayward died, and now
> None passes there because the mist and the rain
> Out of the elms have turned the lane to slough
> And gloom, the name alone survives, Bob's Lane.

This ghostly quality in Thomas's writing – his sense of place as peopled by the past – has affected me profoundly. In 'Hide and Seek' and 'Stray' I pay tribute to it explicitly. Other poems of mine are doubtless 'Thomasy' in other ways – or would like to be, which is of course a different matter.

'Hide and Seek' comes from a collection of poems called *Ginnel* in which I remember my childhood in Headingley, Leeds. 'Ginnel' is a northern dialect word for the narrow alleyways between houses; and in the collection, the word also works a metaphor for the passage between past and present – like Thomas's avenue, 'dark, nameless, without end'. This particular poem was provoked by a recent walk in the local park ('the Hollies') where I played with my sisters as a child. I went there to see if I could find an old stone bath which used to be part of our games. Of course the bath had gone, like Bob's Lane – swallowed up by the undergrowth over a period of thirty years. But a deep hollow nearby remains exactly as I remembered it. In this poem of revisiting, I imagine myself haunting and haunted by this spot twice over – as a child playing, and as an adult remembering.

'Stray' belongs to a later part of my life; but the place it describes is from a much earlier period in history. My room in St Edmund Hall looks out over the graveyard of St Peter in the East, a Norman church which the college converted into a library during the nineteen-seventies. Thomas liked to wander in here as a student, and it was a favourite haunt of his when he was researching for his first commissioned book, *Oxford* (1903). His description of it as 'the peacefullest and homeliest of churchyards' is one of his most evocative pieces of early prose. I often think of it – and him – when I look from my window between tutorials. The grass was probably longer in Thomas's day; and the skyline from the graveyard must have been very different. But 'the melody of the place' is still the same.

HIDE AND SEEK

'No garden appears, no path, no hoar-green bush
Of Lad's-love, or Old Man, no child beside,
Neither father nor mother, nor any playmate;
Only an avenue, dark, nameless, without end.'
    (Edward Thomas, 'Old Man')

Along this stretch of muddy pathway
breasting the Hollies
all's stilled to a hush under dripping trees.
Sun gleams on the flat green oily laurel leaves.

Ivy, bracken, rhododendron,
have long since buried
our stone bath in oblivion,
but the hollow made when there was a river
is a great bin of ferns and stones going on for ever,
where a child can hide.

My eyes are shut behind tight fingers,
and I am counting slowly:
eighteen, nineteen, twenty…
'Coming ready or not!'

Ready or not,
I'm a long way off
like a dream
and my voice in the dream
making no sound.

I call and call down the pathway
to the hollow
through cupped hands.

Lucy Newlyn
from *Ginnel* (Manchester: Carcanet, 2005)

STRAY

It is sweet to enter that peacefullest and homeliest of churchyards, St Peter's in the East, overlooked by St Edmund Hall and Queen's College and the old city wall. There is a peace which only the thrush and blackbird break, and even their singing is at length merely the most easily distinguishable part of the great melody of the place. Most of the graves are so old or so forgotten that it is easy – and in Spring it is difficult not – to perceive a kind of dim reviving life among the stones, where, as in some old, quiet books, the names live again a purged and untroubled existence.

(Edward Thomas, *Oxford*: 1903)

Rain on mottled graves,
and among long soft
fingers of yew. Rain
bending grasses, dark-
ening stones, pocking
grainy lichened tombs.

Often he'd wander in
alone – conjuring
the shades of Aubrey,
Browne and Hearne –
his Welsh soul probing
deep into English soil.

All along the wall
the ivy-leaved toad-flax
hangs its delicate bells.
Fern fronds, heavy
with rain-weight, lie
bowed down low.

On the path, hurrying
the other way,
a young man his age:
hand raised, listening
to his mobile, like
a traveller from afar.

High on the air-waves,
signals weave and dance.
A lone blackbird flicks
between gables – quick
and random as the stray shell
that buried him in France.

Lucy Newlyn

Edward Thomas.

Bernard O'Donoghue

My connection with Edward Thomas is a slight one: he was the Treasurer of the Davenant Society at Lincoln College, Oxford in the 1890s, a role in which I succeeded him in 1966. As I filled in my report in the ancient minutes book, it was an unnerving thrill, and responsibility somehow, to know that Thomas's minutes were within the same covers, fifty pages back. There was a great cult of Thomas at Lincoln in the 1960s, partly stimulated by Faber's 1956 publication together of Helen Thomas's magical paired memoirs *As It Was* and *World Without End*. And, as well as 'Adlestrop', we had all become fixated on Thomas's 'The Owl', with its 'owl's cry, a most melancholy cry'. I think that poem was in my head when I wrote 'The Owls at Willie Mac's', another melancholy story of a slightly mysterious Irish neighbour. I think it was the same feeling of ashamed comfort, put into relief by its absence and vulnerability.

THE OWL

Downhill I came, hungry, and yet not starved;
Cold, yet had heat within me that was proof
Against the North wind; tired, yet so that rest
Had seemed the sweetest thing under a roof.

Then at the inn I had food, fire, and rest,
Knowing how hungry, cold, and tired was I.
All of the night was quite barred out except
An owl's cry, a most melancholy cry

Shaken out long and clear upon the hill,
No merry note, nor cause of merriment,
But one telling me plain what I escaped
And others could not, that night, as in I went.

And salted was my food, and my repose,
Salted and sobered, too, by the bird's voice
Speaking for all who lay under the stars,
Soldiers and poor, unable to rejoice.

Edward Thomas

THE OWLS AT WILLIE MAC'S

Having heard their cries across the fields,
I went outside into their element,
As blind in theirs as they in mine by day.
It was so dark, that late summer night,
I could see nothing of what caused
The ticking, and the steady tread
Of heavy boots towards me down the road
Until his bicycle was right alongside.
Still without seeing, I could smell the warmth
And kind breath of Nugget Plug and Guinness.
And then the voice, as from an invisible flame:

'When I worked at Willie Mac's, you'd hear them
Every night. You'd never see them, even when
They were right on top of you and sounding
Like a screech of brakes.' Who was he,
This dark-dressed, nearly extinct escaper
From the nineteen-fifties Saturday night?

There are some animals, the medievals said,
Whose eyes are so acute that they can, lidless,
Outstare the sun. He walked away from me,
Saving the battery by still not winding on
The squat flashlamp I pictured at the front.
Neither could my defective vision see
Him as he would be three months ahead,
Stretched in the road like the thirsty bittern
By a car that could hardly be expected
To pick him out against a wintering sky.

Bernard O'Donoghue
from *Here nor There* (London: Chatto and Windus, 1999)

Tom Paulin

I quote two lines from 'The Owl' in a poem I wrote to celebrate the 50th anniversary of the founding of Radio Three: 'And salted was my food, and my repose, / Salted and sobered, too, by the bird's voice.' In the poem, I run together various lines of poetry that have been with me my all my life – the poem is a cento with bridge passages. I remember reading Edward Thomas at school in Belfast and studying Frost. Our English teacher at Annadale Grammar School, Eric Brown, had a record of Frost reading 'After Apple-Picking' and I became fascinated by Frost's voice, the rhythm and cadences of his poem. At the same time, I knew some of his prose, as I'd read him on sentence sound – 'a sentence is a sound in itself on which other sounds called words may be strung.' I learnt of the friendship between Frost and Thomas, and read Thomas's biography of the Duke of Marlborough, because I was studying the War of the Spanish Succession for A level. With hindsight, I can see that it was their sentence sound, their use of a vernacular speaking voice, which drew me to the two poets. Another English teacher, Carroll Spence had been at Trinity with Mahon and Longley, and he invited Longley to give a poetry reading in the school. I never read or teach Thomas without recalling those days. It was the time I started to try and write poetry and prose, a very uncertain beginning, but it would have been even more uncertain if I hadn't read Thomas's poetry in my teens.

yet if I wanted to put a date
when this naked shivering self
began to puzzle at print sound
spokensound
the wind in the reeds
or a cry in the street
I'd choose that room for a start
the bangles
the curtain rings
– it's my baby tuckoo
tuckoo tuckoo it is
not the tundish
this is echt British
except that's always fake somehow
it's machinery means of production
not a spring well
– the well of Anglish
or the well of Oirish undefiled
for this isn't when
but where it happened
where ice burned
and was but the more ice
and salted was my food and my repose
salted and sobered too by the bird's call
the golden bird who perched
on his golden bough
to sing that ancient salt
is best packing
that all that is mortal of great Plato there
is stuck like chewed gum
in Tess's hair
which happened – as it had to –
before ever I seen those tinned kippers
packed into boxes
on the quayside
in Cullercoats or Whitley Bay
and my great aunt

takes the penny ferry over the Tyne
and my English not my Scots granny
calls me *hinny*
and it feels
– that houyhnhnm whinny
of the northeast coast
almost like love and belonging

Tom Paulin
from *The Wind Dog* (London: Faber and Faber, 1999)

Peter Porter

In the Summer of 1973 (it might have been '72, but I think '73 is correct), I was with a team of four persons travelling through Oxfordshire and adjacent parts for The Arts Council, reading and performing at schools and halls. One day the novelist Shena Mackay and I were together in a car – I can't recall our destination – when we saw the road sign for Adlestrop. We decided to diverge and visit the village since we were familiar, as most people at that time would have been, with Edward Thomas's poem. Later that year I wrote 'Good Vibes' to record the occasion and to reflect our feelings while in Adlestrop. The dated title springs from a litany of jokey criticism of vernacular cliché which Shena and I had entertained ourselves with on the tour. In my customary fashion I attempted to modulate from the quotidian into the sententious – so death and the rest of his accoutrements are in the poem. It seems it all happened a long time ago, when I read the poem today.

GOOD VIBES
for Shena Mackay

If you hadn't noticed the unprominent sign
We'd have missed Adlestrop, missed the gone
Railway and the bullock raking his back
In the hollow holly-bower. Missed, too, the sky
So intolerably lofty in its beakered blue
And the loping dog which frightened me
(Which is how I know he was friendly) –
Most noticeably missed the station bench
And ADLESTROP, the railway sign, with Edward
Thomas's poem on a plaque for pilgrims.
Not a great poem, but rich in names
And heartache and certainly a focus for
A sinisterly fine October afternoon.
Down one lane adjacent the Home for Children,
(With what impediment we never found),
All the day-labourers of Oxfordshire and Gloucestershire
Were about their honey-making masonry
Of Cotswold stone, and the bullocks were nifty
In the meadow by the creek. There were no
Devils in the landscape, exhalations from
Ponds and dogs' breath and graveyards after rain
Could only be imagined in such unexpected sunshine,
But we felt them, felt a new humidity,
Oppressive like the self. This was a short halt
On two pilgrimages, a look-back out of Hades,
Such as the gods provide for laughter in their
Chronicles. Yet that sound, that risible division,
Strikes mortal earth some otherwise – such as
Gravel flicking from a low-slung bumper,
A trailing jet above, a jostling on the eaves
Of sycamores. It was as if the well-intentioned
Dead were breathing out and blessing everyone,
Vibrations of the minute, without franchise,
A pointless benediction. Thinking again, I feel

Grateful that you saw through uncleaned windows
A name which meant the same to all half-educated
Persons. To have trod on ground in happiness
Is to be shaken by the true immortals.

Peter Porter
from *Living in a Calm Country* (Oxford: Oxford University Press,
1975) and *Collected Poems: Volume I: 1961–1981* (Oxford: Oxford
University Press, 1999)

Jem Poster

The poetry of Edward Thomas has had a significant influence on my own writing, and a number of my poems seem to me to reveal the debt quite clearly. 'Again' hadn't previously struck me as being indebted in this way, but when I came to look for a poem which reflected the concerns of my essay (see 'I Cannot Tell: Edward Thomas's Uncertainties') it seemed an appropriate choice. Like much of Thomas's work, it deals with the elusiveness of our memories and with the resistance of experience to the necessarily crude frameworks provided by words. Both narrator and protagonist find it impossible to comprehend and articulate the essential nature of the experience at the poem's centre, but both implicitly recognise the value – or the necessity, at least – of each renewed attempt to do so.

AGAIN

But if I start with that – the way he breaks
from the coppice, head down, one arm crooked forward, shielding
his face from the stinging twigs – I hit the thing
off-centre. Yes, that's what I best remember,
that and his headlong flight across the blanched
meadows to the garden where his mother
in thornproof gloves, dead-heading the roses, turns
at the click of the gate-latch; but there's something
I've not accounted for, a faint vibration
subtle but too insistent to ignore.
                                                    I'll
start again. He's standing at the muffled
heart of the coppice where the water gathers
in a sullen pool. Honeysuckle and decay; the smell
of his own prickling skin. Above, the leaves
whisper and stir incessantly, but here
nothing moves; unless perhaps a breath
or tremor wrinkling the filmy surface –
                                        Out,
out and running. This time I feel the uneven
ground beneath his plimsolls, feel the barbs
snag the shoulder of his T-shirt as he ducks
under the shivering wire. The blood
sings in his head; and as the gate slams back
on its rusted hinges I see the garden's long
perspective blur and slide.
                        A flurry
of unfocused movement; the gloves flung down
beside the rocking trug, a hand outstretched
to steady him as he reels. He's gasping
something his mother strains to catch but can't
make head or tail of. He'll have to start again.

Jem Poster
from *Brought to Light* (Tarset: Bloodaxe, 2001)

Vernon Scannell

I have always liked Edward Thomas's poem, 'Tall Nettles', admiring its economic and exact observation and the gentle music of the verse-movement, the internal chiming in the last lines of 'dust' and 'lost' and the way the sibilants let us hear that sweetening shower.

Some forty odd years ago I wrote my own poem featuring nettles which, apart from difference in quality, is quite different in intention and execution. My nettles are suburban where Thomas's are rural and they lay claim to symbolic significance while Thomas's are simply and powerfully themselves. Still, I hope he might have been sympathetic to my theme. My poem was written at a time when the Cold War seemed in imminent danger of being ignited and the fear that my young son might be involved in a war is present in the use of military imagery that pervades the poem.

I originally published 'Nettles' in a small collection for younger readers called *Mastering the Craft*, but I hope it holds some interest for readers of all ages.

NETTLES

My son aged three fell in the nettle bed.
'Bed' seemed a curious name for those green spears.
That regiment of spite behind the shed:
It was no place for rest. With sobs and tears
The boy came seeking comfort and I saw
White blisters beaded on his tender skin.
We soothed him till his pain was not so raw.
At last he offered us a watery grin,
And then I took my hook and honed the blade
And went outside and slashed in fury with it
Till not a nettle in that fierce parade
Stood upright any more. Next task: I lit
A funeral pyre to burn the fallen dead.
But in two weeks the busy sun and rain
Had called up tall recruits behind the shed:
My son would often feel sharp wounds again.

Vernon Scannell
from *Mastering the Craft* (Oxford: Pergamon, 1970)

Michael Schmidt

When I was at the Hill School in Pottstown, Pennsylvania, where I studied from the eighth through the twelfth grades, Robert Frost came as a visiting speaker. The experiences recounted in the poem took place there: he delivered an essay entitled 'The Panhandle of Poetry', I think. (Tobias Wolff was at the same school and recounts the visit rather differently. My poem appeared before his account was published.) I had spent some of my early childhood in Capistrano, California – south of Frost's West Coast landscapes, admittedly – and I found his presence, his voice, his manner, quite beguiling. Any teenager with a literary bent, even a wee Modernist like me, would have been taken by the heart by such a man.

When I started research at Oxford, after my B.A., I was working on Edward Thomas, and my first few months were spent comparing the prosodies of Thomas, while freeing himself from the shackles of prose writing, with those of Frost. I was struck by how in the end irritatingly regular the poems in Frost's first three or four books seemed to be, as against the much quieter and more subtle dynamic of Thomas's prosody. It was then that I realised how deeply I loved Thomas, and yet how privately, whereas the love I felt for Frost was a more public, a more common thing. I resented it when other readers moved in on Thomas (I had much the same response to the growing Elizabeth Bishop critical industry in later years), whereas it seemed natural that Frost should be trudged over by hundreds of critical feet. Yet Frost did help give Thomas the confidence to come out of the shade, as he said to Eleanor Farjeon, and trust his movements over a loved ground made more deeply familiar by the language that seemed to come up out of it to greet him.

IT WASN'T SNOWING

It wasn't snowing but it should have been.
You were an old man, nine months from the grave.
Your hand was very dry and very hot
And large, as I recall (I was a boy,
Fifteen years at most, I led you round
Part of the school, your guide; you seemed to listen).
That night you read in a slow, dismissive voice
That left the words like notes on staves hung in the air,
No longer yours, but part of memory –
You talked about Miss Dickinson of Amherst
And said aloud the eight lines of her poem
'The heart asks pleasure first'. And from that night
I've known the poem word-perfect, part of me.

I think you let more lines free into language
And memory with your rusty, lonely voice
Than any other poet of our age.
It must have been like freeing doves
And watching them go off to neighbouring cotes
Or into the low clouds of your New Hampshire
Knowing they'll meet no harm, that they'll survive
Long after the hand that freed them has decayed.

Those lines are wise in rhythm and they lead
Into a clapboard dwelling, or a field,
Or lives that prey upon the land and one another,
Or the big country where we both were children.

Michael Schmidt
from *The Love of Strangers* (London: Hutchinson, 1989)

Peter Scupham

One of Edward Thomas's most fascinating prose pieces is the auto-biographical fragment known as *The Childhood of Edward Thomas*, with its picture of a kind of South London country-boy, roaming the commons and waste land, with forays to Swindon. There is no sentimentality, only an account of the disciplines and freedoms of a stone-throwing, rough-and-tumble boy, who came through heedless cruelties – read how his killing of fish was accompanied by 'a slight suffocation and beating of the heart and clouding of the brain' to an understanding and love of the natural world.

My poem, 'The Map-Maker' re-visits my father's boyhood, a close parallel to Thomas's. Thomas enjoyed map-making as a boy; he was a map-reading Instructor at Hare Hall before he was commissioned. I have the careful map my father made of his own locality. He shared the same pursuits: birds-nesting, butterfly-collecting, fishing. As Thomas says: 'I rapidly learnt the names and seasons of most common moths and butterflies. I learnt to catch and kill and display them in the orthodox manner. To acquire all the tools of the trade I begged from my father and mother and bartered with everybody'. And among the books I have inherited are the three classic accounts of late-Victorian country life by Thomas's admired Richard Jefferies: *The Amateur Poacher, The Gamekeeper at Home* and *Round About a Great Estate*.

My father's map was made in that crux year, 1916, when he was 12, and in this poem my father's map and the vanished English countryside are tangentially interwoven with the landscape of the First World War, in which my father's brother was serving, as Thomas did, in the Artillery. I think of the poem as a celebration of, and elegy for, the richness and harshness of that late Victorian, Edwardian world.

The sound of the paper – surely that's the same?
Open it out. Sprung on my finger ends
the resistance is purposive, a clean flip.
On the obverse, four spots of glue hold nothing, tightly,
their ochres caked and crystalline. He spreads it out
as I spread it now, smoothing its awkward lie.
Folds guide small rivulets of shade, flats cream
under gaslight, or whiten in the profligate sun.

This is how he sees it. Rather, how what he sees
in the beck, the lane, the heat-haze over the wolds
can be dried and certified, held like the moths
in his killing-bottle. Catlike, he marks his journeys.
Ink runs thinly, darkens. He sows words broadcast,
dips the scratch-pen, straight-edges the railway,
As outside, hot verges coarsen with umbellifers:
Lineside. Tiger beetles, flowers, Lepidoptera in general.

His head adrift with flutterings, sheen and texture,
he pushes his way through millions of green and brown,
holding tight to a spinning signpost of names.
His tracks race off the paper through *Nova Scotia,*
J. Scupham, July 9, 1916. In brightest Lincolnshire
my twelve-year-old father carefully encodes
Hill, Clearing, Viper's Bugloss, Yellow Underwings,
ransacks *America* for its *Heaths and Tigers* -

the large Heath *(Epinephele Tithonus),*
the Scarlet Tiger *(Callimorpha Dominula)* –
this Midsummer, his 'Prize for Nature Study'
is Furneaux' *British Butterflies and Moths.*
With bruised laurel, cyanide of potassium,
the countryside may be coaxed into your trap
and, later, secured by silver, black, or gilded pins.
Be sure the poison does not merely stupefy,

leaving you horrified, when your box is opened,
'by the sight of the poor victim struggling to free itself',
a teeming landscape unwilling to lie down.
I refold his paper, packed with nests and burrows,
thickets of skin and fur. Ink and copy-pencil
shine briefly against my lamp, keep the dry glaze
lost by close on a hundred years of eyes.
The dead rustle back to nest with a stir of wings;

the annular rings thicken and simplify.
I could stand there still, lost in a no-man's-land,
holding his childhood's trench-map, think of his brother
laying his gun-sights somewhere on the Somme,
consider how folds of dead ground foster rivulets,
hedges whiten to blackthorn, cream to hawthorn.
As he dies, I ask how he spends the time,
bedbound. 'Oh, just go for walks,' he answers.

Peter Scupham
from *Collected Poems* (Manchester: Carcanet, 2002)

Owen Sheers

Growing up in Wales it was the voices of two other Thomases, Dylan and R.S. rather than Edward, that dominated my early reading. The songs and prayers of these two poets, the immediate vitality of R.S.'s blade-sharp metaphors, the blood-beat of Dylan's percussive rhythms, were particularly seductive to my adolescent ear and eye. For many of their poems this is still the case and the best of their work will always live with me as part of my imaginative DNA. In more recent years, however, Edward Thomas's quieter voice has increasingly made itself heard and has become an equally important poetic touchstone.

One reason for this is Thomas's relationship, as a poet, to the rhythms and potential of everyday speech. Thomas was always interested in the value of speech in poetry. In championing the early work of Robert Frost, perhaps his own most crucial influence, he was at pains to draw attention to how the medium of Frost's poetry, unlike the 'discord and fuss' of recent fashions, 'is common speech.' Similarly, in a review of Yeats's poetry Thomas mentions how 'the best lyrics seem to be the poet's natural speech.' Perhaps we shouldn't be surprised by this emphasis, coming as it does from such a prolific prose writer and chronicler of those he met and listened to along his journeys on the road. What fascinated me on first reading Thomas's poetry, however, was how everyday talk didn't just inform the lyric cadences of his poems, but actually entered them as direct speech, at once energetically lifting the poem while also rooting it in lived, immediate experience. In many of my favourite poems of Thomas's it is direct speech and dialogue that provides the structural thread, the punctuation, the closely observed, quietly spoken pathos. From the early 'Up in the Wind', through 'Home', Jack and George's conversation in 'The Lovers', the entirely spoken 'The Chalk Pit' to the beautiful and, for me, one of the most moving of his poems, 'As the team's head brass', Thomas uses spoken dialogue to pare away the authorial voice and enliven the poem with simple statements of surprising emotional and psychological depths. The language employed is in a conversation of its own with Thomas's skilful prosody, effortlessly suggesting the speaker's hand gestures, intonations and expressions, while still managing to carry Thomas's metres and half-rhymes. The spoken words are often imbued with a sense of inherited wisdom, apparently learnt across generations rather than merely over the course of the speaker's life.

The other striking note that Thomas's poetry rang in me was his ability to notice, seek and *need* solace and direction from the natural world. The birds, plant-life and trees of rural England and Wales are the barometer against which he delicately measures time and the passage of human existence. Even in the final pages of his war diary, among the freezing mud and shell craters of no-man's land, Thomas is observant of the blackbird's song, and the effect upon him of the early morning:

'The morning chill and clear hurts my skin while it delights my mind.'

I can't pretend this following poem was written with Thomas's work in mind, or even that it was informed by anything more than a resonant knowledge of his poems. I do hope, however, that in some way it touches upon the two qualities of Thomas's writing I've mentioned here. The use of direct speech to punctuate or 'turn' a poem, and the perennial surprise and confirmation of nature; of her beauty and endurance against the shorter, confused and interrupting lives of men who only occasionally, in rare moments of understanding, manage to meet her as communicants.

> 'Here, in fact, is nothing at all
> Except a silent place that once rang loud,
> And trees and us – imperfect friends, we men
> And trees since time began; and nevertheless
> Between us still we breed a mystery.'

Edward Thomas, 'The Chalk Pit'

THE LIGHT FELL
i.m. Robert Woof, Director of The Wordsworth Trust

The weather had been confused all day
so who can say why it was just then
the light fell that way –

the sun riding low to burnish for a minute,
no more, the tops of the hills
against a curtain of cloud, ashen with snow.

Or why it was then the deer chose
to show their faces, lift their heads from grazing,
step near, then pause, before coming on again.

'Oh human life, mysterious,' I heard a woman say.
'Not gone, oh no, not gone. There's electrics you know?
I wouldn't say it if I didn't believe it to be so.'

And as the light fell drew our eyes, a thinning seam of amber
compressed between the land and sky,
I could believe it too:

that your guiding hand had motion still
and influence among these hills, to light the Crag and Michael's Vale
just so, according to your will.

And as the soil hit the wood and the gathered crowd moved,
said what they could, wished well and farewell,
that it was just as much you as the still lowering sun

throwing one flank of the valley dark
and leaving the other lit,
to illustrate, as the land here always did,

what we'd but sensed within ourselves.
How at once and from the very same source,
a light could rise, as the same light fell.

Owen Sheers

Penelope Shuttle

During the question and answer session at the Edward Thomas Conference in Oxford, I asked if any of Edward Thomas's poems had been translated into other languages. He is a quintessentially English writer. I was curious to know if his work 'travelled', as it were. I learned that Thomas is translated into Italian and Japanese and was particularly struck by the existence of a Japanese Thomas.

Initially he and Japan seem very far apart, but on further reflection I realized that there are affinities. I thought of the poet-monk Basho, to whom walking was as important as it was to Edward Thomas, and how his poems, like those of Thomas, are created from close observation and experience of landscape; it is only possible to relate to landscape by moving through it at god's speed, at walking pace, three miles an hour.

In his haibun book, *The Narrow Road to the Deep North and Other Travel Sketches*, a mixture of prose and haiku written during his walking journeys to the north of Japan in 1689 and 1691, Basho writes:

> How far must I walk
> To the village of Kasajima
> This endlessly muddy road
> Of the early wet season?

to which, long after, Thomas responds:

> Downhill I came, hungry, and yet not starved...

And when Basho says – Go to the pine if you want to learn about the pine, or to the bamboo if you want to know about the bamboo – I feel Edward Thomas would have seconded that.

Both writers draw upon the power of placenames and in my poem I imagine the evocative power of English place names transposed to the Japanese landscape, how the atmosphere and insight of Thomas's work finds sympathetic readers in Japan, land of the haiku, renga and haibun.

As for Edward Thomas in Italian, I was recently at the Poetry-on-the-Lake Festival in Orta, Italy, and attended a reading by Massimo Boicchiola, the Italian translator of poets from the Great War, including Edward Thomas. After the reading, Massimo told me that the first time he read Thomas's 'Adlestrop' he placed the emphasis on the name thus – AD EL strop, believing it to be a town in Belgium, and the train a troop train going to the front. Further research showed him this was not so, but what a fascinating alternative interpretation of this poem.

EDWARD SAN

Some quiet person
is translating the poems of Edward Thomas
into Japanese

Now it rains in orchards
in the land of the haiku

The bird of the snow
is flying over Tokyo

A pure thrush word
spreads its calligraphic wings
over Kyoto,

an unknown bird
whistles his three lovely notes
in the woods near Kiwa-Cho

All Japan's cherry trees
shed their petals
on the old road to Hiroshima,

where no-one comes for a wedding

The bullet train
doesn't stop at Japan's Adlestrop

but all the birds of Japan's
North Island and South Island
go on singing

Someone is alone
in the new house at Osaka
when the wind begins to moan,

a child with his mother
on the cliffs at Morioka
hears the bell ringing under the sea

and in the mountain gardens
of Kobe, Sapporo and Hokkaido
readers are spellbound

by two voices,
the wind and the rain

Penelope Shuttle

Jon Stallworthy

Asked to advise the staff of the Imperial War Museum on the contents of their 2002 exhibition, 'Anthem for Doomed Youth', I told them that what I (and surely many others) would most want to see displayed was the watch stopped by the blast of the German shell that killed Edward Thomas at 7.36 a.m. on 9 April, Easter Monday 1917.

The exhibition drew 32,000 visitors, and few of its exhibits attracted more attention than Edward Thomas's watch. So, writing my poem in 2003, I thought I knew where it came from. I should have known better; should have remembered how often poems are prompted by memories from both life (frequently conscious) and literature (frequently subconscious). I remembered the first – my gaze returned by the blind white eye of the watch in its glass case. But it was only on the afternoon of the Edward Thomas conference in Oxford in 2005 that I remembered the second:

In Memoriam [Easter 1915]

The flowers left thick at nightfall in the wood
This Eastertide call into mind the men,
Now far from home, who, with their sweethearts, should
Have gathered them and will do never again.

The heart-stopping emblem of Edward Thomas's death at Easter 1917 had clearly summoned up a subconscious memory of his quatrain 'In Memoriam [Easter 1915]': emblem and text together prompting another quatrain, one imaging watch and owner as *sweethearts* – 'Face to face, hand in hand . . . heart to heart'.

My homage came from deeper levels than I knew.

EDWARD THOMAS'S FOB-WATCH

Face to face, hand in hand,
never a day apart
until the last day and
the wordless heart to heart.

Jon Stallworthy
from *Body Language* (Manchester: Carcanet, 2004)

John Stammers

I have made use of the Edward Thomas poem 'And You, Helen' as a general point of departure for one of my own poems: 'Why'. In that poem, I also rehearse the issue of the offer, but from a different angle. There Thomas, more generously than I, considers being able to give Helen gifts from a great store he might be offered. I, on the other hand, am in the passive position of being made an offer. The elliptical nature of the last line in 'Why' is intended to ironise that shift. In formal terms, I have also always been interested in the sustained use of single syllable words in the line. In fact, in the poem in question, Thomas uses these nearly exclusively throughout the whole poem e.g. line 18, 'What you want and want it not too late'. I allude to this in my last line, but insert 'offers' as a kind of Persian-rug intentional flaw. It also, of course, connects thematically to the Thomas.

Helen Noble and Edward Thomas before their marriage (when he was approximately eighteen years old). This is the only known photograph of the two together.

WHY

Above you like a horse, my nostrils fire heat
on the maroon disruption of duvet and bedlinen;
the artery in my neck slams blood up my head.
A voided gin bottle, its final smear in your tumbler,
informs your blowsy mouth with its juniper come-ons.
Veronica, the sparkling of my *Aqua Pura* is the sadder noise—
those *petillant* increments,
the frowns of angels on their pinheads calling:
Beware, beware she dyes her hair – her eyes are green.

I extend my shadow across you;
the bedclothes murmur like rumours.
I put it all down to your henna'y reveal,
your eyes sharp as limes.
Your question undoes me to myself,
offers what I want to have you want me to.

John Stammers
from *Stolen Love Behaviour* (London: Picador, 2005)

Anne Stevenson

For several years now I have been adding sections, one by one, to a long poem called, for want of a better title, *A Lament for the Makers*. Roughly based on Medieval dream sagas, it borrows its form from authors such as Langland, Chaucer, and, of course, Dante. The story follows the author into an underworld where deceased poets are ghosts inhibited by fame and reputation from disappearing into desirable oblivion and the bliss of forgetting. The presiding Virgil is Peter Redgrove who explains to the author how poets live on in the imaginations of their successors and readers. Other poets who speak are Frances Horovitz, Ted Hughes and Edward Thomas. The excerpt printed here has to be read as a fragment of a much longer whole.

Edward Thomas at Berryfield Cottage, Ashford, near Petersfield, in October 1907.

from A LAMENT FOR THE MAKERS
(Edward Thomas speaks)

Well, England must be ugly now.
I died in good time,
escaping the finale of her dotage.

She was a bitch half buried
when I went to war.
I see her struggling to renew herself –

careless of her image,
slipshod, rich and ignorant –
from contaminated soil.

Yet, there must be some who care,
a few who tend her garden
in the wild places, still.

Without me, no doubt,
summer is in spate again,
flowering over England and Wales.

Time's wheel will still be turning
on the axle of its arrow.
The redstarts will be back from Africa

breeding among the crab apples.
Foxgloves must be burning
up the long wires of their stems.

Lovely, head-high unclaimed grasses –
they are lucent and astir,
each one tasselled according to its kind.

Anne Stevenson

Seán Street

One of the things which makes Edward Thomas such a pivotal figure for modern poetry is the absorption of the cadence of the spoken word into his writing. It was something about which he and Robert Frost had long conversations, language and the various music of it, and it runs through Thomas's writing like a stream, from the exchange between the poet and the ploughman in 'As the team's head brass', the voices in 'Lob' and 'A Gentleman' to his imagined words set to a bugle call and the monologues where he himself talks to his family one by one. In the use of these audible voices, there is the skill at disguising rhyme and structure in the colloquial, making so many of his poems masterclasses of miniature aural dramas.

Thomas would have understood the special relationship that exists between poetry and radio, two forms where the power comes from the imaginative interaction between reader/poet and listener/speaker. Of course times change and language changes with the times according to purpose; these days journalism, TV and radio's necessity for compressed messages, the clichés and stylistic short-cuts of rolling news formats surround us, and threaten to undermine language with artificiality. Thomas would have noted and deplored it, and would probably have parodied it.

His landscape is a peopled one, full of real voices. It is also a place where weather happens, and that weather is a part of the place and the men and women who people it. We are shaped by where we are, what we do, and by how our climate affects us. Thomas's 'Wild Girl' in 'Up in the Wind' and my ailing weather girl may seem culturally far apart, but they are both trapped by elements, place and circumstance, and their voices reflect that.

THE DYING WEATHER GIRL

Rain again. In February the weather
becomes a state of mind. The savoury
part of the year; broken gardens blow about,
it's hard to hold to a purpose just now.

Anticyclone – the lines come in closer.
I remember my greatest forecasts, weather
as news breaking storm warnings and the charts
burst colour of exclamatory symbols.

Brute images beyond the map earnest
in my eyes, see rain and the sea collide
and I stroke, caress chromakey blue, conjuring,
conducting elements to camera,

meteorological mime, my making.
Structural damage is inevitable,
the cold front floods through, the burst water rising
shorting out time until all screens blacken, still.

Isobars compress round the bed, weather
rises, tapping, tapping in from the west
hard against glass. I stumble as the glass falls,
falling, broken gardens fly off and away

into February, black and unseen tides.
Tonight there is heavy rain again, storm force,
there is a deceptive wind-chill factor.
Cold. Clouds deepen, make it grow night too early.

Seán Street
(uncollected; first published in *The Interpreter's House* magazine,
20, ed. Merryn Williams, Summer 2002)

Kim Taplin

At least half of Edward Thomas's poetry, probably more, comes pretty directly out of the experience of walking in the countryside. The same is true for me. What I owe him as a poet is not about style. It is confirmation that this matter of nature and being human in it is neither escapist nor utopian but central. Never more so than now when human beings pose an unprecedented threat to nature.

I share his love of the insignificant aspects of the natural world – even those such as nettles and mud that are not obviously beautiful – and his pleasure in place-names.

I love his honesty too, though I'm not sure I agree with him about rhetoric. His desire to eradicate it, to 'wring the necks of my rhetoric, the geese', is doomed to defeat. Rhetoric is inseparable from speech, inevitable as sin. Man is an image-making animal. We cannot speak with the innocence of birds because we know we are naked. Having said that, the instinct was a noble one; and the deep delight in reading Edward Thomas's poetry can be compared with drinking clear, pure, mountain water when one is very thirsty. And these days we are parched.

The book-length poem *Goodfellow* from which my contribution is taken is, like Thomas's 'Lob', an exploration of an archetype.

from GOODFELLOW

it's then I catch the whiff of Herb Robert
    a stench some people can't abide
and others love because it seems to them
    the quintessence of English country summer
Mabey says maybe it got its name
    as a Goodfellow flower 'because of the smell'
– the sweat of a strong goblin toiling?
    or is it the smell of mortality?
you do think of a small corpse at first

in Burwash Common he leads me a dance
    astray among single species lawns
and spick brick security alarmed
    gates with wrought iron called 'The Heights'
where people daily disinfect for demons
    and a path sneaks out beyond the houses
unmarked and nettly and peters out. . .

it's par for the course it always happens
Puck has a passion for red herrings
Burton's *Anatomy* classes him
as one of the ancient *Ambulones*
that walk about Midnight on great Heathes
& desart places. . . & draw men out of the way
Please trespass! wrote Edward Thomas

sweating I complete the magic circle
try another path, further west
    and come on a Private Farm Road
        No walkers
        No dogs
        No horses

    leaping dogs muddy my map and legs
but they don't bark or bite, he calms them
    scratched and slipping on the Wealden clay

where it stays always miry under the trees
    I finally come into the potent place

the field like the name is set aside
    a wide stretch of tall feathery grasses
hedged to the south by rangy hollies
    and as I eat my sandwich on a stile
two bronze deer, one with antlers,
    stare long & stockstill from the summit
before turning and racing into the trees

from *Goodfellow* (Kidlington: Field Cottage, 2006)

Edward Thomas in 1913.

Charles Tomlinson

In reading Thomas, I find myself often returning to 'The Path'. It is the energy of the poem's syntax that impresses, by creating a distinctive path of its own. Without such a sense of direction, what would all the detail of place and colour (gold, olive, emerald) amount to? The numerous drafts of the poem, in R. George Thomas's splendid edition, evolve towards that creation of 'articulate energy' in Donald Davie's phrase. After all its pauses and accelerations, even its fanciful glance sideways at the wood as a possibly 'legendary or fancied place', we are still on track. And all this energy is directed towards that sudden closure of arrival as the path 'ends where the wood ends'. It would be too crude to call this ending a surprise. For what it does is to leave us with a reverberation of kinetic details echoing in the mind. Technically 'The Path' has much to offer to a poet.

THE PATH

Running along a bank, a parapet
That saves from the precipitous wood below
The level road, there is a path. It serves
Children for looking down the long smooth steep,
Between the legs of beech and yew, to where
A fallen tree checks the sight: while men and women
Content themselves with the road and what they see
Over the bank, and what the children tell.
The path, winding like silver, trickles on,
Bordered and even invaded by thinnest moss
That tries to cover roots and crumbling chalk
With gold, olive, and emerald, but in vain.
The children wear it. They have flattened the bank
On top, and silvered it between the moss
With the current of their feet, year after year.
But the road is houseless, and leads not to school.
To see a child is rare there, and the eye
Has but the road, the wood that overhangs
And underyawns it, and the path that looks

As if it led on to some legendary
Or fancied place where men have wished to go
And stay; till, sudden, it ends where the wood ends.

Edward Thomas

OLD MAN

Old Man, or Lad's-love, – in the name there's nothing
To one that knows not Lad's-love, or Old Man,
The hoar-green feathery herb, almost a tree,
Growing with rosemary and lavender.
Even to one that knows it well, the names
Half decorate, half perplex, the thing it is:
At least, what that is clings not to the names
In spite of time. And yet I like the names.

The herb itself I like not, but for certain
I love it, as some day the child will love it
Who plucks a feather from the door-side bush
Whenever she goes in or out of the house.
Often she waits there, snipping the tips and shrivelling
The shreds at last on to the path, perhaps
Thinking, perhaps of nothing, till she sniffs
Her fingers and runs off. The bush is still
But half as tall as she, though it is as old;
So well she clips it. Not a word she says;
And I can only wonder how much hereafter
She will remember, with that bitter scent,
Of garden rows, and ancient damson-trees
Topping a hedge, a bent path to a door,
A low thick bush beside the door, and me
Forbidding her to pick.

                        As for myself,
Where first I met the bitter scent is lost.
I, too, often shrivel the grey shreds,
Sniff them and think and sniff again and try

Once more to think what it is I am remembering,
Always in vain. I cannot like the scent,
Yet I would rather give up others more sweet,
With no meaning, than this bitter one.

I have mislaid the key. I sniff the spray
And think of nothing; I see and I hear nothing;
Yet seem, too, to be listening, lying in wait
For what I should, yet never can, remember:
No garden appears, no path, no hoar-green bush
Of Lad's-love, or Old Man, no child beside,
Neither father nor mother, nor any playmate;
Only an avenue, dark, nameless, without end.

Edward Thomas

OLD MAN, OR LAD'S-LOVE

It was that child – and you, Edward Thomas –
preoccupied my thoughts,
forbidding her to pick the shoots
from the bush she passed whenever she
went in or out of the house ... Years later
I met her, both of us adult by now.
The first thing that came into my mind
was to exclaim my fascination with that poem she,
as a child, had inhabited. 'I'll let you have'
she replied 'a sprig from that same bush.'
And so she did. I planted it
outside my own front door
and over the years I came to be
the guardian of four identical plants,
recalling Thomas to me each time I
passed in or out, recalling the way his lines
would grow then change direction
in a living flow of contradiction unforeseen
and 'Old man, or lad's-love,' – the names
come back to me each time
I encounter those green growths (and your name too
with its Welsh intonation, Myfanwy),
as I look out from this Cotswold corner to see
a landscape opening beneath me
into both space and time, beckoning out of Wales which is
the place of origin for all Thomases.

Charles Tomlinson

Edward Thomas in 1913.

John Powell Ward

Edward Thomas's writing was often curiously elusive. This doesn't at all mean obscure, for we get his small natural scenes clearly and at once. But something in the trees, weeds or garden fences was just out of reach; by the nature of the case he can't pass that on to the reader in itself, and so instead he turns it into an aesthetic equilibrium of some kind – a poem – which just stays there itself and so lasts. His shy melancholy could embarrass or suffocate but it seems not to. So it is still positive.

Occasionally he ties this sense of elusive place to time. For instance he began his poem 'The Parting' by saying: 'The Past is a strange land, most strange. / Wind blows not there, nor does rain fall'. The first of my two poems, 'The Present', was written at a cottage in west Wales, I imagine not unlike various places where Edward Thomas lived at one time or another; although of course he never lived in Wales. Wind blew and rain fell in abundance; but this place had the same sense of nature as local; the beds of nettles, jam-jars for wasps, rain on the cow-parsley, and brambles outside the back door, rather than the big mountains or valley plains of the grander vista. I don't know what Thomas would have made of the place poetically, but he would surely have loved it.

My second poem needs little introduction. Certainly in any terms of what Edward Thomas would have done with such a notion. There was no environmental threat in his time, or at least none perceived. In that respect we have left his world behind, for better or worse. We articulate nature overtly, globally, and even clear-eyed, marshalling evidence as ecological challenge to world crisis; we have a strong and multi-faceted communications and travel technology; and our range is galactic. The one item in Thomas's poetry overtly to do with mechanised travel, the railway train at Adlestrop, is seen as a wayside interlude. The emotion that nature engendered was perhaps the pathetic fallacy, while today it is more likely to be anger. No doubt he would have shared it.

THE PRESENT
(*for S*)

We twist our heads out through the bedroom window
And wait. There is night and the blackness under.

There is dew, endless and level, no matter how
The empirical tide has dusted our minds dry now.

There is darkness, and an autumn smell, which no
                                     doubt
Humans could easily learn to live without.

It's dark out here; my legs and stomach feel warm,
Though. Is this past night still doing our cheeks harm?

Certainly now we could pull back our heads and say
'You're so real, love, and sex is here to stay.'

Certainly we could; and couldn't we once declare
Nature was womb and the big lay everywhere?

An owl hoots. Yes, you can hear them here still.
Time's not a thing, it is we who fill

It seeking an existence where we can belong.
Is sniffing a leaf, in nineteen-eighty, wrong?

Asking, we pull our heads back in from the darkness.
There's dew on your hair. You undress.

John Powell Ward
from *Selected and New Poems* (Bridgend: Seren Books, 2004)

HURRY UP PLEASE, IT'S TIME

They trapped the rain in butts; took pulp and jars
To the new recycling plant; they halved
Their electricity and bore the single bulb
Of a furtive lamp; they adapted the car
To clean-fuel specification. They grew carrots
And turned the Sunday papers into compost.
They walked or bicycled instead of drove;
They put on heavy sweaters and thick
Socks and thus cut down their central heating.
They considered the lilies, how they grew,
And read their secondhand books, still wondering
If even Solomon's wisdom could suffice
To save the human venture that began
In Eden; its art, its buildings and its law.

But I can't tell you how this all worked out;
Its hour had not yet come; only
The unaborted children who survive
Will know of that, staring at their hands
Like monkeys, asking what to do next.

John Powell Ward
from *Selected and New Poems* (Bridgend: Seren Books, 2004)

Robert Wells

Edward Thomas's poems were given to me by a friend of my father's, a poet called Hal Summers (there is a poem of his in Philip Larkin's *Oxford Book of Twentieth-Century English Verse*). I was a few weeks short of my fourteenth birthday, and it was the first book of poems by a twentieth-century poet that I possessed. Pinned to the flyleaf was a note, which ended, 'If you don't care for them – not to worry: try them again at five-year intervals!' Forty-five years later, I realise that I have followed this gentle injunction, more or less. I didn't care for the poems at first; in some ways, which cease to matter when I think of the best poems, I still don't. As Thomas wrote in 'Old Man', 'I cannot like the scent'. Yet I found something in them which continued to draw me back. I felt it chiefly in the way that things are allowed to exist for themselves in the poems, and in the accompanying sense of release. I understand this now as an aspect of what for me is Thomas's outstanding quality, the truth-to-occasion of his poems and their clear prose sense. What I might perhaps have learned from Thomas came to me, so far as it did, largely in other ways. Yet I like to think that the poem given below might be described as 'Thomasy'. It describes a remembered meeting, which seems at once slight and essential; and the setting is a rural one, as yet mostly untouched by mechanised modernity, but changing, and far more vulnerable than it knows. The poem is in eleven-syllable pentameters. The word '*tepe*' means hillock in Persian, and in archaeological parlance, a mound formed by successive layers of occupation.

BREAD AND BROTHERHOOD

IN LURISTAN

He came out of the house with bread in his hand.
His mother had just baked it, as he told me
(I happened to be walking by); and, tearing
Half the strip off, he offered it with a smile,
The flat uneven *nan*, mottled with scorch-marks,
Still warm and moist in its first freshness.
                                        We stood
In the dusty track before his curtained door,
Munching companionably and looking out
At the morning and the land, the nearby spring,
The grove it watered, acres of corn and beans,
Then arid pasture with clusters of black tents:
Encampments of village families, for whom
 – A generation's stone-throw from nomadism –
The habit of mud walls and poplar rafters
Proved hard in summer, in spite of planted fields.

Off to one side and out of view, the *tepe*:
Our excavation all but finished, the mound
Of habitations sifted now, dug-down-through
Past layers of burning, resettlement, neglect,
To the first ground-plan, the original floor,
Its beaten earth uncovered and newly swept...
I'd stretched out there as if to claim possession.

His name was Karim.
                        True, we liked each other
Though hardly in a way that had been tested
Beyond good nature's limit; were the same age,
Had shared a season's labour. But that meeting
 – Call it the moment of bread and brotherhood –
Comes back persistently across thirty years
In its first freshness; not as more than itself,
If vivid, scarcely a parable – and yet
The sum of what can humanly be hoped for.

Robert Wells
from *The Day and Other Poems* (Manchester: Carcanet, 2006)

Clive Wilmer

Several of my poems are indebted to Edward Thomas, but the poem I offer here, 'Dog Rose in June', is the only one written in conscious emulation. I doubt if it was conscious from the start, but as soon as the third line came to me I knew from the word 'sniff' that I was thinking of 'Old Man'.

My poem is in important ways unlike Thomas. For one thing, it is in free verse, though some of the lines resolve themselves into pentameters and there is something in their movement that calls Thomas to my mind. This may be an association of rhythm with subject-matter: the quiet naturalness of Thomas's tone and his passionate absorption in slight experiences – looking at a flower, listening to a bird, pausing at the end of a footpath. The other big difference is that my poem is erotic and Thomas never deals with erotic themes. This seems so remarkable a lacuna that I wonder if it is not significant. Thomas's poems are involved with his need for solitude, so perhaps by extension a freedom from sexual want. It could be that his intensity is due in part to a transfer of sexual emotion.

If this is so, my poem may have picked it up like a stray radio-signal. 'Old Man' is a poem of passionate desire: the desire for death. 'I sniff the spray,' he says, 'And think of nothing; I see and I hear nothing . . .' 'No garden appears . . . / Only an avenue, dark, nameless, without end.' Both Eros and Thanatos can occasion a paradox that sometimes makes for poetry: that the poet seeks to make conscious and articulate a longing for silence or oblivion. For this purpose, sex is often much the same as death.

DOG ROSE IN JUNE

Pink petals flare in the hedge:
Rosa canina, rose of the dog-days.
Gently I splay the petals, bend and sniff.
The whole flower gives off sweetness,
Pungency deeper in.
Such heat this evening, come away from the path.

Clive Wilmer
from *The Mystery of Things* (Manchester: Carcanet, 2006)

2/Lt. P. E. Thomas.

Afterword

MICHAEL LONGLEY

Several years ago my wife and I and our friend Ronald Ewart visited Edward Thomas's grave at Agny on the outskirts of Arras. Suddenly, shockingly, we found his headstone in the small cemetery. We stood just feet away from the skull that had contained the brain that had produced the lines that had filled our minds for many years. In that moment we loved him and mourned him, and tried to hold back our tears. Listening to the birdsong and the rustle of the surrounding trees, we wrote our names in the visitors' book. Edna added the four lovely lines of 'Thaw'. By the time we returned to Agny three years later, I had visited the *Anthem for Doomed Youth* exhibition in the Imperial War Museum, and had gazed at Thomas's crinkled notebook and his pocket watch, stopped at the instant of his death in a shell-blast at the beginning of the battle of Arras on 9th April 1917. The more one learns, the more painful the fact of his death becomes. Walking away from the poet's narrow plot was more difficult this second time. I want to go back to Agny.

*

Like everyone else I have suffered periods of writer's block, two of them protracted and painful. I have no idea where poetry comes from or where it goes when it disappears. It is a mystery most vividly brought home to us by Edward Thomas's life and achievement. He made his living as a writer of prose – country books, criticism, biographies, anthologies – and a ferocious routine of reviewing. Some of this huge output is good and the best of it nourished the poems that were waiting to be born. But he considered himself a hack, a drudge. As we know, he was released into his true calling by, first of all, Robert Frost's friendship and then by the Great War, the muse that killed him. The poetry existed as a subterranean current. It had to come. So, strangely, Edward Thomas's poetic career *began* with writer's block. A mountain of prose ended up meaning less than a book of poems. The one hundred and forty poems he wrote in the last two years of his life are a miracle. I can think of no body of work in English that is more mysterious.

*

When he first came to Belfast in 1973 to give a reading, I took Douglas Dunn to the Crown for a drink. 'What's Edna working on just now?' he asked. 'She's preparing an edition of Edward Thomas's poems.' 'Och,' Douglas exclaimed: '"Tall Nettles" – that's the sort of poem you dream about writing.' I have read 'Tall Nettles' hundreds of times. It is brand new every time – 'worn new'. Somehow 'the dust on the nettles' seems capable of registering everything. 'Anything however small,' Thomas wrote, 'may make a poem. Nothing however great is certain to.' 'Aspens', for instance, celebrates the tree itself but also manages to be an *ars poetica* and an elegy that covers the war and 'village' England – 'the inn, the smithy and the shop.' The weaving syntax communicates psychological commotion and foreboding. (And who has used adverbs more compellingly than Thomas does in the penultimate line: 'ceaselessly, unreasonably'?) He is a master of the short lyric. His quatrain poems contain whole worlds: 'Thaw' with its dizzying alternation of perspectives; 'The Cherry Trees' and 'In Memoriam: Easter 1915', which are compressed lamentations for the dead and missing of the Great War. *Multum in parvo*. Better than any other poet, Edward Thomas shows that miniature is not the same as minor.

*

In April 2004 I sat beside Edna at a heavy mahogany table in the New York Public Library's marvellous Berg Collection. A white-gloved attendant brought us the field notebooks into which Edward Thomas had scribbled nature-notes for his prose works. New York seemed a strange setting in which to follow the poet-to-be as he wandered in pre-war Hampshire, Wiltshire or Gloucestershire, scrutinising the birds and the flowers and obsessively describing the weather of nearly a hundred years ago. I got an electric charge touching the pages he had touched. Almost as exhilarating was my unexpected ability to decipher his tiny, cursive script. I felt at home with his handwriting. I was able to help Edna decode several knotty passages. I was taken back thirty years to when she was working on her annotated edition, *Poems and Last Poems*, and I helped her to transcribe material from files of newspaper cuttings in the Thomas archive in Cardiff. Now, waiting in an airport coffee shop to fly back to Europe, I wrote this quatrain and called it 'Footnote':

> I deciphered his handwriting for Edna
> In the Berg Collection, and helped them both

To rise above the table-top's green baize
When Edward 'grasped the stile by the holly.'

*

We went on a pilgrimage to Thomas territory in March 2004. In Wiltshire we walked around Stonehenge, and spent the night in Manor Farm in the middle of the Avebury Stone Circle. We must have looked like house-hunters or nosey parkers as we inspected Thomas's Hampshire homes: Berryfield Cottage, Yew Tree Cottage and Wick Green (The Red House). We took a bunch of Mothering Sunday daffodils to the memorial stone above Steep. And on the crest of a muddy Gloucestershire hillock planted with cabbages we looked down on Oldfield House, where Thomas stayed in August 1914, and beyond it, across dips in the landscape, to Little Iddens where Robert Frost then lived. Past those hedges and along those lanes the two poets had strolled together and talked 'of flowers, childhood, Shakespeare, women, England, the war'. When Frost returned to Little Iddens as an old man in 1957, he could not bring himself to cross the threshold. Lovers of Thomas's poetry stand waiting behind him. His 'Iris by Night' complements Thomas's 'The sun used to shine':

> Then a small rainbow like a trellis gate,
> A very small moon-made prismatic bow,
> Stood closely over us through which to go.

*

I felt honoured to be one of several poets who read their poems and talked about Thomas at the Conference held in St Edmund's Hall in March 2005. On that day we were this great poet's posterity and in our different ways we showed that Edward Thomas's presence is everywhere: 'The past hovering as it revisits the light'.

Seven Poems by Michael Longley

MOLE

'Does a mole ever get hit by a shell?'
Edward Thomas in his diary, 25.2.17

Who bothers to record
This body digested
By its own saliva
Inside the earth's mouth
And long intestine,

Or thanks it for digging
Its own grave, darkness
Growing like an eyelid
Over the eyes, hands
Swimming in the soil?

from *Man Lying on a Wall* (London: Victor Gollancz, 1976);
Collected Poems (London: Jonathan Cape, 2006)

EDWARD THOMAS'S WAR DIARY
1 January – 8 April, 1917

One night in the trenches
You dreamed you were at home
And couldn't stay to tea,
Then woke where shell holes
Filled with bloodstained water,

Where empty beer bottles
Littered the barbed wire – still
Wondering why there sang
No thrushes in all that
Hazel, ash and dogwood,

Your eye on what remained –
Light spangling through a hole
In the cathedral wall
And the little conical
Summer house among trees.

Green feathers of yarrow
Were just fledging the sods
Of your dugout when you
Skirted the danger zone
To draw panoramas,

To receive larks singing
Like a letter from home
Posted in No Man's Land
Where one frantic bat seemed
A piece of burnt paper.

from *Man Lying on a Wall* (London: Victor Gollancz, 1976);
Collected Poems (London: Jonathan Cape, 2006)

When he was billeted in a ruined house in Arras
And found a hole in the wall beside his bed
And, rummaging inside, his hand rested on *Keats*
By Edward Thomas, did Edmund Blunden unearth
A volume which 'the tall, Shelley-like figure'
Gathering up for the last time his latherbrush,
Razor, towel, comb, cardigan, cap comforter,
Water bottle, socks, gas mask, great coat, rifle
And bayonet, hurrying out of the same building
To join his men and march into battle, left
Behind him like a gift, the author's own copy?
When Thomas Hardy died his widow gave Blunden
As a memento of many visits to Max Gate
His treasured copy of Edward Thomas's *Poems*.

from *The Weather in Japan* (London: Jonathan Cape, 2000);
Collected Poems (London: Jonathan Cape, 2006)

THE MOUSTACHE

The moustache Edward Thomas grew to cover up
His aesthete's features, the short-back-and-sides hair-do
That moved him to the centre of modern times, recall
My father, aged twenty, in command of a company
Who, because most of them shaved only once a week
And some not at all, were known as Longley's Babies.

from *The Weather in Japan* (London: Jonathan Cape, 2000);
Collected Poems (London: Jonathan Cape, 2006)

THE WAR GRAVES

The exhausted cathedral reaches nowhere near the sky
As though behind its buttresses wounded angels
Snooze in a halfway house of gargoyles, rainwater
By the mouthful, broken wings among pigeons' wings.

There will be no end to clearing up after the war
And only an imaginary harvest-home where once
The Germans drilled holes for dynamite, for fieldmice
To smuggle seeds and sow them inside these columns.

The headstones wipe out the horizon like a blizzard
And we can see no farther than the day they died,
As though all of them died together on the same day
And the war was that single momentous explosion.

Mothers and widows pruned these roses yesterday,
It seems, planted sweet william and mowed the lawn
After consultations with the dead, heads meeting
Over this year's seed catalogues and packets of seeds.

Around the shell holes not one poppy has appeared,
No symbolic flora, only the tiny whitish flowers
No one remembers the names of in time, brookweed
And fairy flax, say, lamb's lettuce and penny-cress.

In mine craters so vast they are called after cities
Violets thrive, as though strewn by each cataclysm
To sweeten the atmosphere and conceal death's smell
With a perfume that vanishes as soon as it is found.

At the Canadian front line permanent sandbags
And duckboards admit us to the underworld, and then
With the beavers we surface for long enough to hear
The huge lamentations of the wounded caribou.

Old pals in the visitors' book at Railway Hollow
Have scribbled 'The severest spot. The lads did well'
'We came to remember', and the woodpigeons too
Call from the wood and all the way from Accrington.

I don't know how Rifleman Parfitt, Corporal Vance,
Private Costello of the Duke of Wellingtons,
Driver Chapman, Topping, Atkinson, Duckworth,
Dorrell, Wood come to be written in my diary.

For as high as we can reach we touch-read the names
Of the disappeared, and shut our eyes and listen to
Finches' chitters and a blackbird's apprehensive cry
Accompanying Charles Sorley's monumental sonnet.

We describe the comet at Edward Thomas's grave
And, because he was a fisherman, that headlong
Motionless deflection looks like a fisherman's fly,
Two or three white after-feathers overlapping.

Geese on sentry duty, lambs, a clattering freight train
And a village graveyard encompass Wilfred Owen's
Allotment, and there we pick from a nettle bed
One celandine each, the flower that outwits winter.

from *The Weather in Japan* (London: Jonathan Cape, 2000);
Collected Poems (London: Jonathan Cape, 2006)

EDWARD THOMAS'S POEM

I

I couldn't make out the minuscule handwriting
In the notebook the size of his palm and crinkled
Like an origami quim by shell-blast that stopped
His pocket watch at death. I couldn't read the poem.

II

From where he lay he could hear the skylark's
Skyward exultation, a chaffinch to his left
Fidgeting among the fallen branches,
Then all the birds of the Western Front.

III

The nature poet turned into a war poet as if
He could cure death with the rub of a dock leaf.

from *Snow Water* (London: Jonathan Cape, 2004);
Collected Poems (London: Jonathan Cape, 2006)

A GUST
for Eddie Linden at 70

I'm thinking of the pope and you, Eddie,
As I dander towards the New York Public
Library to peek at the field note-books
Of Edward Thomas wandering in England
In pursuit of spring before poetry and war.
Somewhere between Dorval and La Guardia
I encountered John Paul among the clouds
Like a surge of energy from the engines.
Now he lies stiff and full of chemicals
In precarious white hat and purple slippers
Saying the rosary over and over.
It all depends on the embalmer's craft.
The Poles cry out for his leathery heart.
John Paul was *musarum sacerdos* (part-time)
And you, Eddie, are a priest of the muses too
(Aquarian Order), your Vatican City
All the practitioners, the bad and good.
A shell blast killed Edward Thomas, a gust
That still riffles the pages in the library
On this bright popeless early April day.
Through the Door of the Sacraments I follow
John Paul and Edward and Eddie Linden.

(first published in *London Review of Books*)

Notes on the Poems

Abse

Betjeman wished to recite Thomas's 'Adlestrop': in 1940, Betjeman produced a programme called 'Back to the Railway Carriage' for the BBC Home Service (broadcast on 10 March, and reprinted in *The Listener*, 28 March) in which he read out 'Adlestrop', and said that it describes 'the deep heart of English country'. The BBC 'commissioned him to dwell on calming and homely topics while the threat of Invasion lingered on'. See John Betjeman, *Coming Home*, ed. Candida Lycett Green (London: Methuen, 1997).

Bugan

Hawthornden Castle: Thomas was intrigued by 'Drummond of Hawthornden' – William Drummond (1585–1649), who lived at Hawthornden Castle. Thomas's story 'Hawthornden' (published in 1910 and reprinted the following year in *Light and Twilight*) is not directly concerned with Drummond of Hawthornden, but it clearly draws on Drummond's desire to 'rest in honourable leisure' at Hawthornden. It is a story about yearning and home. In the title-essay of *Horae Solitariae* (1902), Thomas notes that 'Elia himself has confessed a love – "shall I be thought fantastical?" – for the names of certain poets. "The sweetest names, and which carry a perfume in the mention, are Kit Marlowe, Drayton, Drummond of Hawthornden and Cowley"'. Twice in 1907, Thomas reviewed Drummond's *A Cypress Grove* (1623).

Constantine

'elected friends': see Frost's poem 'Iris by Night'.
the hand: Thomas's poem 'The long small room', from 1916, describes

> this my right hand

> Crawling crab-like over the clean white page,
> Resting awhile each morning on the pillow,
> Then once more starting to crawl on towards age.
> (ll. 12–15)

Crawford

Norman MacCaig: born 1910, died 1996.

Kathleen Jamie: born 1963.

Mandelstam: Osip Mandelstam (1892–1938). Russian poet, and victim of Stalinism.

'somehow someday I shall be here again': 'A month or two [ago] I dreamt we were walking near Ledington but we lost one another in a strange place & I woke saying to myself "somehow someday I shall be here again" which I made the last line of some verses'. Edward Thomas, *Elected Friends: Robert Frost and Edward Thomas to One Another*, ed. Matthew Spencer (New York: Handsel Books, 2003), p. 83. The poem 'A Dream' ends: 'I awoke from waters unto men / Saying: "I shall be here some day again."'

the Turl: Lincoln College in Oxford is on Turl Street. Thomas was a history scholar at Lincoln 1898–1900.

St Louis: T. S. Eliot was born in St Louis, Missouri.

Crossley-Holland

The closing quatrain on p. 102 is 'Watercolour', also published in *The Language of Yes*.

pulk: a marsh pool.

Dale

Logan Pearsall Smith: Logan Pearsall Smith (1865–1946) famously said in *Afterthoughts* (1931) that 'People say that life is the thing, but I prefer reading'.

Hill

A. E. H.: A. E. Housman (1859–1936), poet and classical scholar. Housman was from Bromsgrove, Worcestershire, but wrote *A Shropshire Lad* (1896).

Bateson Memorial lecture: see 'Gurney's "Hobby"', *Essays in Criticism*, xxxiv, 2 (April 1984), pp. 97–128.

'steeped in Auden': *The Collected Poems of Drummond Allison*, edited and introduced by Stephen Benson, 'published privately in an original run of 300', Bishop's Stortford College, 1994, p. 23. The other quotation is from p. 16.

Jenkins

the touch of rain / on the spike: possibly a faint echo of Thomas's poem 'Like the touch of rain' (also known as 'Go now'), which begins 'Like the touch of rain she was / On a man's flesh'.

Mackinnon

This poem was written after a visit to Steep in September 2005.

McNeillie

Gerard Manley Hopkins: Hopkins (1844–89) studied theology at St Beuno's in North Wales 1874–77.

Ivor Gurney: Gurney (1890–1937) was a poet and composer who fought on the Western Front, and spent many years in a mental institution. He was a great admirer of Thomas's poetry.

Muldoon

Killdeer: a large American plover, *Charadrius vociferous*, with a plaintive song.

O'Donoghue

The Davenant Society: an undergraduate literary society at Lincoln College. William Davenant (1606–68) was godson of Shakespeare, an undergraduate at Lincoln and unofficial Poet Laureate. In a wooden box known as 'The Ark', the society kept 'The Regalia' (now missing), which included an early copy of Davenant's *Gondibert* and a small silver owl. On 24 April 1899, in 'fear and trembling', Thomas delivered a paper to the Society entitled 'The Relation of Prose to Poetry in the XIXth Century'; and the minutes of the meeting record that this was followed by 'an absorbing discussion' (*Lincoln Archive*).

Paulin

'A sentence is a sound…': Robert Frost, *Selected Letters* (London: Jonathan Cape, 1965), p. 110.

Porter

Shena Mackay: born in Edinburgh in 1944, is the author of, among others, *Redhill Rococo* (1986), *Dunedin* (1992), and *The Orchard on Fire* (1995).

Schmidt

This poem was first published as one in a sequence, numbered 'XV'.

Tobias Wolff: born in Alabama in 1945, he is a novelist and short-story writer, best known for his memoir of childhood, *This Boy's Life* (1989).

Elizabeth Bishop (1911–79): American poet, whose *Complete Poems* (1927–1979) were published in 1983.

'Miss Dickinson of Amherst': Emily Dickinson (1830–86), American poet, at first regarded as minor and eccentric, but now considered a major writer of great originality.

Shuttle

Basho: the pseudonym of Matsuo Munefusa (1644–94), Japanese poet, considered the finest writer of Japanese haiku during the formative years of the genre. Basho's work here is translated by Nobuyuki Yuasa: *The Narrow Road to the Deep North* (Penguin Classics).

Stevenson

Peter Redgrove (1932–2003): prolific British poet, who wrote numerous volumes, the most recent being *From the Virgil Caverns.*
Frances Horovitz (1938–83): British poet, well known for writing about landscape, who published four collections of poems, including *Water Over Stone* (1980) and *Snow Light, Water Light* (1983).

Taplin

'wring all the necks of my rhetoric, my geese': Letter from Edward Thomas to Robert Frost, 19 May 1914. Thomas is translating one of Verlaine's injunctions in 'L'Art Poetique'; see *Elected Friends: Robert Frost and Edward Thomas to One Another*, p. 10.

Tomlinson

Thomas wrote a number of poems for (or featuring) his daughter Myfanwy. 'The Path' and 'Old Man' are two of them. Charles Tomlinson uses his observations on the syntax of 'The Path' as an implicit commentary on the form of his own poem.

Longley

'the tall Shelley-like figure': Longley is quoting from Barry Webb, *Edmund Blunden: A Biography* (New Haven and London: Yale University Press, 1990), p. 56.

Notes on Contributors

Dannie Abse was born in 1923 and went to school and university in Cardiff before moving to London. He became a doctor, and was a specialist in charge of the chest clinic at the Central Medical Establishment in London. His first collection of poetry was published in 1948, and his *New and Collected Poems* in 2003. An autobiography, *Goodbye Twentieth Century*, was published in 2001, and he is the author of *The Two Roads Taken: A Prose Miscellany* as well as several other works of prose. He is a Fellow of the Royal Society of Literature, and President of the Welsh Academy of Letters.

Carmen Bugan was born in Romania in 1970, but her parents became political dissidents during the time of Ceausescu. She has lived in the United States and Ireland, and now lives in Oxford. She has a doctorate from Oxford University, for a thesis on the work of Seamus Heaney. Her poetry appears in the anthology *Oxford Poets 2001*, *The Tabla Book of New Verse 2004*, The Forward Book of Poetry 2006, *PN Review*, and *Harvard Review*; and her collection *Crossing the Carpathians* was published in 2004. She is Creative Arts Fellow at Wolfson College, Oxford.

Polly Clark was born in Toronto in 1968 but she grew up in Lancashire, Cumbria and the Borders of Scotland. She has a degree in English and Philosophy from Liverpool University, and an MA in English Literature from Oxford Brookes University. She has worked at Edinburgh Zoo, which features in some of her poems, and taught English in Hungary; and she now works in publishing. In 1997, she won an Eric Gregory Award, her work appeared in *New Blood* in 1999, and her first collection of poems was *Kiss* (2000).

Gillian Clarke was born and brought up in Cardiff, and read English at Cardiff University. She is President of Ty Newydd, the writers' centre in North Wales which she co-founded in 1990, and a tutor on the M.Phil. course in Creative Writing, the University of Glamorgan. Her poetry is studied for GCSE and A Level throughout Britain. She lives with her husband (an architect) on a small-holding in Ceredigion. Recent books include *Collected Poems*, 1997, and *Making the Beds for the Dead*, 2004, both published by Carcanet. The *Irish Times* once commented that she 'beautifully achieves an Edward Thomas-like perspective.'

David Constantine was born in Salford in 1944. He studied Modern Languages at Wadham College, Oxford, before becoming a lecturer at Durham University in 1969, and since 1981 he has been a Fellow of The Queen's College, Oxford. He is a translator of Hölderlin and other German writers, and an editor of *Modern Poetry in Translation*. His *Collected Poems* appeared in 2004. He has won a number of prizes, including the Alice Hunt Bartlett Prize and the European Translation Prize. In 2004, his *A Living Language: Bloodaxe/Newcastle Poetry Lectures* was published, and he has also given lectures on Edward Thomas.

Robert Crawford was born in Scotland in 1959. He was an undergraduate at Glasgow, and has a D.Phil. from Balliol College, Oxford. He has taught at the University of St Andrews since 1989. He is now a Professor of Modern Scottish Literature. His critical works include *The Savage and the City in the Work of T. S. Eliot* (1987), *Devolving English Literature* (2000) and *The Modern Poet* (2001). His poetry collections include *Selected Poems* (2005), a Poetry Society Special Commendation, and *Apollos of the North* (2006). He co-edited *The Penguin Book of Scottish Verse* (2006).

Kevin Crossley-Holland was born in 1941, grew up at the foot of Whiteleaf Cross on the Chiltern Hills, and read English at Oxford. He has been Gregory Fellow in Poetry at Leeds University, editor at Macmillan and editorial director of Victor Gollancz, and has taught in Minnesota. Author of seven collections of poems, he has translated *Beowulf* and retold the Norse myths, while his children's books have been widely translated and won the Carnegie Medal and Guardian Children's Fiction Prize. He is a Fellow of the Royal Society of Literature and Honorary Fellow of St Edmund Hall.

Guy Cuthbertson was born in Solihull in 1975. He was an undergraduate at the University of St Andrews and then a graduate student at the University of Oxford, at The Queen's College. At Queen's, he wrote a doctoral thesis entitled 'The Literary Geography in Edward Thomas's Work'. He has been a lecturer at St Edmund Hall and Merton College, Oxford, and at the University of Swansea; and he currently teaches at the University of St Andrews. He has published a number of articles on Thomas, and he is editing Thomas's Autobiographies for Oxford University Press.

Peter Dale was born in 1938 and studied English at the University of Oxford. He co-edited the poetry journal *Agenda*, and was a secondary school teacher. His first collection of poetry, *Walk from the House*, was published in 1962, and his other collections include *One Another: A Sonnet Sequence*, published in 1978 and republished in 2002, and *Edge to Edge: New and Selected Poems*, published in 1996. He was awarded an Arts Council Bursary in 1970. He has also translated Dante, Corbière, Villon, Laforgue and Tamil poetry. His latest book of verse, *Under the Breath*, appeared in 2002.

Jane Draycott was born in 1954, and has worked as a teacher in a number of places, but she is now based in Oxfordshire. She is currently a tutor at the University of Oxford and Lancaster University. She has also worked as Poet in Residence at Henley's River and Rowing Museum. Her collections of poetry include *Prince Rupert's Drop*, *Tideway* and *The Night Tree*. In 2002, she won the Keats-Shelley Prize, and her first two collections were shortlisted for the Forward Poetry Prize. She was included in the Next Generation Poets 2004.

Jonty Driver was born in Cape Town in 1939. He later lived in Grahamstown, before attending the University of Cape Town. He was elected President of the National Union of South African Students (NUSAS) in 1963 and 1964. He then moved to England (and was prohibited from returning to South Africa). He read for an M.Phil. at Trinity College, Oxford, and later taught at Sevenoaks School. He was the Master of Wellington College from 1989 until 2000. He has produced novels and a biography as well as several collections of poetry, including *So Far: Selected Poems 1960-2004*.

U. A. Fanthorpe, born in Kent in 1929 and educated at Oxford, taught English for sixteen years before becoming a clerk-receptionist in a Bristol hospital. Since 1978 she has published nine collections of poetry; *Collected Poems* came out in 2003. She has been awarded a number of honours: a Fellowship of the Royal Society of Literature in 1988, a CBE for services to poetry in 2001, and the Queen's Gold Medal for Poetry in 2003. She lives in Gloucestershire, and as an Honorary DLitt of the University of Gloucestershire, delivered the Laurie Lee Memorial Lecture on 'Dymock: The Time and the Place'.

Helen Farish was born in 1962 and grew up in Cumbria. Her first collection, *Intimates* (2005) won the Forward Prize for Best First Collection and was short-listed for the T. S. Eliot prize. In 2004 she completed a doctorate on the poetry of Louise Gluck and Sharon Olds. She is now Senior Lecturer in English at Sheffield Hallam University where she also runs the MA in Creative Writing.

Michael Foley was born in Derry in 1947, and was educated at St Columb's College and Queen's University, Belfast, where he studied Chemistry. He moved into the field of computing science, and now teaches at the University of Westminster in London. His poetry collection *True Life Love Stories* was published in 1976. His most recent collection is *Autumn Beguiles the Fatalist*, published in 2006. He has published four novels, and edited *The Honest Ulsterman*.

John Fuller was born in 1937 in Ashford, Kent. He was an undergraduate at New College, Oxford, and became a Fellow of Magdalen College in 1966. He has written at length on the poetry of W. H. Auden. His collections of poetry include

Fairground Music, Epistles to Several Persons and *Ghosts*. He has also written fiction, including the successful novel *Flying to Nowhere*, and more recently *Flawed Angel* (2005). He has won the Newdigate Prize, a Gregory Award, the Geoffrey Faber Memorial Prize, the Forward Poetry Prize and the Whitbread First Novel Award.

Elizabeth Garrett was born in London in 1958, but grew up in the Channel Islands. At the University of Oxford, she wrote a doctoral thesis on 'poetic identity and the role of the clown in modern poetry'. She has worked for the Bodleian Library and the Voltaire Foundation. Her first collection, *The Rule of Three* (1991), won a Southern Arts poetry prize, and followed a pamphlet of her poems, *The Mortal Light* (1990). Her poetry also appeared in Carol Rumens's *New Women Poets* in 1990. In 1994, she was one of the New Generation Poets, and her next collection, *A Two-Part Invention*, was published in 1998.

Jane Griffiths was born in Exeter in 1970, but grew up in Holland and is of Welsh ancestry. She read English at the University of Oxford, where she won the Newdigate Prize. She later wrote a doctoral thesis at Oxford, on John Skelton. She was a Fellow and Stipendiary Lecturer in English at St Edmund Hall, Oxford, and she is now a lecturer at the University of Edinburgh. She has also worked as a bookbinder, and for the *Oxford English Dictionary*. In 1996, she won an Eric Gregory Award. Her poetry has been published in a number of periodicals, and as *A Grip on Thin Air* and *Icarus on Earth*.

David Harsent was born in Devon in 1942. He has published nine collections of poetry. The most recent, *Legion*, won the Forward Prize for best collection in 2005 and was shortlisted for both the T. S. Eliot and Whitbread Awards. His work in music theatre has involved collaborations with a number of composers, but most often with Harrison Birtwistle, and has been performed at the Royal Opera House, Carnegie Hall, the Proms and on BBC 2 and Channel 4 TV. A new opera, *The Minotaur* (also with Birtwistle) will open at ROH in 2008. He is a Fellow of the Royal Society of Literature and in 2005 was appointed Distinguished Writing Fellow at Sheffield Hallam University.

Seamus Heaney was born in 1939. He was an undergraduate at Queen's University, Belfast, and later worked there as a lecturer. He has been a professor at Harvard University, and was Oxford University's Professor of Poetry from 1989 to 1994. His *Death of a Naturalist* won the Somerset Maugham Award in 1967, *North* (1975) won the W. H. Smith Award and the Duff Cooper Prize, and *The Spirit Level* was 1996 Whitbread Book of the Year. He was awarded the Nobel Prize for Literature in 1995. In addition to poetry, he has produced a number of other books, including *Preoccupations* (1980), and, jointly, *Homage to Robert Frost* (1998).

Geoffrey Hill was born in 1932 at Bromsgrove, in Worcestershire. He was an undergraduate at Keble College, Oxford, and then taught at the University of Leeds for many years. He is a Professor Emeritus at Boston University, and he has also taught in Bristol, Cambridge, Michigan and Nigeria. He has won a number of prizes, including the W. H. Heinemann Award for *The Triumph of Love* in 1999, the Duff Cooper Memorial Prize for *Tenebrae* in 1979, the Alice Hunt Bartlett Award and the Whitbread Award for Poetry for *Mercian Hymns* (1971), and the Hawthornden Prize for *King Log* in 1969.

Matthew Hollis was born in Norwich in 1971. *Groundwater* (2004), his first full-length collection, was a Poetry Book Society Recommendation and was shortlisted for the Whitbread Prize for Poetry, the Guardian First Book Award and the Forward Prize for Best First Collection. He is co-editor of *101 Poems Against War* (2003) and *Strong Words: Modern Poets on Modern Poetry* (2000), and works as a poetry editor at Faber and Faber. In 2005–6 he was Writer-in-Residence at the Wordsworth Trust in Grasmere.

Jeremy Hooker was born in Hampshire in 1941. He was a student at the University of Southampton and then a lecturer at the University College of Wales, Aberystwyth. He has since taught at several other universities, and is now Professor of English at the University of Glamorgan. His critical works include studies of John Cowper Powys and David Jones, *Writers in a Landscape* (1996) and *Imagining Wales* (2001). *The Cut of the Light: Poems 1965–2005* represents his ten collections of poetry. He has edited selections of Richard Jefferies's essays and Edward Thomas's stories. His *Welsh Journal* was published in 2001.

Nigel Jenkins was born in 1949, and brought up on a farm in Gower. He worked as a newspaper reporter, and was then a student at Essex University. He now teaches creative writing at the University of Wales Swansea, and lives in Mumbles. He has also worked on a circus. He has written several books of poetry, including *Song and Dance* (1981), *Acts of Union* (1990), *Ambush* (1998) *Blue* (2002), and *Hotel Gwales* (2006). He is also a playwright, editor and translator, and his prose works include *Footsore on the Frontier: Selected Essays and Articles* (2001). He has won several prizes, including an Eric Gregory Award and the Welsh Arts Council's Book of the Year Award.

P. J. Kavanagh was born in 1931. He was educated abroad, and at Merton College, Oxford. He is a Fellow of the Royal Society of Literature. He has produced several collections of poetry, including *Edward Thomas in Heaven* (1974) and *Collected Poems* (1992). He has also written novels, including *A Song and Dance* (1968), which won the Guardian Fiction Prize, and his volume of autobiography, *The Perfect*

Stranger, won the Richard Hillary Prize. He has edited *The Collected Poems of Ivor Gurney* (1982) and (with James Michie) *The Oxford Book of Short Poems* (1985).

Grevel Lindop was born in 1948 in Liverpool. He read English at Wadham College, Oxford, and later at Manchester University, where he became Professor of Romantic and Early Victorian Studies. Since 2001 he has been a freelance writer. He has published six collections of poems, including *Selected Poems* (2000) and *Playing with Fire* (2006). His other books include *A Literary Guide to the Lake District* (revised edition 2005), and editions of Chatterton's poems, Robert Graves's *The White Goddess,* and (as General Editor) *The Works of Thomas De Quincey.* He is currently writing a biography of Charles Williams.

Edna Longley was born in 1940, and studied at Trinity College, Dublin. She is now Professor Emerita at Queen's University, Belfast, where she taught for many years. One of her earliest publications was an edition of Edward Thomas's *Poems and Last Poems,* and she also edited the selected prose of Edward Thomas. There are essays on Thomas in *Poetry in the Wars* and *Poetry and Posterity.* She has also produced a study of Louis MacNeice, and a number of other books and articles and she edited *The Bloodaxe Book of Twentieth-Century Poetry from Britain and Ireland.* She is married to Michael Longley.

Michael Longley was born in Belfast in 1939, and educated at Trinity College, Dublin, where he read Classics. He has published eight collections of poetry including *Gorse Fires* (1991) which won the Whitbread Poetry Award and *The Weather in Japan* (2000) which won the Hawthornden Prize, the T. S. Eliot Prize and the Irish Times Poetry Prize. His most recent collection *Snow Water* (2004) was awarded the Librex Montale Prize. His *Collected Poems* appeared in 2006. In 2001 he received the Queen's Gold Medal for Poetry, and in 2003 the Wilfred Owen Award. He and his wife, the critic Edna Longley, live and work in Belfast.

Lachlan Mackinnon was born in 1956, and read English at Christ Church, Oxford. He has written three books of poems, *Monterey Cypress* (1988), *The Coast of Bohemia* (1991), and *The Jupiter Collisions* (2003); two critical books, *Eliot, Auden, Lowell: Aspects of Baudelairean Inheritance* (1983) and *Shakespeare the Aesthete: An Exploration of Literary Theory* (1988); and a biography, *The Lives of Elsa Triolet* (1992). He has reviewed extensively in the national press. He teaches at Winchester College.

Glyn Maxwell was born in 1962 in Welwyn Garden City, where he went to school. He was an undergraduate at Worcester College, Oxford, and then studied poetry and theatre at Boston University. He is a playwright, as well as a poet. He has taught at Amherst College in Massachusetts, and lives in the United States. He won a Somerset Maugham Award, the Geoffrey Faber Memorial Prize and the E. M. Forster Prize. His books include *The Breakage* (1998), which features 'Letters to Edward Thomas', *The Nerve* (2002), *The Sugar Mile* (2005) and *The Boys at Twilight: Poems 1990–1995* (2000).

Peter McDonald was born in Belfast in 1962, and read English at University College, Oxford. He has taught at the universities of Cambridge and Bristol, and he is now Christopher Tower Student and Tutor in Poetry in the English Language at Christ Church, Oxford, where he runs Tower Poetry. He has written a study of Louis MacNeice, and edited MacNeice's plays and poems, and has also written two important books on contemporary poetry. He won the Newdigate Prize for poetry as an undergraduate, and his first full collection of poems was *Biting the Wax* (1989). *Pastorals* was published in 2004.

Patrick McGuinness was born in 1968 in Tunisia. He is now a Fellow of St Anne's College, Oxford, where he teaches French, but he lives in Cardiff. He has produced a number of translations and editions, as well as *Maurice Maeterlinck and the Making of Modern Theatre* (2000) and *Symbolism, Decadence and the 'Fin de Siècle'* (2000). His collection of poetry, *The Canals of Mars*, was published in 2004. In 1998 he won an Eric Gregory Award and in 2001 he won the Levinson Prize for his poetry.

Jamie McKendrick was born in Liverpool in 1955. He studied at the University of Nottingham, and taught at the University of Salerno in Italy. He now lives in Oxford, and has been Poet in Residence at Hertford College, Oxford. His collections of poems include *The Sirocco Room*, *The Marble Fly*, which won the 1997 Forward Prize for Best Collection, and *Ink Stone*, which was shortlisted for the T. S. Eliot Prize. *Sky Nails: Poems 1979–1997* was published in 2000. He has edited *Twentieth-Century Italian Poems*, and translated the poetry of Valerio Magrelli.

Andrew McNeillie was born in North Wales in 1946, attended the John Bright Grammar School in Llandudno, and later read English at Magdalen College, Oxford. He is now the Literature Editor at Oxford University Press. His poetry collection called *Nevermore* (2000) was shortlisted for the Forward Prize for Best First Collection. He has since produced another two collections of poetry, *Now, Then* in 2002 and *Slower* in 2006. He has also written a prose memoir, *An Aran Keening* (2001), and he founded the Clutag Press in 2000. His biographical memoir of his father *Ian Niall: Part of His Life* came out in 2007.

Esther Morgan was born in 1970 in Kidderminster, and read English at Newnham College, Cambridge. She worked as a volunteer at the Wordsworth

Trust in Grasmere, before taking an MA in Creative Writing at the University of East Anglia. She has taught creative writing at that university and is currently a tutor on the MSt in creative writing at Oxford University. In 1998 she won an Eric Gregory Award. Her first collection, *Beyond Calling Distance*, was published in 2001 and won the Aldeburgh Poetry Festival First Collection Prize and was shortlisted for the John Llewellyn Rhys Memorial Prize. Her second collection, *The Silence Living in Houses*, was published in 2005.

Andrew Motion was born in 1952. He read English at University College, Oxford, during which time he won the Newdigate Prize, and then, as a graduate student, he studied Edward Thomas. He became a university lecturer, and he is now Professor of Creative Writing at Royal Holloway College, University of London, a Fellow of the Royal Society of Literature and the Poet Laureate. His first collection, *The Pleasure Steamers*, was published in 1977, and many other collections have followed, including *Dangerous Play*, which won the *Mail on Sunday*/John Llewellyn Rhys Prize, and *Natural Causes*, which won the Dylan Thomas Award. His non-fiction works include biographies of Philip Larkin and John Keats, *The Poetry of Edward Thomas* (1980), and a childhood memoir, *In the Blood*.

Paul Muldoon was born in Portadown, County Armagh, in 1951, and grew up in the countryside, near Moy. He studied at Queen's University, Belfast – where he was taught by Seamus Heaney, and became friends with a number of other Belfast poets – before working for the BBC and as a freelance writer. He has lived in the United States since 1987, but he was Professor of Poetry at Oxford from 1999 to 2004. His first collection was *New Weather*, and later collections include *Why Brownlee Left*, *Meeting the British*, *Madoc: A Mystery* and *The Annals of Chile*. He has won many major prizes.

James Nash was born in west London in 1949, where he grew up; but he has lived for many years in Leeds. Having taught in inner-city schools, he now works as a journalist, writing for the *Leeds Guide*, and editing the books page for the arts magazine *Northern Exposure*. He is Writer in Residence in the Faculty of Education at Leeds University, and for High Schools in Calderdale. He has also taught creative writing at HM Prison, Wakefield. He has published three collections: *Deadly Sensitive* (1999), *In Transit* (2000), and *Coma Songs* (2003), all with Grassroots Press. He has recently turned to prose, and a story of his appeared in *Four Fathers* (2006).

Lucy Newlyn was born in Uganda in 1956, and grew up in Leeds. She is a Professor of English Language and Literature at Oxford University, and a Fellow and Tutor in English at St Edmund Hall. She has published widely on English Romantic Literature, including three books with Oxford University Press, and

The Cambridge Companion to Coleridge. Some of her poems appeared with Carcanet in the *Oxford Poets Anthology, 2001*; and her first collection, *Ginnel,* appeared in 2005. She edited Edward Thomas's *Oxford* (2005); and she is the general editor of the forthcoming *Edward Thomas Selected Prose,* to be published with Oxford University Press.

Bernard O'Donoghue was born in Cullen, County Cork, in 1945, later moving to Manchester. He studied Medieval English at Oxford University, where (as a graduate student) he was a member of Edward Thomas's college, Lincoln. He is now a Tutor and Fellow in English at Wadham College. He is the author of *Seamus Heaney and the Language of Poetry* (1995); and he has published five collections of poetry: *Poaching Rights* (1987); *The Weakness* (1991); *Gunpowder* (1995), winner of the 1995 Whitbread Poetry Award; *Here Nor There* (1999); and *Outliving* (2003). His latest work is a verse translation of *Sir Gawain and the Green Knight* (2006).

Tom Paulin was born in Leeds in 1949, grew up in Belfast, and was educated at the universities of Hull and Oxford. As a graduate student, he was a member of Lincoln College, where Edward Thomas read History. He has published seven collections of poetry as well as a *Selected Poems 1972-1990,* two major anthologies, two versions of Greek drama and several critical works, including *Thomas Hardy: the Poetry of Perception, The Day-Star of Liberty: William Hazlitt's Radical Style,* and *Crusoe's Secret: The Aesthetics of Dissent* (2005). His most recent collections of poetry are *The Wind-Dog* and *The Invasion Handbook* (2004), and *The Road to Inver* (2004). Well-known for his appearances on the BBC's *Late Review,* he is the G. M. Young Lecturer in English Literature at Hertford College, Oxford.

Peter Porter was born in Brisbane, Australia in 1929. His first collection of poetry, *Once Bitten, Twice Bitten,* was published in 1961, and *The Cost of Seriousness* in 1978. *Collected Poems* (1983) won the Duff Cooper Prize and *The Automatic Oracle* (1987) won the Whitbread Poetry Award. His collection of poems, *Max is Missing,* was published in 2001, and won the Forward Poetry Prize. Peter Porter was awarded the Gold Medal for Australian Literature in 1990; and the Queen's Gold Medal for Poetry in 2002. His most recent collection, *Afterburner* (2004), was shortlisted for the T. S. Eliot Prize.

Jem Poster was born in 1949, and educated at Cambridge. He directed the creative writing diploma at Oxford University's Department for Continuing Education before moving to Aberystwyth, where he is Professor of Creative Writing. He is the author of a collection of poetry and two novels, *Courting Shadows* (2002) and *Rifling Paradise* (2006). Other publications include *George Crabbe: Selected Poetry* (1986) and *The Thirties Poets* (1993), as well as a range of articles on twentieth-century poetry and fiction.

Vernon Scannell was born in 1922, served in the Gordon Highlanders in World War Two and was a professional boxer and a teacher before becoming a full-time writer in the 1960s. He wrote an introduction for *Elected Friends*, an anthology of poems written to, for, and about Edward Thomas, edited by Anne Harvey. He has published novels, criticism, four autobiographical prose books and over a dozen books of poetry. His *New and Collected Poems 1950–1980* was published in 1980. He has received the Heinemann Award, the Cholmondeley Poetry Prize and is an Honorary Fellow of the Royal Society of Literature.

Michael Schmidt was born in Mexico in 1947 and studied at Harvard and Oxford before settling in England. A founder and editorial director of Carcanet Press, he has also been editor of *Poetry Nation Review* for thirty years. He is Professor of Poetry at the University of Glasgow. His first collection, *Black Buildings*, was published in 1969; more recently he has published a *Selected Poems, 1972–1997* (1997). *Lives of the Poets* (1998) presents a comprehensive overview of six centuries of British poetry, and *The Story of Poetry: From Caedmon to Caxton* (2001) combines history, criticism and anthology. His latest book, *The First Poets: Lives of the Ancient Greek Poets*, was published in 2004.

Peter Scupham was born in Liverpool in 1933, and was an undergraduate at Emmanuel College, Cambridge. He now lives in Norfolk. He founded the Mandeville Press with John Mole, and also started a catalogue book business with Margaret Steward. Ten volumes of his poetry were published by Oxford University Press, and his poetry has also been published by Mandeville, Anvil, Carcanet and others. His *Collected Poems* includes his poetry from 1972 to 2001. He is a Fellow of the Royal Society of Literature.

Owen Sheers was born in 1974 in Fiji, but grew up in Abergavenny and went to university at Oxford. He won an Eric Gregory Award and the Vogue Young Writer's Award, and his debut prose work, *The Dust Diaries* (2004), was short-listed for the Ondaatje Prize and won the Welsh Book of the Year 2005. His first collection of poetry was *The Blue Book* (2000), and his second collection, *Skirrid Hill*, won the 2006 Somerset Maugham Award. In 2004 he was Writer in Residence at The Wordsworth Trust and was selected as one of the Poetry Book Society's 20 Next Generation Poets. His first novel, *Resistance*, was published in 2007.

Penelope Shuttle was born in Middlesex in 1947. She has published eight collections of poems as well as a *Selected Poems* (1998). She is also the co-author of two prose works, *The Wise Wound* and *Alchemy for Women*, dealing with the psychology and creative aspect of menstruation. She has lived in Cornwall since 1970. Her work has been widely anthologised. Her most recent collection is *Redgrove's Wife*

(2006), shortlisted for The Forward Prize. She is a Hawthornden Fellow, and a Tutor for The Poetry School.

Jon Stallworthy was born in London in 1935, and was an undergraduate at Magdalen College, Oxford. Until his retirement, he held a Readership (and subsequently a Professorship) in Modern English Literature at Oxford University, and he is a Fellow Emeritus of Wolfson College. His biography of Wilfred Owen won the Duff Cooper Memorial Prize, the W. H. Smith Literary Award and the E. M. Forster Award. His first collection of poetry appeared in 1961, and *Rounding the Horn: Collected Poems* was published in 1998, in the same year as his autobiography.

John Stammers was born in Islington in 1954, where he lives and works as a freelance writer and teacher of creative writing. He read philosophy at King's College London and is an Associate of Kings' College. He achieved a commendation in The National Poetry Competition of 2000 for his controversial poem *On Love*. His first collection, *Panoramic Lounge Bar* (2001) was awarded the Forward Prize for Best First Collection and shortlisted for the Whitbread Poetry Award; his second, *Stolen Love Behaviour* (2005) is a Poetry Book Society Choice. It was shortlisted for the T. S. Eliot Prize 2005, and the Forward Prize for Best Collection 2005. He is the convenor of the British and Irish Contemporary Poetry Conference.

Anne Stevenson was born in 1933. She grew up in the States but has lived in Britain for most of her adult life. She has published twelve collections of poetry, a book of essays, *Between the Iceberg and the Ship* (1998), a critical study, *Five Looks at Elizabeth Bishop* (1998) and a biography of Sylvia Plath, *Bitter Fame* (1989). Her most recent collections are *Granny Scarecrow* and *Report from the Border* (2003). Northern Arts Literary Fellow in 1981 and writer-in-residence at Edinburgh University in 1989, she was the inaugural winner of the Northern Rock Foundation Writer's Award in 2002. Her *Poems 1995–2005* was published by Bloodaxe Books in 2005.

Seán Street has published six collections of poetry, including *Figure in a Landscape* (1981) and *A Walk in Winter* (1989). He has worked in radio as a writer, producer and presenter for more than thirty years and his work is frequently to be heard on BBC Radios 3 and 4. His prose includes a number of texts on radio history, as well as an anthology of recollections of country life, and books on Gerard Manley Hopkins and the Dymock Poets. He is Professor of Radio in the Bournemouth Media School at Bournemouth University; and he has written a history of British radio. His most recent collection is *Radio and Other Poems*.

Kim Taplin was born in 1943. She read English at Oxford, and lives in Oxfordshire. She has written a number of books that celebrate the natural world, and walking in it, some of which refer to or discuss Edward Thomas. She has also written frequently about the countryside for *The Countryman* and other publications. Her poetry publications include *By the Harbour Wall* (1990), *For People with Bodies* (1997) and *From Parched Creek* (2001). She is also the author of two critical studies that bring together her interests in ecology and literature: *Tongues in Trees* (1989) and *The English Path* (2000).

Charles Tomlinson was born in Stoke-on-Trent in 1927. He taught at the University of Bristol from 1956 until his retirement. He has published many collections of poetry as well as volumes of criticism and translation, and has edited the *Oxford Book of Verse in English Translation* (1980). His poetry has won prizes in Europe and the United States, including the New Criterion Poetry Prize, 2002. His latest volume is *Cracks in the Universe* (2006). He is an honorary fellow of the American Academy of the Arts and Sciences and of the Modern Language Association. He was made a CBE for his contribution to literature in 2001.

John Powell Ward was born in Suffolk in 1937, and studied at the universities of Toronto, Cambridge and Wales. He worked for many years at the University of Wales, Swansea. He was editor of *Poetry Wales* from 1975 to 1980, and he is the editor of the Border Lines series. (A special centenary issue of *Poetry Wales* was devoted to Edward Thomas in 1978, containing important articles on his Welsh connections.) In addition to several volumes of poetry, Ward has published on individual writers such as Wordsworth and R. S. Thomas, as well as on more general topics. His many books include *The English Line: Poetry of the Unpoetic from Wordsworth to Larkin* (1991) and *The Spell of the Song: Letters, Meaning, and English Poetry* (2004). Seren Books have recently published his *Selected and New Poems*.

Robert Wells was born in Oxford in 1947. He has worked as a woodman on Exmoor, a teacher in Italy and Iran, and in publishing. He now lives in France. He is the author of *The Winter's Task* (1977), *Selected Poems* (1986), *Lusus* (1999); as well as two verse translations: Virgil's *Georgics* (1982) and Theocritus's *Idylls* (1988). His latest collection, *The Day and Other Poems* was published in 2006.

Clive Wilmer was born in Harrogate in 1945, and grew up in London. He lives in Cambridge, where he is a Fellow of Sidney Sussex College. He has published six collections of poetry, including *The Falls* (2000) and *The Mystery of Things* (2006). He has written extensively on the work of John Ruskin and William Morris, interviewed poets for the BBC, edited an anthology about Cambridge, and, with George Gömöri, translated poems from Hungarian.

Edward Thomas's Poems: Index